The Boxing Scene

D1566651

BOOKS BY THOMAS HAUSER

GENERAL NON-FICTION

Missing
The Trial of Patrolman Thomas Shea
For Our Children (with Frank Macchiarola)
The Family Legal Companion
Final Warning: The Legacy of Chernobyl (with Dr. Robert Gale)
Arnold Palmer: A Personal Journey
Confronting America's Moral Crisis (with Frank Macchiarola)
Healing: A Journal of Tolerance and Understanding
Miscellaneous
With This Ring (with Frank Macchiarola)
A God to Hope For

ABOUT BOXING

The Black Lights: Inside the World of Professional Boxing
Muhammad Ali: His Life and Times
Muhammad Ali: Memories
Muhammad Ali: In Perspective
Muhammad Ali & Company
A Beautiful Sickness
A Year at the Fights
Brutal Artistry
The View from Ringside
Chaos, Corruption, Courage, and Glory
The Lost Legacy of Muhammad Ali
I Don't Believe It, But It's True
Knockout (with Vikki LaMotta)
The Greatest Sport of All
The Boxing Scene

FICTION

Ashworth & Palmer
Agatha's Friends
The Beethoven Conspiracy
Hanneman's War
The Fantasy
Dear Hannah
The Hawthorne Group
Martin Bear & Friends
Mark Twain Remembers
Finding the Princess

The Boxing Scene

THOMAS HAUSER

TEMPLE UNIVERSITY PRESS
Philadelphia

Temple University Press
1601 North Broad Street
Philadelphia PA 19122
www.temple.edu/tempress

Copyright © 2009 by Thomas Hauser
All rights reserved
Published 2009
Printed in the United States of America

∞ The paper used in this publication meets the requirements of the
American National Standard for Information Sciences—Permanence of
Paper for Printed Library Materials, ANSI Z39.48-1992

Library of Congress Cataloging-in-Publication Data

Hauser, Thomas.
    The boxing scene / Thomas Hauser.
        p. cm.
    Includes bibliographical references.
    ISBN 978-1-59213-976-7 (cloth : alk. paper) — ISBN 978-1-59213-977-4
(pbk. : alk. paper) 1. Boxing. 2. Professional sports. I. Title.
    GV1133.H343 2009
    796.83—dc22

2 4 6 8 9 7 5 3 1

For Larry Merchant, Jim Lampley, Arthur Curry, and Dave Wolf
Four of the best

Contents

II. Curiosities, Issues, and Answers

Author's Note

*T*he Boxing Scene contains the articles about professional boxing that I authored in 2007. The articles I wrote about the sweet science prior to that date have been published in *Muhammad Ali & Company*; *A Beautiful Sickness*; *A Year at the Fights*; *The View from Ringside*; *Chaos, Corruption, Courage, and Glory*; *The Lost Legacy of Muhammad Ali*; *I Don't Believe It, But It's True*; and *The Greatest Sport of All*.

Special thanks are due to Secondsout.com under whose aegis most of the articles in this book first appeared.

I

Fights and Fighters

As 2007 began, the ice that Evander Holyfield was skating on seemed dangerously close to cracking.

Evander Holyfield and the Impossible Dream

Boxing isn't like other sports. When aging players in other professional athletic endeavors can't perform anymore, the system forces them out. In boxing, there's always money to be made off an aging fighter; either as an opponent to pad a young prospect's record or as a "name" that sells tickets and engenders pay-per-view buys.

Evander Holyfield is an aging fighter. He's forty-four years old and has amassed a professional record of forty wins against eight losses and two draws over twenty-two years. "I've had a lot of good things happen to me in my career," he says. "Making the United States Olympic team [in 1984] was my greatest moment. Beating Buster Douglas [in 1990] to become undisputed heavyweight champion of the world for the first time was a high point. And knocking out Mike Tyson [in 1996] is up there with those two."

Then Holyfield utters the words that have become the mantra of his fistic faith: "But the best is yet to come. I'm not going to retire until I'm the undisputed heavyweight champion of the world again."

Reality would seem to dictate otherwise. In the past six years, Holyfield has won just three fights. In 2004, he fought a journeyman boxer named Larry Donald at Madison Square Garden and lost eleven of twelve rounds. He was so outclassed that the New York State Athletic Commission put him on indefinite medical suspension for what it called "poor performance" and "diminished skills." Evander subsequently passed a series of medical tests, at which point the commission removed him from its medical suspension list and placed him on administrative suspension. He has fought twice since then, both times in Texas, winning, but looking his age.

Is Holyfield's pursuit of the heavyweight championship a noble quest, or is he the victim of delusional self-indulgence? Is his impossible dream within reach; or is he like Sisyphus, the Corinthian King of Greek mythology, condemned to roll a large boulder up a hill for eternity?

Given the myriad world-sanctioning organizations and competing promotional interests that rule boxing today, it would be hard for anyone, let alone a forty-four-year-old man, to unify the heavyweight crown. But that doesn't keep Holyfield from saying, "In boxing, it's all or nothing. You're either on top or you're just one of the guys in line trying to get there. I plan on getting to the top again. I'd like my next fight to be a championship fight. But if that's not available to me, I'll take a non-title fight to stay busy and keep my reflexes sharp. If I had a choice, I'd rather that someone else unify the titles and then fight me. One shot, one win, and I could retire as undisputed heavyweight champion of the world. But I'll fight them all one at a time if I have to. The only way they can keep me from achieving my goal is to not let me participate."

What sort of man is driven like this? Emanuel Steward, who trained Holyfield for two fights in 1993 (including his winning effort against Riddick Bowe), offers the first clue: "People who don't know Evander think he's a humble guy," Steward says. "But I've never met anyone with an ego like his. Evander is very nice and very polite, but his ego drives him. He loves being the center of attention as much as anyone I know. It might not seem that way, but he loves the spotlight."

Holyfield also loves a challenge. During his career, he has fought twenty-one fights against fourteen men who have held a version of the heavyweight crown. "I fight people who fight back," he says. "My whole career, I've fought people when they were at their best. You can't prove anything to me by doing it to someone else. You got to do it to me. And I don't look to beat somebody because he makes mistakes. I want to be better."

Holyfield is particularly fond of the challenge inherent in taking on bullies. "Evander was obsessed with beating Mike Tyson," says Steward, "because Tyson was a bully."

"All through high school, I ran from bullies," Holyfield acknowledges. "But if they caught me, I beat them up. I looked at Mike Tyson and I said to myself, 'This man is good. There ain't no sense in wishing him away. You got to fight him to become champion.' But I knew could break him."

In their first encounter, Holyfield knocked Tyson out in the eleventh round. "I'm really not interested in being the baddest man on the planet," Evander said afterward. "My only interest is being the best man in the ring."

The next time they met, Tyson was disqualified in the third stanza when he bit off part of Holyfield's ear. "Today's a great day," Evander said the morning after that fight. "I'm still the heavyweight champion of the world; I just got paid $33 million; and I only had to fight three rounds. The only bad part is that one ear is a little pointy."

Determination is another facet of Holyfield's character. Lou Duva and George Benton trained Evander from his first pro fight through Holyfield–Bowe I in 1992. "One thing you have to realize," says Duva, "is that there are better boxers than Evander and bigger punchers than Evander, but no fighter ever has invested more of himself in winning. No fighter that I know has Evander's drive and willpower. No fighter is as competitive. No fighter has his heart."

Evander's determination is coupled with total belief in himself and faith in God. It makes for a compelling package. And many people think there's another motivation for his continuing to fight. Money.

Logic says that Holyfield should be extraordinarily wealthy. Between 1990 and 1995, he had lucrative title fights against James "Buster" Douglas, George Foreman, Bert Cooper, Larry Holmes, Ray Mercer, Michael Moorer (two times), and Riddick Bowe (three times). Then, beginning with the first Tyson–Holyfield fight in 1996, he fought eleven times under the Don King Productions (DKP) banner for gross purses in excess of $123 million.

But earning the money was only half the battle. The other half was keeping it. Holyfield has eleven children by seven different women (including five out of wedlock). He provides generously for all of them. There have been two costly divorces. It requires more than $1 million a year to maintain the mansion that he lives in. For a while, there was a serious gambling problem. And his business judgment has not been good.

For many years, Holyfield was represented in boxing matters by an Atlanta attorney named Jim Thomas, who has a well-deserved reputation for integrity and intelligence. Thomas won't discuss the particulars of Evander's finances for reasons of attorney–client confidence, but he does say, "Fighters should have a simple philosophy when it comes to business away from boxing. Each deal should be money in, no money out. You license your name and put in some time in exchange for a percentage of the company and maybe an up-front payment. You do not—I repeat, you do not—put your own money into the ventures."

Holyfield didn't adhere to Thomas's philosophy. He didn't want to retire from boxing with $20 million in the bank. He wanted to be a billionaire. As a result, he lost millions of dollars in a rhythm-and-blues-gospel record company and tens of millions of dollars in a black family-oriented television channel.

"I'm not fighting for the money," Evander says. "If someone gave me a billion dollars tomorrow, I'd keep fighting. I have a goal, and that goal is to become undisputed heavyweight champion of the world again."

But the fact of the matter is that Holyfield doesn't have significant income apart from boxing. And his most recent fight (against Fres Oquendo in November 2006) engendered fewer than 40,000 pay-per-view buys. Adding insult to injury, while Evander received a $250,000 advance from promoter Murad Muhammad, the $1,175,000 check that he was given after the fight bounced. The financial issues surrounding Holyfield–Oquendo are still unresolved.

Holyfield is currently trained by Ronnie Shields, who assisted Lou Duva and George Benton for much of their time with Evander. Shields knows something about fighters past their prime, having trained Mike Tyson for his 2002 knockout loss at the hands of Lennox Lewis.

"I have no reservations about Evander continuing to fight," Shields says. "He's slower now than he was before. His reflexes aren't what they once were. But he trains hard; he does everything I ask him to do; he knows his way around a boxing ring; his heart hasn't changed. And one thing more," Shields continues. "Evander has faith. God says you can have a goal and, through prayer and working for that goal, you cannot be stopped. Telling Evander he shouldn't fight is like telling Noah, 'You're crazy, don't build an ark.' I honestly believe that Evander can be heavyweight champion of the world again."

But Holyfield's past trainers take a contrary view. Don Turner began working with Evander in 1994. They were together for sixteen fights; a run that ended after Holyfield was knocked out by James Toney in October 2003.

"Evander only hears what he wants to hear," says Turner. "And if you don't tell him what he wants to hear, you're gone. I'm a big fan of reality; and the reality is that Evander isn't what he used to be. I told him so and got fired. But I'd rather lose my job than go to a funeral."

"Evander had a great career," Turner continues. "But the time has come. The second Lennox Lewis fight [which Holyfield lost] was his last good fight, and that was seven years ago. I'm sure Evander believes he can win the championship again. When he was little, his mother told him that he could accomplish anything he wanted if he tried long and hard enough, and he believed her. It's unfortunate sometimes that people have such strong beliefs, but that's the way it is. Evander knows fighting. And the way the heavyweights are these days, in his mind, he thinks he can beat them. But what you think and what you can do are two separate things. A person can believe anything he wants, but nature has a way of telling you the truth. I just don't think he should be fighting anymore, and I hope something happens to get him out of boxing before he gets carried out."

Emanuel Steward is in accord, reminiscing, "The first time I saw Evander, he was a thirteen-year-old kid fighting in tennis shoes. What fuels him now is that he has total belief in himself; more self-belief than I've ever seen in any other fighter including Muhammad Ali. He's courageous, he has good boxing skills, and the fear factor is totally absent so it's hard to discount him completely; especially since, outside of Wladimir Klitschko, the heavyweights today aren't much. But a lot of people who like Evander and care about boxing are unhappy with his continuing to fight. I'm one of them, but there's nothing we can do about it."

"I saw Evander in San Antonio when he fought Fres Oquendo," adds Lou Duva. "It was sad. Evander was doing the best he could but he was fighting from memory; and at the championship level, you don't win fights from memory. Was he a great champion? Yes. Was he a credit to the sport? Yes. But anyone who knows boxing knows that he's not anything close to what he once was. He's fighting bums now, and he can't even look good against them.

If he keeps fighting, it's not going to end well. There's no better representative for boxing in the world today than Evander Holyfield. If he stops fighting now, he could be our greatest ambassador. But when he keeps fighting, it downgrades the sport. And God forbid something really bad should happen to him."

Very few fighters walk away from boxing when there's big money to be made. Lennox Lewis and Rocky Marciano retired while they were on top. Marvin Hagler and Michael Spinks were still marketable when they left the ring after losses in mega-fights. But these men are the exception rather than the rule. Most fighters stay on too long.

A fighter is at risk every time he steps into the ring. Holyfield is now at greater risk than he has ever been before. Outrageous self-belief lifted him to extraordinary heights and fueled his greatness as a fighter. Now that same self-belief threatens to destroy him.

Lennox Lewis is uniquely situated to comment upon Holyfield's continuing quest. Like Evander, he once reigned as undisputed heavyweight champion of the world. They fought each other twice. Their first bout was declared a draw despite the opinion of most onlookers that Lewis had won. In their second encounter, Lennox emerged with a unanimous-decision triumph.

The Lewis–Holyfield relationship was marked by acrimony at the time they faced each other in the ring. Evander called Lennox "arrogant," while Lennox labeled his opponent a "hypocrit." But those days are gone. Lewis now calls Holyfield "the best fighter I ever fought." Evander responds in kind, saying, "Riddick Bowe might have been the best at the time I fought him, but Lennox is the smartest fighter I ever fought. If I was going to war, Lennox is definitely one of the people I'd want fighting beside me."

"You have to know when to call it a day," Lewis says when asked about his own decision to retire. "It was easy for me because I had achieved all my goals. Before Tyson would have been too early. I had to fight Tyson to secure my legacy and be regarded by everyone everywhere as the true undisputed heavyweight champion. But once you've been undisputed champion, there's no higher goal in boxing. And no matter how good you are, you know that someday you'll have to give the championship up. So what you're really doing from that time on is boxing for money."

"After Tyson," Lewis elaborates, "any time was a good time to retire. After the Klitschko fight, I discussed my situation with a lot of people, including my mum. Being my mum, she knew which way I was leaning but she never said she'd like me to retire. She said she was with me either way. There were people who urged me to keep fighting, but there was something in it for them. My mum was only concerned about me."

Then Lewis's thoughts turn to Holyfield. "He has a big ego," Lennox says. "I don't. He misses the glory. I don't. I'm sure he has people around him who are telling him that he can still do it. You can always find yes-men who tell you what you want to hear and fire the ones who don't. They're getting paid, and you're the one who's getting damaged. Evander is an old fighter.

He's past his time. What he's trying to accomplish might not be totally unattainable given the heavyweight division today. But he's at a point now where he's taking serious chances with his health. I don't think he should be in the ring anymore."

"Let's say you have a friend whose girlfriend has broken up with him and married someone else," Lewis continues. "Your friend is devastated, so you say to him, 'Cheer up, there are other possibilities. There's a whole ocean of women out there.' I look at Evander and I say, 'Okay, your girl was boxing. It was great for a while and now she's treating you badly.' But there are other things that Evander can do in life; giving back, creating. There are plenty of fish in the sea. Evander is trying to accomplish at age forty-four what he already accomplished when he was in his twenties. I can't make judgments for other people. But I think it's sad when a person has the same goals at age forty-four that he had when he was in his twenties."

Holyfield knows what the boxing community is saying. "If other people want to put me down, that's their choice," he acknowledges. "But I think it's sad that people are painting a picture of me that I'm not smart enough to know when to quit. I watch tapes of my fights. There are times when I say to myself, 'I know what I should be doing but it's not happening. It's embarrassing to be in the ring with somebody, and you know you're better than he is but he's getting the best of you. I fought a few times when I shouldn't have because of injuries. That's the biggest problem I've had. But life is full of disappointments, and I can handle anything that comes my way. I truly believe that, if I do everything in my power to achieve my goal, God will help me to become undisputed heavyweight champion of the world again."

Having shared that thought, Evander turns to evaluating the current heavyweight champions. "The giant [Nikolai Valuev] would be the most difficult for me because of his size. You got to stand tall to get to him and he's in good shape. Klitschko is big and strong. He has a good right hand, good reflexes, and decent skills, so I'd say he's number two. Maskaev is what he is. I don't see him being a problem. Briggs would be the easiest. He has a breathing problem, asthma. Briggs can't go five rounds if someone fights him. But I can beat all of them."

Then Holyfield is asked, "What would it take to get you out of the ring? What would you construe as a sign from God that he wants you to do other things?"

"I already know that God wants me to do other things," Evander answers. "But he wants me to do this first."

"Is there a time when you might say to yourself, 'It doesn't look as though I'm going to be successful in my quest to become undisputed heavyweight champion of the world again. It's time to put boxing behind me.'"

"No. You don't dictate a timetable to God."

I've written about John Duddy several times. When John fought Anthony Bonsante at Madison Square Garden, I opted for a different kind of story.

John and Grainne: A Love Story

Fans watch fighters in the ring and see the blows. That's very different from getting hit. And while fans often identify with fighters, they rarely consider what watching a fight is like for someone who has close personal ties to one of the combatants and loves him.

Grainne Coll loves John Duddy, the Irish middleweight with piercing blue eyes who is unbeaten in nineteen fights and is causing a sensation in America. Like Duddy, she's a native of County Derry, Ireland. Her mother works at The Harbour Museum in Derry. Her father is a retired bus driver. Grainne is twenty-six years old; pretty with long brown hair and partial to casual clothes. "But I wear dresses when necessary," she says.

John and Grainne met seven years ago. The first time they saw each other was at a credit union in Derry. Grainne was working as a sales assistant at Marks & Spencer and went there to deposit her pay. John had a job as a lifeguard at a swimming pool around the corner.

"I was walking out of the credit union just as John was coming in," Grainne remembers. "He was wearing a lifeguard uniform, and I thought he was gorgeous. We stopped, looked at each other, and said hello. And that was it. He was coming; I was going; so I went back to Marks & Spencer."

Grainne couldn't have known it at the time. But after John put his pay in the credit union, he went back to the swimming pool and told one of the other lifeguards, "Something strange just happened. I saw this girl. We stopped and said hello. All we said was 'hello,' and it was a crazy feeling."

"A month or two later," Grainne recounts, continuing the story, "I went to a bar called The River Inn with my friend Kristy. We walked in and, right away, I saw John sitting at the bar with some friends. He was wearing a blue shirt and his arms were folded. I told Kristy, 'I don't care what it takes, I'm going to get him.' So I walked over and sort of shoved against him, which got his attention, and said, 'Hello, how are you?' "

"I'm good. How are you?" Duddy answered.

But still, there was no exchange of names or telephone numbers.

"After that," Grainne continues, "we passed each other one more time on the street. It was driving me mad. Then, finally, finally, John came around Marks & Spencer with a friend. He'd found out where I worked and he asked me if I wanted to go to a barbeque with him. My face turned bright red and I said, 'Yes, of course.' "

"She had a nice face and a nice smile," Duddy reminisces. "I said to myself, 'I'd like to get to know this person.' "

At the time, Duddy was boxing as an amateur. "I thought he was just a lifeguard," Grainne recalls. "He didn't tell me for a couple of weeks that he was a boxer. And when he did, I thought, 'He must not be very good because I've never heard of him.' We were into football in our house. I'd never been to a fight in my life."

John and Grainne grew close to one another. They were a good fit. But in the ring, Duddy was struggling. He was suffering from burnout and the feeling that he was going nowhere, that he had learned all he was going to learn. "He was thinking seriously about giving up boxing," Grainne remembers. "Then, one night, he said to me, 'I think I should go to America. That's the only way I can learn my trade. Do you want to come with me?' "

"No problem," she answered.

In 2003, John and Grainne relocated in New York. They're now engaged and live together in Queens (one of the city's five boroughs).

"It takes a lot of dedication to be a fighter," Grainne says. "You can have all the talent in the world, but you have to want it and work really hard for it. I've never met a man who wants something so bad as John wants to succeed in boxing."

"In the days before a fight," Grainne continues, "John gets really quiet. He stays in the house and doesn't go out or talk to people much. I understand it. He's focusing on what he has to do. The night before a fight, I pretty much leave him alone. We don't talk much. John reads or watches a film and goes to bed early. The day of a fight, I get up, get my breakfast, give John a kiss, and leave the house. I don't see him again until he's walking to the ring that night."

As for the rest of their time together, Grainne says, "John is genuine, down-to-earth, loyal, thoughtful, considerate, and good fun. There's nothing phony about him. What you see is what you get. It's half-and-half with the housework. He does the laundry and some of the cooking. He loves reading and watching old black-and-white movies. John wants to be a poet. John wants to be a writer. He has a way with words; he could do those things. He just has to believe in himself."

"Grainne knows the best and worst of me," Duddy notes in response. "She sees me when I come home from a bad day at the gym. As much as she'd like to think that I'm thinking of her twenty-four-seven, she knows that, coming up to a fight, my mind is somewhere else. It's frustrating for her when I go into my shell, but she understands what I'm going through. And I wouldn't be where I am today if it weren't for Grainne. She saw me through when I was down as an amateur and not feeling very good about myself. People ask me sometimes whether I'm married or single. I just tell them I'm in love with Grainne."

When will they get married?

"Maybe next year," Duddy answers. "We're in no rush. We're as good as married now."

But Grainne isn't the only one with affection for John. There are times when it seems as though all of Ireland in America is in love with Duddy.

Perhaps the most remarkable thing about "Duddy-mania" is that Team Duddy is building a star without broadcast television, HBO, Showtime, or a big-name promoter. A lot of savvy marketing has gone into the process. Eddie McLoughlin is John's promoter. Anthony McLoughlin (Eddie's brother) is the manager of record. They began by building alliances in the local Irish-American community and selling tickets in bars; the way ring heroes were developed in the 1930s and 1940s when boxing mattered.

The coming out party for Team Duddy occurred on March 16, 2006 (the night before St. Patrick's Day), when Duddy scored a first-round knockout over Shelby Pudwill. The fight took place at The Theater (a 4,955-seat venue adjacent to the main arena in Madison Square Garden). It was only the second time in history that The Theater sold out for a fight.

"A lot of people came from Ireland," Duddy remembers. "There were people who came from Scotland that I didn't even know. I thought I was prepared for it. But after the fight, it was a tidal wave of people going crazy, screaming my name and jumping for joy. It wasn't a dream come true because I never dreamed such a thing. It was more than I could ever dream of. It was a very special moment for me."

Two months later, Duddy flew to Las Vegas to attend the annual Boxing Writers Association of America awards dinner. "I can't believe it," he said during the cocktail hour. "Wayne McCullough [a silver medalist for Ireland at the 1992 Olympics and later the World Boxing Council bantamweight champion] came over and said hello to me. I remember watching him on television when I was a boy."

"I've heard a lot about John and wanted to meet him," McCullough said afterward. "He's a nice fellow."

The next day, they were text-messaging back and forth.

"I think we're doing a pretty good job on the promotional end," says Eddie McLoughlin. "But the reason for the success we're having is John. He's the whole package, in and out of the ring. He has this charisma about him."

Well and good. But once the bell rings, charm and charisma don't matter. The key to it all is that Duddy is an exciting fighter who has survived every ring challenge to date. His sternest test came last September when he triumphed over veteran Yory Boy Campas in a scintillating brutal twelve-round slugfest. John suffered deep gashes above each eye; the first time he'd been cut since being hit by an elbow while sparring as an amateur. He was also wobbled by Campas's punches and, at one point, appeared on the verge of being knocked out.

"I'd never been in a position like that before," Duddy acknowledges, "where my back was against the wall and I was fighting an opponent who took everything I threw at him and hit just as hard as I did. That's the first time I was ever really asked in the ring, 'Do you want to be a professional fighter?' And the answer was 'yes, I do.'"

Duddy walked through the fire against Campas and emerged with a unanimous-decision triumph. "Now the snowball is getting bigger," he says. "Things are catching on. I won't use the word 'star' but I know that, as of late, I've become an attraction."

The cuts that Duddy suffered against Campas kept him out of action for five-and-a-half months. The obvious coordinates for his return to the ring were the night before St. Patrick's Day 2007 and Madison Square Garden. Equally obvious (but unanswered) were the questions, "What had John learned from the Campas fight?" and "Could he correct the flaws that allowed Campas to hit him so hard and so often?"

"The Campas fight showed me that I have to fight with my brain, not just my heart, and make defense more of a priority," Duddy acknowledged. "Yory taught me with his fists, 'Look, kid, you can't fight like that or you're going to lose.' I'm trying to break some of my bad habits. Hopefully, in my next fight, I'll show a bit more experience and maturity. I have a good boxing brain, but I don't always use it as well as I should. The smart thing would be to use my boxing skills a bit more; so I guess, this time, we'll see how smart I am. I know Harry [trainer Harry Keitt] can teach me. The question is, 'Can I learn?' I've got to fight smart. That's what makes champions."

The opponent chosen for Duddy's 2007 St. Patrick's Eve test was Anthony Bonsante; a tough gritty club fighter with twenty-nine victories to his credit. Two years ago, Bonsante achieved a measure of fame as one of the boxers on the television reality show *The Contender*. The highlights of his career were a win over Matt Vanda and a draw against Prince Badi Ajamu. But he came up short against Kingsley Ikeke and Allan Green, lost four times to *Contender* opposition, and (more troubling) was defeated by Danny Thomas and Tocker Pudwill.

Duddy arrived at his dressing room for the Bonsante fight at 8:00 P.M. "The weather is terrible," he said. "Sleet, snow, rain, everything." Wearing black sweatpants and a long-sleeved gray shirt, he did several minutes of stretching exercises; then took off the gray shirt and put on a white T-shirt with large green letters that read, "Legalize the Irish.org." Beneath that, in smaller type, the message continued, "Irish Lobby For Immigration Reform."

Duddy likes a quiet dressing room where he can sit alone with his thoughts. His team leaves him alone in the hours before a fight. But the higher a fighter climbs, the more intrusions there are.

At 8:10, referee Steve Smoger entered the dressing room to give Duddy his pre-fight instructions. Smoger was followed by representatives of the World Boxing Council and International Boxing Association, both of which had belts on the line. Then an MSG Network camera crew taped an interview that would air during the telecast.

At 9:00, the interruptions ended and Duddy was alone. The solitude of his dressing room contrasted markedly with the scene outside.

Duddy–Bonsante had become more than a fight. It was a celebration. The Theater was sold out. Joe Frazier and Jake LaMotta were at ringside. So was novelist Tom Wolfe. Irish dancers performed in the ring between bouts accompanied by Irish musicians who stood on a stage behind the press section.

Two months earlier, Duddy had noted, "I have people calling to complain to me that they can't get tickets for the fight. That's because tickets aren't on sale yet." Now John said simply, "Seeing all the excitement on a night like tonight, knowing that I'm responsible for a large part of it; that's a good feeling."

The crowd had become a character in the drama.

At 9:30, Grainne entered the arena, wearing a black skirt, a red-and-black silk blouse, and high-heeled red shoes. Her parents, who had come from Ireland for the fight, were with her. Making her way past well-wishers, she settled in a third-row ringside seat beside her father.

The arena was jammed; every seat taken. The undercard fights had been what are known in the trade as "cowboys and Indians." In each bout, there had been a clear favorite whom the promoter expected would win. Six of the bouts featured an Irishman against a lesser foe. Now, to the consternation of many in The Theater, one of the "Indians" triumphed. Five-time Irish National Amateur Champion James Clancy (9–0 as a pro) was knocked woozy by Rodney Ray of Brooklyn at 1:20 of the second round.

It was a reality check for the crowd and for Grainne. This is boxing. Anything can happen. The fights aren't scripted, and the brutality is real.

Normally, Grainne laughs a lot. Now there was nervous chatter. "I'm completely nervous; I can't concentrate," she told her father.

At 10:20, the singing of the Irish and American national anthems began.

At 10:32, almost unnoticed, Anthony Bonsante walked to the ring.

"When I'm watching John fight," Grainne had said earlier, "there's every type of emotion. As soon as I hear the bagpipes, I get nervous and have butterflies in my stomach. Then the fight starts and I'm scared. I think of the worst that might happen. But it's exciting to see your man up there doing what he loves to do and hear the crowd shouting his name."

At 10:34, Duddy began his walk to the ring. Bagpipes sounded and, as John came into view, the crowd exploded.

A rhythmic chant of "Duddy! Duddy!" filled the air.

The fighters were introduced. There were boos for Bonsante and a thunderous roar for John.

Grainne clasped her hands and rubbed her palms together nervously. No matter how stable an environment a fighter tries to create, he is forced by his trade to live life on the edge. One moment of violence can change everything.

As for the fight, Bonsante threw only a handful of punches in the early going, opting for a defensive strategy that allowed Duddy to move forward with abandon. Anthony is a survivor but he lacks power. John is relentless against opponents of that caliber and was the aggressor from the opening bell.

Grainne leaned forward in her chair during the fight, fidgeting with her fingers and watching intently. She was largely silent but joined in when the crowd chanted, "Duddy! Duddy!" An occasional "Ohhh" escaped her lips when either fighter landed solidly. "I think I'm sweating more than John," she said at one point. Then she cupped her hands on either side of her mouth and shouted, "C'mon, John."

Duddy showed the same defensive flaws he's shown in the past. He didn't move his head enough or bend at the knees. There wasn't much need to retreat, but when he did, he often moved straight back while standing straight up.

In round four, there was an accidental clash of heads and Bonsante emerged with an ugly gash high on his forehead. The cut bled for the rest of the fight, dripping into his eyes and onto his gloves whenever he tried to clear his vision.

"He kept wiping the blood away with his gloves," Duddy said afterward. "Every time he hit me, I got splattered with his blood."

In the middle rounds, Bonsante landed some good shots (better than John should have allowed), but they didn't have much effect. Meanwhile, Anthony's blood was streaming down his face. It stained both fighters' trunks, their socks, even the undersoles of their shoes as they moved around the blood-splattered ring canvas. After round nine, the cut had worsened to the point where Bonsante was no longer able to continue. Because it had been caused by an accidental head-butt, the winner was determined by the judges' scorecards. This observer gave every round to Duddy. The judges favored him by a 90–81, 89–82, and 88–83 margin.

When the decision was announced, a happy smile crossed Grainne's face. Then she put two fingers between her teeth and let out an ear-splitting whistle.

But there was an unanswered question: "What had Duddy learned from fighting Yory Boy Campas?" Bonsante didn't truly test him. Eddie McLoughlin says that he wants John fighting in the main arena at Madison Square Garden for the middleweight championship of the world on St. Patrick's Day weekend 2008. But despite the hype, Duddy isn't a legitimate title contender yet.

"We're not jumping over mountains here," trainer Harry Keitt said in the dressing room after the fight. "We take things one fight at a time. A win is a win. John did what he had to do tonight."

Meanwhile, Grainne was on her way to a nearby bar to have a beer with her father. "John has to change clothes and talk to the writers and television people," she said. "If I'm there, I'd just be in the way. A beer with my da will calm me down." She fingered her cell phone. "I'll wait for the call; John saying, 'It's over. Meet me out back; we're going home.' "

In a sport hungry for attention, Oscar De La Hoya versus Floyd Mayweather Jr. shaped up as the event of the year.

Boxing Awaits De La Hoya–Mayweather

The tagline for the fight ("The World Awaits") is a bit pretentious. The world hasn't paid much attention to boxing lately. The days of Louis–Schmeling II and Ali–Frazier I (when the world really awaited a prize fight) are gone. But boxing is waiting for Oscar De La Hoya versus Floyd Mayweather Jr. like a drowning man who sees a log floating in his direction. The log won't solve all of his problems but it will keep him afloat for a while.

Oscar De La Hoya is the last of boxing's crossover stars. He won a gold medal at the 1992 Barcelona Olympics and has compiled a professional record of thirty-eight wins against four losses with thirty knockouts. Mayweather settled for bronze in 1996 in Atlanta, but is undefeated in thirty-seven fights with twenty-four knockouts as a pro.

De La Hoya and Mayweather each won his first world title at 130 pounds; Oscar in 1994 and Floyd in 1998. Mayweather has captured belts at 130, 135, 140, and 147 pounds. Oscar has annexed belts in the same weight divisions plus 154 and 160 pounds. Some of their titles lacked credibility. For example, De La Hoya's middleweight laurels WBO version were overshadowed by the fact that Bernard Hopkins held the WBC, WBA, and IBF crowns at the same time. But Oscar is a superb fighter and one of boxing's greatest attractions ever, while Floyd is regarded in most circles as the sport's reigning "pound-for-pound" monarch. Their May 5 match-up is likely to be the biggest event that the sweet science hosts for a while.

De La Hoya versus Mayweather will feature boxers with contrasting personalities and markedly different ring styles. When Oscar turned pro, promoter Bob Arum christened him "The Golden Boy," a name that dates to a 1937 play about a violin-playing boxer and the 1939 film of the same title that made William Holden a star.

Despite the demands of his trade, De La Hoya works hard to cultivate a clean-cut corporate-friendly image. He wears impeccably-tailored suits, is unfailingly polite, never swears in public, and eschews bling. He'll be paid roughly $30 million for fighting Mayweather, but two other incentives are also on his mind.

First, for all his accomplishments, De La Hoya has never been acknowledged as boxing's "pound-for-pound" king. A victory over Mayweather could earn him that honor. And second, Oscar loves the limelight, the big event. And right now, it doesn't get any bigger than De La Hoya versus Mayweather. As Patrick Kehoe wrote recently, "These bits of stardust are what Oscar lives for."

Mayweather, by contrast, cultivates a gangsta persona that, by some accounts, is more than just image. He goes by the nickname "Pretty Boy." That's a tip of the hat to Charles "Pretty Boy" Floyd, a Depression-era bank robber. But Mayweather takes his craft seriously and is a fervent defender of the sweet science. "Anybody can put tattoos all over his body and go out and street-fight for twelve minutes," Floyd says of mixed martial arts. "It takes dedication and talent to be a professional boxer. It's an art."

Mayweather is also conscious of his place in history. "In basketball, you get a new record every year," he observes. "In football, you get a new record every year. In every other sport, you get a new record every year. In boxing, your record stays with you forever." And it aggravates him that, despite being undefeated and "pound-for-pound," he has been accorded second billing to an opponent who has won only two fights (against Felix Sturm and Ricardo Mayorga) over the past four years.

"I'm a throwback fighter," Mayweather says. "I'm always in shape. I bust my ass. I work hard. I've dedicated my life to boxing. You could have Bill Gates's money, and you couldn't buy this talent. I've never lost, never been down, never been hurt. Like me or not, you got to respect my fighting."

Mayweather is enjoying the promotion for the May 5 fight. And he's bringing a decidedly different vibe to the proceedings than Oscar is. On February 20 in New York (the first of eleven kick-off press conferences), Floyd gyrated down the red-carpeted runway at the Waldorf Astoria, wearing black pants and a multi-colored warm-up jacket. Then Oscar entered, looking very much like the successful businessman he is. As De La Hoya approached, Mayweather took off his jacket. Now he had a different look. Black jeans and a black T-shirt. Seconds later, Floyd removed his shirt. His message was clear: "I'm here to fight." In response, Oscar took off his jacket and lifted his shirt to show off his abs. But that meant, for the rest of the press conference, the Golden Boy sat at the dais with his shirt hanging out of his suit.

"Shit happens," Mayweather told the assembled media. "Floyd Mayweather gives it to you raw and uncut. If you want fake shit [he pointed at Oscar], here it is. If you want real shit [pointing to himself], here it is." When it was De La Hoya's turn to speak, Floyd mocked him with physical gestures and repeatedly interrupted him. Oscar cut his remarks short after thirty seconds.

Then came the posed staredown, and Mayweather was in De La Hoya's face; pushing forward chest-to-chest, touching, trash-talking. Oscar stayed calm. By his reckoning, "Things like this get my blood boiling and motivate me." But to most observers, it seemed as though Mayweather had won the round by taking Oscar out of his game plan and having his way.

"I had to tone it down a bit to get him to take the fight," Mayweather said afterward. "Once I got his name on that contract, it freed me."

As for the fight itself, Mayweather has opened as a 2-to-1 betting favorite. "I'm going to stand toe-to-toe with Oscar," Floyd says. "He has my word on that. I'll be right there in front of him. It will be a toe-to-toe battle and, absolutely, I'll knock him out."

But as a general rule, one can discount (if not totally disregard) anything that a fighter says about strategy prior to a fight. No one expects Mayweather to stand toe-to-toe with De La Hoya. He simply has to outbox him.

De La Hoya has been in the ring with the likes of Pernell Whitaker, Fernando Vargas, Ike Quartey, Félix Trinidad, Shane Mosley, and Bernard Hopkins. But the results have been mixed. He has three wins and four defeats against those fighters in the seven biggest challenges of his career. He triumphed over Whitaker, Vargas, and Quartey, but lost to Trinidad, Hopkins, and Mosley (twice). One can argue that Oscar deserved the decision against Trinidad and Mosley (the second time around). But one can also argue that he lost to Whitaker and Quartey.

Mayweather is faster than any of the aforementioned fighters (including Mosley, whose quickness gave Oscar trouble). He's smaller than De La Hoya, but here the thoughts of Emanuel Steward are instructive: "I know people are saying Oscar is the naturally bigger man," Steward said last month. "But he's never been a particularly physical fighter. Even at 154 pounds, Floyd Jr. is as physically strong as Oscar and maybe even better suited for any rough stuff."

Also, De La Hoya has won only one fight since decisioning Felix Sturm almost three years ago. That was his May 6, 2006, knockout of Ricardo Mayorga. Did Oscar look good in that fight? Absolutely. But Mayorga is the perfect opponent for building illusions.

"I don't care what big fights Oscar has been in," Mayweather says. "I could have done the same thing to an old Camacho. I could have done the same thing to an old Whitaker. I could have done the same thing to an old Chavez. Oscar is straight up and down with no special effects. And he's never been in with Floyd Mayweather Jr."

"Oscar has never fought anyone like Floyd,' adds Leonard Ellerbe (Mayweather's friend, confidante, and assistant everything). "There isn't anyone like Floyd. Besides, Oscar is a part-time fighter. How the hell is a part-time fighter going to be competitive with the best fighter in the world?"

However, the other side of the coin is that Mayweather isn't invincible. He battered Diego Corrales, beat José Luis Castillo twice, and did nicely against Zab Judah. But it's a reasonable assumption that De La Hoya would have beaten all of the men that Mayweather has fought. And where common opponents are concerned (Genaro Hernandez and Arturo Gatti), Oscar disposed of each man more quickly than Floyd did.

De La Hoya–Mayweather is a step up for Floyd. It's easy to say that he'll outspeed and outbox Oscar. But De La Hoya has experience and power. He's tougher than a lot of people give him credit for being. Floyd's hands might cause him trouble, as they have in the past. And Mayweather is coming up in weight. Oscar found that his power didn't carry well to 160 pounds (he couldn't hurt Sturm or Hopkins). He believes that Floyd will suffer from a similar fate and that this is an instance where a younger, smaller, faster man will be beaten by size and strength.

To neutralize Mayweather's speed, De La Hoya will have to attack, apply pressure, and make Floyd fight. He must be in shape to do it for twelve full rounds. And he has to be willing to walk through fire, which means taking two or three punches on occasion to land one.

But there's a story line to De La Hoya versus Mayweather that goes beyond the actual fight. One of the things that makes the business of boxing unique in the world of sports is that a promoter can conceive of a big fight (sometimes even a historic event) and bring it to fruition in a matter of months. *Field of Dreams*. Build it and they will come.

De La Hoya–Mayweather has the potential to become the most lucrative event in boxing history. Let's start with some numbers. The previous record for a live gate was $16,860,300 for the November 13, 1999, rematch between Lennox Lewis and Evander Holyfield. For De La Hoya–Mayweather, the MGM Grand Garden Arena will be configured to hold 15,799 customers. Tickets are priced at $2,000, $1,500, $1,000, $750, and $350. Most of those tickets were purchased by the MGM Grand, competing casinos, and sponsors before any public sale. Others were reserved for HBO, Golden Boy, and the Mayweather camp. On January 27, the remaining tickets went on sale to the public and sold out within three hours. Golden Boy says that the live gate will be $19.3 million.

The all-time pay-per-view buy record for a fight is 1,990,000 for the 1997 rematch between Evander Holyfield and Mike Tyson. Lewis–Tyson came close with 1,930,000 buys and grossed a record $112 million in pay-per-view dollars. Oscar De La Hoya versus Félix Trinidad generated the non-heavyweight-record of 1.4 million buys. Three other De La Hoya fights (Mosley II, Hopkins, and Vargas) also eclipsed the one-million-buy mark.

"Our goal," says Golden Boy CEO Richard Schaefer, "is to break all records. This fight will be unlike any fight anyone has ever seen. The promotion of this fight, from the initial press conference to fight night will be unprecedented in its scope. We have no doubt this will be the biggest boxing event of all time."

Thus, in early February, the world was treated to Oscar and Floyd publicizing their upcoming confrontation while at the Super Bowl. HBO announced its intention to air a four-part prime-time countdown series in the weeks lead-ing up to the fight. And the New York City kick-off press conference opened with Schaefer talking, not about the competitive merits of the fight, but about dollars.

First, Schaefer cited the live gate. Then he moved on to television. The bout will be seen in 176 countries. In addition to regular pay-per-view, it will be shown at 1,200 closed-circuit locations in the United States. A $17 million marketing budget is expected to generate hundreds of millions of impres-sions. Tequila Cazadores is the presenting sponsor. The secondary sponsors are Tecate Beer, Rockstar Energy Drink, and Southwest Airlines. Merchan-dising sales are expected to top $3 million.

Money was also the focal point of bickering between De La Hoya and his now-former trainer, Floyd Mayweather Sr.

Floyd Sr. was in prison on drug charges when Floyd Jr. competed in the Olympics. He trained his son early in his pro career, but was replaced by Roger Mayweather (Floyd's uncle), who is now in jail on domestic abuse charges. Uncle Roger is expected to be released before the fight.

Fathers coach against their sons in team sports from time to time, but boxing is different. That plus the much-publicized estrangement between Floyd Sr. and Floyd Jr. offered the promotion yet another marketing angle. But Mayweather Sr. (who had received a reported $250,000 fee for each of Oscar's previous eight outings) decided that he wanted $2 million to train Oscar to fight his son. De La Hoya countered with an offer of $500,000 plus a $500,000 bonus if he won. That led to some unscripted media outbursts.

"Oscar and little Floyd are getting much more than they normally get, so why can't I get mine?" Floyd Sr. told TheSweetScience.com. That was fol-lowed by a statement to MaxBoxing.com: "These motherfuckers must think I'm crazy. A million dollars ain't shit these days. I told them to give it to some-body else and have a good day." *USA Today* was advised, "If Oscar doesn't use me, it won't be because I'm not a great trainer. What I'm asking for is nowhere near what he's going to make. There's too much money for me to take chits and bits." There were also words for the *Las Vegas Review–Journal*: "It's obvious that Oscar is super-tight. What comes first in this particular situ-ation; greed or the fight?"

On January 30, 140 members of the media listened in on a teleconference call to hear De La Hoya announce that Freddie Roach would train him for the fight.

"Oscar did not want to be in a position where he added fuel to the fire of a father-and-son dispute," Richard Schaefer explained to the media. Schaefer added that Floyd Sr. being in the corner opposite his son would have intro-duced an unwanted "circus atmosphere" to the proceedings.

De La Hoya, for his part, said that the economics of Floyd Sr.'s $2 million demand had "no impact whatsoever" on his decision to work with Roach. Rather, he took the demand as a sign of Floyd Sr.'s ambivalence with regard to training a fighter to beat his own son.

Mayweather Sr. (who bills himself as "the world's greatest trainer") derided the choice of Roach as "a move from first class to coach" and appeared at his son's side when the press tour reached Las Vegas. It's unclear what role, if any, he will play with regard to Floyd Jr.'s preparation for the fight.

Over the next two months, interest will rise as De La Hoya versus Mayweather draws closer. Newspapers that haven't staffed a fight since Lewis–Tyson in 2002 will start paying attention. Casual sports fans who rarely follow boxing will become at least vaguely aware that a fight of significance is about to happen.

But a word of caution is in order. As a fight, De La Hoya–Mayweather is no more important than De La Hoya–Trinidad, Lewis–Tyson, Holyfield–Tyson, Lewis–Holyfield, Trinidad–Hopkins, or a half-dozen other encounters of the past decade. It's also unclear how good a fight it will be. Some mega-fights live up to the hype. Others don't.

However, as an event, De La Hoya–Mayweather is exceedingly important; primarily because today's heavyweight division is in such poor health. "This fight," says HBO Sports president Ross Greenburg, "has the potential to break through and reconnect boxing with sports fans around the country." Toward that end, it's important that De La Hoya–Mayweather be seen as a platform for boxing to build on, not an end unto itself.

No one begrudges Golden Boy its high ticket prices for the fight. The market bears what the market bears. Similarly, $54.95 is a bit much for pay-per-view, but no one is required to buy the fight unless he or she wants to. If the sponsors are willing to part with millions of dollars, fine.

However, a lot of writers who've covered Golden Boy since its inception (and are one of the reasons for the company's success) seem to have been left to fend for themselves when it comes to securing rooms for fight week. Others are concerned that they might not be credentialed for the fight. There have been lavish promotional expenditures in some areas and questionable cost-cutting in others. If Golden Boy's intention is to squeeze every last dollar out of De La Hoya versus Mayweather without regard to the future, it might wind up strangling the goose that lays boxing's golden eggs.

This article touched on one of the many sidelights that accompanied the "superfight" between Oscar De La Hoya and Floyd Mayweather Jr.

Floyd's World

The May 5 fight between Oscar De La Hoya and Floyd Mayweather Jr. might turn out to be the largest-grossing fight in the history of boxing. Over the next few months, thousands of articles will be written about the combatants. Their respective psyches will be thoroughly explored. I don't claim intimate knowledge of either man, but one experience with Mayweather stands out in my mind.

On Tuesday, March 30, 2004, I was at the ESPN Zone in New York to attend the kick-off press conference for the fight between Mayweather and DeMarcus Corley. Marilyn Cole Lownes and I were writing a feature story on "Boxing Bling-Bling" for the *Observer Sports Monthly*. Holger Keifel was with us as our photographer. We were hoping to photograph Floyd with at least some of his jewels.

Mayweather entered the restaurant wearing blue jeans, a T-shirt, and denim jacket accessorized with a diamond-studded watch, necklace, and ring. Holger asked if he'd be willing to take the jacket and T-shirt off. Floyd demurred. "What's this for, anyway?" he queried.

We told him.

Mayweather weighed his options; then decided that, if there was going to be a photo shoot of his bling, it should be captured in all its glory. He snapped his fingers and instructed an entourage member: "Bring it here."

The aide handed Mayweather an unobtrusive black-leather attaché case. Floyd opened it up and began to remove the treasures inside. Pendants, chains, watches, bracelets, rings; most of them gold and platinum with large-carat diamonds embedded within.

The press conference was about to start.

"Let's do this afterward," Floyd said.

During the next hour, Mayweather talked with the media about the fight, made faces while Corley spoke, and doodled on a pad like a child with attention deficit disorder. But when you're an undefeated world champion, you get away with that sort of thing.

When the press conference ended, Floyd returned to our camera. "I'm the master," he told us. "I know all about jewelry. People say I'm cocky and arrogant, but I say I'm confident and slick. And my lifestyle is flashy. I like flashy jewelry and flashy cars; that's me. There's never too many diamonds." But beyond that, he was totally disinterested in talking about his bling. He only wanted to show it off. The bling speaks for itself.

At most photo shoots, the model follows direction. Here, Floyd directed the entire shoot in the manner of Orson Welles directing and starring in *Citizen Kane*. He didn't want Holger touching or positioning his bling. "I do this all the time," he told us. "I know how to do it better than anyone."

Mayweather was in charge. Everyone present bowed to his will. The entourage members whose salaries he pays, the photographer who wanted the pictures, and us.

"Gimme the horse."

A "Ferrari horse" fashioned from 600 black, white, and yellow diamonds appeared.

"Gimme the glove."

A bejeweled boxing glove was placed in his hand.

One of Mayweather's friends had been wearing a diamond-studded money bag on a gold chain around his neck and had assured us that it was his own.

Mayweather snapped his fingers: "Gimme my bag."

The bag was removed from its wearer's neck and handed to the champ.

Holger asked Floyd if he'd be willing to wrap some of the chains, bracelets, and other bounty around his fist and hold it out against the white backdrop. Mayweather complied. But everyone present understood that the bling wasn't wrapped around a model's hand. It was wrapped around the fist of its owner, who happened to be the best pound-for-pound fighter in the world.

De La Hoya–Mayweather was a major financial success and a good (but not great) fight.

De La Hoya–Mayweather in Perspective

At 5:00 P.M. on Wednesday, May 2 Floyd Mayweather Jr. was holding court at the Mayweather Boxing Club, the storefront gym in Las Vegas where he trains. In three days, "Pretty Boy" would enter the ring to face Oscar De La Hoya. The final pre-fight press conference at the MGM Grand had ended several hours earlier.

"Oscar's lip was twitching at the staredown," Mayweather said glee-fully. "We did eleven cities [on the pre-fight publicity tour], eleven stare-downs, and Oscar was never like he was today. Oscar is worried; Oscar can't sleep nights; Oscar knows he's got a problem. And to me, it's just another fight. I ain't worried about Oscar at all."

Mayweather grew up in a quintessential dysfunctional family amidst chaos and conflict. His mother was a drug addict. His father spent five and one-half years in prison for cocaine trafficking. An uncle (Roger Mayweather, who is now Floyd's trainer) recently served a six-month prison term for domestic violence. One of Floyd's aunts died of AIDS.

"Before people criticize me, they should walk in my shoes," May-weather told the handful of people gathered around him by the ring apron. My mommy on drugs; my daddy a hustler. When I was little, I lived seven deep in a one-bedroom apartment. Seeing somebody shot, seeing a gun; that was normal for me."

"Pretty Boy" struts and swaggers through life. He lives large and speaks his mind. Boxing is his enabler. He resides in a 12,000-square-foot-home, owns a dozen cars, wears millions of dollars worth of bling, and walks around with tens of thousands of dollars in his pocket on an average day. He's a frequent visitor at the Las Vegas sports books, often winning or losing as much as $10,000 on a single football, basketball, or baseball game. His Super Bowl wagers run as high as $100,000.

Mayweather bristles when his chaotic personal life (and particularly his relationship with his father) is referenced in the media. "Me and my dad's personal business is our personal business," he said when the subject arose during a late-March conference call designed to promote his May 5 bout against De La Hoya. "When you interview me, I don't ask you what's going on with you and your dad or you and your mom." At the final pre-fight press conference, he cautioned, "Before you guys judge me and write bad things about me, go home and look at yourself in the mirror."

When Floyd looks in the mirror he sees a man who pled guilty to two counts of domestic violence in 2002, and two years later was found guilty of misdemeanor battery for striking two women in a Las Vegas nightclub. A felony indictment for allegedly beating the mother of one of his children was dismissed in 2005 when the woman (who had filed a criminal complaint against him) refused to cooperate with the prosecutor's office.

The knock on Mayweather is that he shows little respect for other people. But there's one area where Floyd is reverential. He respects boxing and is totally dedicated to his craft.

Most great fighters define themselves by the sweet science. Muhammad Ali did when he was young. Roy Jones Jr. did (and still does). So does Mayweather. At an age when most children are learning the alphabet, Floyd was being taught to box. The sport was his refuge from the world-at-large (which says all one needs to know about the world he came from). The only positive paternal attention that he received as a child and the only stability in his life revolved around boxing.

Mayweather has gymnastic-like coordination and strength. He's not just always in shape; he's always in fighting shape. Great athletes have a persistent work ethic. Michael Jordan was legendary among his peers for his training regimen. The same is true of Tiger Woods. Among today's elite fighters, only Bernard Hopkins has a training regimen that rivals Mayweather's. But Hopkins does it because he has to. Floyd does it because he loves to. "You have to be in the ring with him to appreciate his skills and understand how good he is," Carlos Baldomir (who Mayweather defeated in 2006) said recently.

"Boxing is an art, and I'm an artist," Floyd says. "I've been boxing my whole life. I don't know life without boxing. I'm an honest fighter; I work hard at it. I'm a student of the game, and I study the game well. My job is to go out there and be Floyd Mayweather. Judge me for how I do my job."

Standing by the ring at the Mayweather Boxing Club," Mayweather was more than willing to assess his own job performance.

"They told Ali, 'Joe Louis was better than you.' They told Joe Louis, 'Jack Johnson was better than you.' I keep hearing about Sugar Ray Leonard. All Ray Leonard heard about was Sugar Ray Robinson. Twenty years from now, there will be another great fighter, and people will tell him 'Floyd Mayweather was better than you.' "

Then came a question.

"Floyd, suppose you got in the ring on Saturday night; and instead of De La Hoya, you were looking at a 22-year-old 154-pound Roy Jones Jr. What happens in that fight?"

Mayweather's eyes lit up at the thought of the challenge.

"Wow, that's a tough one. Roy's height would be hard for me. Same for his speed and power. Mentally, I'd have the edge, and my fundamentals are better than Roy's. But that's a tough, tough fight."

"Who else would give you trouble?"

"Aaron Pryor at 140 pounds would have been tough for me. I do better against him at 147. And Pernell Whitaker in his prime would have been a challenge. Pernell knew the ring. He didn't knock many guys out, but Pernell was beautiful."

Welcome to "The World Awaits," also known as "Golden Boy vs. Pretty Boy" and "The Fight to Save Boxing"—an event that witnessed fighters and promoters measuring themselves against history as much as against one another.

De La Hoya versus Mayweather was boxing's Super Bowl for 2007 and the first mega-event for the sport since Lennox Lewis battered Mike Tyson into submission five years ago. Security at the February 20 kick-off press conference in New York was akin to a presidential luncheon, and things got bigger from there. Oscar was the primary drawing card, but Mayweather did his part to stir the promotional stew. Among the words of wisdom that Floyd uttered in the weeks leading up to the fight were:

- "Lights and fame have nothing to do with boxing skills. I'm the master when it comes to getting in that square circle. Everyone knows that Oscar is gonna get beat. The only question is how."
- "This guy doesn't pose no threat to me at all. De La Hoya's got one style; he's straight up and down. There's nothing special about him, but he's never seen a style like mine. I make A-class fighters look like D-class fighters. I'm a fighter with special effects."
- "This ain't *Rocky*. This is real life. I'm going to dominate. I'm the best at talking trash, but I'm also the best at going out there and backing it up. I'm gonna ice that motherfucker."

There were personal assaults: "Oscar is about Oscar. He's greedy; he's ungrateful. Oscar ain't real, but you all keep believing the stories he's telling you. Any dirt on me, they put it on the front page. Any dirt on Oscar, they sweep it under the rug and seal it in court."

And there was the allegation that De La Hoya lacked heart. In a pointed reference to the Oscar's 2004 knockout loss at the hands of Bernard Hopkins, Mayweather declared, "There's two things we know about Oscar. We know he gets tired and we know he will lay down. If you can bang on the canvas, you can get up."

Needless to say, De La Hoya took offense at Mayweather's remarks. "I truly feel that he needs a humbling experience," Oscar declared. "He really is a little brat. Ever since we went on tour and he started talking all that trash, I've lost respect for him. He can get up on the podium and say a few nice things and then his real side will come out. He starts talking about I'm nothing and I haven't fought anybody and this and that. It's uncalled for; it's unnecessary. What comes out of his mouth is garbage."

"Then do something about it on May 5th," Mayweather countered.

Whether Oscar would be able to do that something was open to question. De La Hoya didn't become a star without being a superb fighter. But against Mayweather, he was still seeking the magnificent victory that eluded him against Félix Trinidad, Shane Mosley, and Bernard Hopkins.

"Mayweather's speed is his biggest asset," Freddie Roach (De La Hoya's trainer) said in an April 18 conference call. "He's very, very quick and he uses his speed very well, and speed will take you a long way. We have to set things up and take advantage of his mistakes at the right time. We're working on it every day."

"We know he's fast," De La Hoya added. "But how fast is he at 154? That's something that we'll see on May 5th. People are talking about speed, how it's going to be a big factor. People are going to be very surprised at how I'll be able to match his speed."

But size and strength shaped up as De La Hoya's biggest edge. It had been six years since Oscar fought at a weight lower than 154 pounds, while Floyd was fighting at 135 less than four years ago. Mayweather had never faced anyone who punched as hard as De La Hoya. And while Oscar would be fighting in the division that's right for him, Floyd was moving above his best weight.

"It doesn't matter," a Mayweather partisan told Freddie Roach. "Floyd has a good chin."

"How good are his ribs?" Roach countered.

Still, the prevailing view was that, when boxing's biggest star faces boxing's best fighter, the best fighter wins. Mayweather's style in the ring is stick, move, and bang. He's technically sound, and his speed makes him special.

In the weeks leading up to the fight, no one made the case for a Mayweather victory more vehemently than Floyd himself:

- "Strength doesn't win fights. Weight doesn't win fights. Ability wins fights. Just because the other guy's got more fat cells, that doesn't mean he's a better fighter."
- "Oscar keeps talking about being in the best shape of his life. Before every fight, he says the same thing. He might come out fast; there are a lot of fighters that are front-runners. But Oscar gets tired, and there's no gas station in that ring."
- "My biggest asset is that I'm a thinking fighter. I'm smart; I'm intelligent; I know my way around the ring much better than Oscar. All the fighters that Oscar beat; I'm a totally different fighter."

- "Oscar can apply pressure. Oscar can throw the big left hook. It ain't gonna work. He'll never hit me with the hook. He'll never hurt me with the hook. You all write, 'This is gonna happen; that's gonna happen.' Trust me, it ain't gonna happen."

"You can apply pressure," Emanuel Steward observed one day before the fight. "You can be aggressive. But if you can't catch the guy you're fighting or if the other guy gets off first, it won't work. Speed has always given Oscar trouble, and Oscar has lost some of his own speed. That comes with age, and it could be a problem. Floyd's speed might make Oscar look even older than he is."

Mayweather is thirty. De La Hoya is thirty-four. Floyd is at his peak as a fighter. Oscar peaked some time ago. Thus, it was instructive to compare De La Hoya with another mega-star who became a part-time fighter in his later years. Sugar Ray Leonard was thirty-four when he was knocked down twice and beaten up by Terry Norris.

And there was one more factor at work. For most of his career, Mayweather had chaffed at being number two at Top Rank (which, for years, promoted both fighters). "I got sick of being behind Oscar," Floyd said recently. "If I had the right promotion behind me from the beginning, I'd be as big as Oscar."

With that in mind, consider Lennox Lewis pursuing Mike Tyson and Antonio Tarver's obsession with Roy Jones Jr. Resentment over being number two can be powerful motivation for a fighter. De La Hoya–Mayweather was the fight that Floyd had wanted for his entire professional career.

Meanwhile, as a commercial venture, De La Hoya–Mayweather was moving into the stratosphere. Boxing was hungry for a big event, and Golden Boy Promotions (together with HBO) had created the most extensive marketing campaign ever for a fight.

The 12,000-seat Mandalay Bay Events Center was sold out for a closed-circuit telecast of the bout. More than 60 percent of the seats in the MGM Grand Garden Arena had a $2,000 price tag attached to them. There were more than 800 requests for media credentials. Three hours before the 2:30 P.M. Friday weigh-in (which was open to the public), 2,000 fans were standing in line to get into the arena. Ultimately, more than 7,000 people watched Oscar tip the scales at 154 pounds while Floyd weighed in at 150 (giving new meaning to the term "weight-watchers"). Several thousand fans were turned away.

"I like people," Freddie Roach said. "But there are crowds everywhere we go and it gets to be a bit much. It's okay for a while. Then you want to go back to quiet."

Something special was building. But there was also a fear factor. Only a handful of mega-fights have lived up to their hype once the bell rang. And it was understood that De La Hoya–Mayweather might fall short of the mark as sports drama.

Floyd isn't interested in entertaining; he's interested in winning. That was also true of his pound-for-pound predecessors (Roy Jones Jr. and Pernell Whitaker). Winning is a champion's bottom line.

Thus, speaking for many in the boxing media, Matt Wells wrote, "Expectations for the success of this fight seem to be running a notch too high. Or perhaps the excessive hyping is a sign of the desperation of boxing's backers in the face of an increasingly disinterested sport-watching public. These two won't collide in the center of the ring the way Diego Corrales and José Luis Castillo did. This will not turn into the sort of brawl that non-boxing fans typically want. Tactically, it could be interesting; but a tactical fight is not worthy of the hype being generated by this event. In a cluttered media world, boxing does not have a lot of chances to get things right."

In other words, no one expected Hagler–Hearns. But beyond that, there was concern that De La Hoya–Mayweather might be a lousy fight. One could envision headlines reading "Golden Boy Lays An Egg" and "Gold-Plated, Not Solid Gold."

By fight night, the odds (which opened at 2-to-1) had dropped to 8-to-5 in Mayweather's favor. In his dressing room, Oscar refused to get on the HBO scale. Presumably, there was a ten-pound weight differential between the fighters; maybe more.

Mayweather entered the ring first, accompanied by rap artist 50 Cent, who was performing his new song, *Straight to the Bank*, in front of a live audience for the first time. Floyd's trunks and robe were red, green, and white (Mexican flag colors), and he was wearing a sombrero. The pro-Oscar crowd didn't like it. Boos as loud as any that have been heard recently in Las Vegas sounded. Then, to the roar of the adoring crowd, De La Hoya came into view. "There were 16,000 people rooting for Oscar and 300 rooting for me," Floyd later acknowledged.

"The best fight I ever fought," Oscar once said, "was my first fight against Julio César Chávez. It was like in *The Matrix* where you could see the bullets coming. Everything Chávez did seemed like it was in slow motion. I knew the punches he was going to throw before he threw them. That had never happened for me before and it has never happened since."

It certainly didn't happen on May 5. To beat Mayweather, De La Hoya had to fight much of the fight the way he fought the last round against Ike Quartey; not the way he fought the last round against Félix Trinidad. It wasn't to be.

Mayweather spent most of the night circling in the center of the ring (where his speed gave him an advantage) and getting off first when it mattered. If a superior boxer goes toe-to-toe with his opponent, it evens out the odds. Floyd had no intention of doing that.

Oscar moved methodically forward. When he did it behind his jab, he was effective. When he stopped jabbing, Floyd peppered him at will. On those occasions when De La Hoya got Mayweather against the ropes, he tried to maul him and hook to the body. But while Oscar threw more body punches than in any of his previous fights, Floyd blocked most of them with his arms.

Mayweather landed the sharper blows; but at 154 pounds, he lacked concussive power. Also, while he often made De La Hoya miss (Oscar landed only 21 percent of the punches he threw), Floyd didn't make him pay as often as he should have. A smirk is not a scoring blow.

After eight rounds, the fight was even on the judges' scorecards. Then, as has happened before, De La Hoya tired down the stretch. Mayweather won a 116–112, 115–113, 113–115 split decision. This observer gave Floyd the nod by a 115–113 margin. Oscar made the fight with his constant aggression but Mayweather won it, outlanding De La Hoya 207-to-122 (70 percent more punches landed).

Floyd did what people thought he would do. Oscar did a bit more than was expected of him. It was a good fight, not a great one.

So, what did we learn from De La Hoya–Mayweather?

First, it's clear that there's still a market for properly promoted match-ups between quality fighters, particularly if one of the fighters is named Oscar.

De La Hoya–Mayweather generated 2.4 million pay-per-view buys for a domestic gross of $134 million in pay-per-view revenue. Those numbers constitute single-fight records and vaulted Oscar past Mike Tyson into the number-one slot in terms of lifetime buys (12,590,000) and PPV revenue ($610,600,000). De La Hoya is the Golden Boy with the golden touch.

Second, we learned that Oscar is still a very good fighter. But he has won just seven fights over the past eight years and lost three of his last five. He's competitive in mega-fights, but doesn't win them. Budd Schulberg once wrote, "The great legends of boxing fought the last round as if their lives depended on it." De La Hoya falls short of that standard. And he has never beaten a great fighter in his prime.

Mayweather showed the world that he might someday be a fighter of legendary proportions, but he's not there yet. "It was a masterpiece of boxing," Floyd chortled after the fight. "I showed you why I'm the best fighter of this era."

But like De La Hoya, Mayweather has yet to beat a great fighter in his prime. Seven years ago, Shane Mosley beat a twenty-seven-year-old Oscar more decisively than Floyd beat the thirty-four-year-old model. And the jury is still out on whether Mayweather will be willing to walk through fire if that's what it takes to win.

"I don't want to have to prove my greatness by having my eyes bleeding and getting knocked down and having to get up to win," Floyd told Tim Smith of the *New York Daily News*. "That doesn't make any sense. People that talk like that just want me to take an 'L.'"

Meanwhile, boxing is in better shape today than it was two weeks ago. A boring fight, a crazy stoppage, or an unjust decision would have further soured mainstream America on the sport. But most people were satisfied with what they saw. And for a while at least, the sweet science was front and center in the public mind.

Naysayers proclaim (and it's true) that boxing has become a niche sport in the United States. But boxing isn't dying. It's a rapidly globalizing sport. Boxing in what was once the Soviet Union isn't at risk. Boxing in Germany isn't at risk. Boxing in the Philippines isn't at risk. In those places, the sport is thriving.

In a way, boxing is like live theater. When motion pictures became popular, social commentators warned that theater would die. It didn't. Then television swept into American homes. Surely, that would be the death knell for live theater. But theater survived.

So will boxing.

I like taking an event that thousands of people are writing about and finding a different angle.

First Bout at 3:05 P.M.

Boxing's historical record, like most forms of history, centers on the exploits of kings, not foot soldiers. But the sweet science is about more than great champions. Journeymen, faceless opponents, and young fighters with optimism are an integral part of the game.

On Saturday, May 5, 2007, Oscar De La Hoya and Floyd Mayweather Jr. met in the ring after the most extensive marketing campaign in the history of boxing. Five hours earlier, on the same square of illuminated canvas, two unknown fighters faced off against one another in an eight-round lightweight contest. This is the story of those preliminary-bout fighters.

Ernest Johnson is a twenty-seven-year-old African-American from Chula Vista, California. His father is a boxing trainer. His mother works for GMAC Financial Services in foreclosures and loans.

Growing up, Johnson played sports year-round. He began boxing at age thirteen, compiled a 68–11 amateur record, and was good enough to be invited to the 2000 Olympic trials. But boxing was sandwiched between track (400 meters was his specialty), football (he started in high school as a wide receiver), and baseball (pitcher and centerfield). Ernest also wrestled at 125 pounds, fashioned a 101–19 record, and was offered a wrestling scholarship to Cal State Fullerton. But he turned it down to pursue a career in boxing.

"I decided to take boxing seriously when I got out of high school," Johnson says. "You can't make a living wrestling."

To make ends meet, Johnson manages a gym and works as a personal trainer for fifteen to twenty hours a week. "I want to go back to school someday," he says. "Get into physical therapy and maybe open my own gym."

Johnson's best weapons as a fighter are his speed and his jab. Prior to his May 5 bout, his record stood at sixteen wins against two losses with seven knockouts. But only three of his victories had come against opponents with a winning ledger. And on the two occasions when he stepped up in class, he'd lost unanimous ten-round decisions.

"The first loss," Ernest says, "I took the fight on six days notice and it was close. The second one, I overtrained because of the first loss. I had no snap on my punches and my shoulder was bothering me because of tendonitis and a slight muscle tear."

After his second defeat (in November 2004), Johnson took twenty-six months off for physical therapy and to let his shoulder heal. This would be his second fight after the layoff.

Johnson had been in a big-fight atmosphere before. Six years earlier, he'd made his pro debut on the undercard of Floyd Mayweather Jr. versus Diego Corrales. Not long after that, he ran into Mayweather at a supermarket in Las Vegas. "I introduced myself and he was nice," Ernest remembers. "Just to be part of something like this is huge. You never know who might see you or put you on another card. This is a stepping stone that I hope will lead to something bigger."

On the afternoon of May 5, Johnson arrived at the MGM Grand Garden Arena at 1:45 P.M. He and four other fighters had been assigned to dressing room 2. Ernest was wearing black sweatpants, a black T-shirt, black warm-up pants, and a black Everlast ski cap. His father, Ernest Johnson Sr., was with him.

There were six rectangular tables in the room; one for Nevada State Athletic Commission officials and one for each fighter's camp. John O'Donnell and John Murray (two Brits with undefeated records who were scheduled to fight in the second and third bouts) were already there. Johnson sat on a chair and adjusted the earpiece on his MP3 player, then scanned the display window to decide what to listen to next.

A commission inspector came into the room.

"Should we go ahead and wrap?" Ernest Johnson Sr. asked.

"Yes."

Johnson began taping his son's hands. Eric Gomez (the matchmaker for Golden Boy) entered. "You're the first fight," he told the Johnsons. "Be ready to go at three o'clock." Then Gomez turned to the inspector. "Walk him out at three o'clock sharp."

At 2:15, the taping was done. Around the room, other fighters were being primed for battle. Johnson found a small square of unoccupied space and shadow-boxed for several minutes.

Referee Vic Drakulich came in and gave Ernest his pre-fight instructions.

The fighter began hitting warm-up pads with his father.

It was 2:55 P.M. "Get your robe on, Johnson," the inspector ordered.

At three o'clock sharp, Ernest left the dressing room and was escorted through a brightly-lit corridor to the arena floor. There was no ring-walk music. When he stepped into the ring, he looked across the enclosure and saw a young man named Hector Beltran.

Beltran was born in Mexico and came to the United States with his family at age two. His stepfather is a truck driver; his mother works for a catering service. A long ugly scar runs across his abdomen. "I was a miracle baby," Hector says. "When I was two months old, the doctor told my mom there was only a small chance I'd live. My organs were all tangled up, so they did the surgery. I'm here, so I'd say it came out pretty good."

Beltran began boxing at age twelve. "I was riding my bike past a gym," he remembers. "The door was open, so I stopped and looked in. The coach asked if I wanted to come inside, but I rode away. The next week, the same thing happened, only this time I went in. It was something to do and it kept me out of trouble."

A year later, Beltran had his first amateur fight. "I was nervous," he recalls. "But a few days before, I had a puppy three months old that was stolen. Just before the bell rang, my coach told me, 'See that guy across the ring. Pretend like he's the guy that stole your puppy.' That got me going."

Beltran graduated from high school and now works as an inventory clerk in shipping and receiving for the Winn Meat Company in Dallas. His record as he stood across from Johnson was 10-and-1 with 9 knockouts, but the numbers were deceiving. The fighters he'd beaten were, for the most part, "professional losers." In his only bout against an opponent with a winning record, Hector had lost a six-round split decision.

"The fight I lost," Beltran says, "my son, Hector Jr., was born six days before it. And two days after he was born, I broke up with my girlfriend. My head wasn't into boxing. I only sparred one day for that fight."

The loss was followed by two knockout wins, but Beltran was inactive for seventeen months after that. Then, in late April, he was offered the opportunity to fight on the undercard of De La Hoya versus Mayweather.

"This caught me off guard," Hector acknowledged one day before the fight. "I took some time off from boxing to get my life in order, and I have responsibilities to my son. It's hard to work nine-to-five, share custody of my boy, and be in the gym, all at the same time. I've only sparred for a week for this fight. But I'm a much better fighter than what I get credit for. I'm young [twenty-two years old]. I have good power and mental toughness. This is a break-out opportunity for me."

"By the way," Beltran added. "My puppy that was stolen; it was a pit-bull. I don't want anyone thinking it was a poodle."

The first time that Johnson and Beltran saw each other was on Friday afternoon at two o'clock when they reported for their pre-fight physicals in Studio 1 at the MGM Grand Garden Arena. They sat side by side, filling out forms at a Nevada State Athletic Commission table and barely glanced at one another. Each man is likeable, soft-spoken, and polite, but they didn't speak.

"It's a little awkward," Johnson said afterward. "You know you're going to fight this guy tomorrow, so you kind of size him up. Anyone who says he doesn't is lying."

What did he think of Beltran?

"They say he's a puncher, but I've never seen him fight or watched tapes. He's taller than I thought. I was expecting a shorter fighter."

After their physical examinations, each man weighed in at 137 pounds. The highlight of the day for Beltran was that he got to shake hands with De La Hoya when Oscar came in for his own physical. "Oscar is my hero," Hector said. "I grew up watching him fight, and I admire the way he has control of his whole life. When we shook hands, he seemed real nice."

On the afternoon of the fight, Beltran entered dressing room 4 at 1:20 P.M. A "participant" credential hung from a chain around his neck. Trainer Dennis Rodarte and assistant trainer Pablo Cortez were with him.

The dressing room was empty. Hector sat on a straight-backed chair and text-messaged a friend. Then he lay down on the carpeted floor, put a rolled-up towel beneath his head, and stared at the ceiling. Several minutes later, he crossed his arms across his chest, turned his head to the side, and closed his eyes.

Each of the five fighters assigned to dressing room 4 was an underdog. The fights had been made for their opponents to win.

At two o'clock, Hector stood up, took a pair of worn red boxing shoes out of a red gym bag, and put them on. The room was beginning to fill up with other undercard fighters and their cornermen.

Rodarte taped Beltran's hands. When he was done, Hector put on his red velvet trunks and gloved up.

At 2:35, Eric Gomez entered the room. "We walk at three," he told Rodarte. "You've got twenty-five minutes."

Beltran went into the adjacent shower room and began hitting warm-up pads with Cortez. After he fought, Hector would take a shower. Thereafter, the shower room floor would be wet and useless to the other fighters for warm-up purposes.

Rodarte put Vaseline on Beltran's face.

Ring announcer Lupe Contreras came into the dressing room and asked Hector how he'd like to be introduced.

"Handsome."

"Handsome Hector Beltran?"

"Yes, sir."

"Out of Dallas?"

"Right."

The doors to the arena had yet to open when Beltran and Johnson made their way to the ring. There were no paying spectators in the stands. The only people present were HBO technicians, ushers, Nevada State Athletic Commission personnel, and a few others with jobs to do.

Contreras took the microphone. "Ladies and gentlemen," he intoned. "Welcome to the MGM Grand Garden Arena for one of the most anticipated nights in the history of boxing."

Beltran was introduced first: "In the blue corner, fighting out of Dallas, Texas, Handsome Hector Beltran."

Johnson's introduction followed. At precisely 3:05 P.M., the bell for round one rang. The doors were now open. There were fourteen paying customers in the stands.

Beltran came out firing power shots early in round one, while Johnson tried to establish his jab. Hector won the round on each judge's scorecard. Then things fell into a pattern. At the start of each round, Beltran was an effective aggressor, but he would tire at which point Johnson fired back. Ernest should have forced Hector to work harder. By not pushing him, he allowed Beltran to rest when he needed to.

Each man's corner shouted encouragement throughout the fight, but the crowd was silent because there was no crowd. Beltran was the harder puncher. Occasionally, he turned southpaw, looking for different angles. After round six, Rodarte put a big gob of Vaseline on Hector's cheek, possibly hoping that Drakulich would order him to wipe it off, thereby giving his fighter an extra ten seconds of rest. But the referee let it go.

Round seven belonged to Johnson. Then Beltran dug deep and rallied to win the final stanza. The decision of the judges was a draw.

In his dressing room afterward, Johnson was disappointed. "His switching back and forth caught me off guard," Ernest admitted. "I didn't know he did that. And I was anticipating his getting tired, but he did and then he didn't."

In dressing room 4, Beltran was in a happier mood. "I know I should stay in the gym more," he acknowledged. "But when you don't get a fight for a while, you don't train like you should. This was good. It's something to build on."

A commission inspector approached with pen and paper in hand.

"Hector, do you want to sign for your check?"

A smile crossed Beltran's face.

"Yeah, I do want that."

Across the room, Lorenzo Bethea, a junior welterweight from Atlantic City, was readying for battle. Bethea had lost four of his previous six fights and, in a matter of minutes, would enter the ring to match his skills against John Murray (who was undefeated in twenty bouts and being groomed for stardom). An hour later, Bethea would be in an ambulance on his way to the hospital with bleeding in his brain.

Meanwhile, upstairs, a mass of humanity had entered the MGM Grand Hotel and Casino. The passageway leading from the hotel registration desk to the casino floor was like a New York City subway platform at rush hour. Every gaming table was full. Bettors were lining up to walk into the sports book and move within view of the odds boards and giant television screens. The big fight was four hours away. The MGM Grand was the place to be.

Shannon Briggs has frustrated admirers and critics alike for years. June 2, 2007, was no exception.

The Enigmatic Shannon Briggs

Perpendicular to the boardwalk in Atlantic City, a four-story shopping mall called The Pier Shops at Caesars extends across a narrow beach and juts out over the Atlantic Ocean. Standing at the eastern end of the mall, one can gaze at the ocean and see Herman Melville's "great shroud of the sea" as it rolled on thousands of years ago.

But turn away from the ocean and a vastly different scene beckons. Large gaps of urban decay are visible between the hotel casinos that mark the skyline. Tourists walking along the boardwalk are solicited by panhandlers. The Miss America Pageant (once Atlantic City's showcase event) is gone. Seedy shops and 99-cent discount stores proliferate.

When Shannon Briggs and Sultan Ibragimov came to Atlantic City to fight for the WBO heavyweight title on June 2, the metaphor was obvious. There was a time when great heavyweight champions were viewed as forces of nature and the most compelling of their battles stirred passions across the ocean. But the phrase "world champion" is now an anachronism. Boxing has WBC champions, WBA champions, WBO champions, and IBF champions, but most of them are "WHO?" champions.

The heavyweight division epitomizes boxing's plight. Since Lennox Lewis retired in 2004, thirteen men have claimed a portion of the throne. Don King looks at the bright side and declares, "The heavyweights aren't down and out. The heavyweights are in a state of glorious equal opportunity." But in truth, the heavyweight division has come to resemble a bizarre game of musical chairs with four belts being passed from fighter to fighter. Whoever holds a belt when the music stops is anointed a champion.

Briggs came to Atlantic City as the WBO champion. Despite occasional outbursts of grumpiness and self-pity, Shannon is personable and articulate. A dozen years ago, he was young and full of hope; a highly-touted amateur who won his first twenty-five professional fights (twenty by knockout with fifteen KOs in the first round). That led to an appearance on HBO's *Night of the Young Heavyweights,* but he faltered and was stopped by Darroll Wilson in three rounds. Then, in November 1997, Shannon fought George Foreman for the "lineal" heavyweight crown (Foreman had beaten Michael Moorer but was stripped of the WBA and IBF titles for refusing to fight mandatory opponents). George won the fight but Briggs got the decision. In the new champion's next outing, he lost to Lennox Lewis on a fifth-round stoppage.

Briggs is now thirty-five years old. The one inexcusable defeat on his record is a loss by decision to Sedrick Fields. He also came out on the wrong end of the verdict in a 2002 bout against Jameel McCline. But Shannon has forty-eight victories, the most important of which occurred on November 4, 2006. That night, trailing on the judges' scorecards, he rallied to stop Sergei Liakhovich with one second left in the twelfth round and annex the WBO crown.

Briggs's critics say that his career has been built on smoke and mirrors; that other than Foreman and Liakhovich, he has never beaten a world-class fighter; that his reputation as a puncher (forty-two KOs) is based largely on blasting out guys who can't take a punch. But more significantly, Shannon has been known throughout his career as a fighter who isn't willing to pay the requisite price for greatness, either in training camp or in his fights.

The two things that most boxers like least are training and getting hit. Briggs, it is said, goes to extreme lengths to avoid both. His detractors claim that, whatever expectations his fans have of him, he always disappoints.

Briggs rejects such criticism, particularly when it comes from the media. "The sky fell down on me when I lost to Darroll Wilson," he says. "Ever since then, people have been ragging on me, saying, 'Shannon Briggs doesn't have it.' But most of the people who write bad about me don't know the first thing about what it means to be a fighter, so it doesn't matter what they say. I've learned over time that I'm a much tougher person than I thought I was. I always knew I was physically tough, but mentally is something else. I don't let the negative things that people say about me hurt me anymore."

"And I fight with a disease," Briggs continues. "People don't understand that. I have asthma. When the asthma is bad, I can't walk up a flight of stairs without being out of breath. When a football player or basketball player has an asthma attack, he comes out of the game and sits on the bench. That option isn't available to me, so I have to pick up the newspapers and read all the idiots who write, 'Shannon is out of shape; he got tired in the first round.' Is anyone really stupid enough to believe that I'd be gasping for air in the first round if I didn't have asthma? Do they really think that I don't train enough to get through one round without breathing hard?"

Briggs's health was part of the storyline leading up to the fight. He and Ibragimov had originally been scheduled to meet at Madison Square Garden on March 10, but a brush with pneumonia forced Shannon to withdraw from that encounter. Ultimately, the match was rescheduled for Atlantic City. Warriors Boxing (which has promotional rights to Sultan) was the promoter by virtue of a $2.5 million purse bid that was divided $1,875,000 to Team Briggs and $625,000 to the Ibragimov camp. It's unclear how much of Briggs's purse went to Don King, but King had a rooting interest in the outcome of the fight since he holds promotional rights to Shannon.

When Briggs met Ibragimov for the first time (at the kick-off press conference for their planned Madison Square Garden confrontation), he voiced pleasure at how small Sultan was. There was a four-inch, fifty-pound differential between them. And Ibragimov doesn't look like a fighter. At best, he conjures up images of a linebacker for an Ivy League football team.

Moreover, although Ibragimov was coming into the fight with a 20–0–1 (17 KOs) ledger, he had never beaten a world-class fighter. The toughest opponent on his record was Ray Austin, who Sultan battled to a draw in July 2006. Given Austin's performance against Wladimir Klitschko earlier this year, that left a lot to be desired.

"Ibragimov doesn't belong in the same ring as me," Briggs declared as the fight neared. "He got rated because of who he's associated with." When informed (inaccurately, as it turned out) that Mike Tyson would be in Sultan's corner as one of his seconds on fight night, Shannon responded, "It doesn't matter to me. He can have Jesus in his corner for all I care."

But Ibragimov (a silver medalist for Russia in the 2000 Olympics) was a 9-to-5 betting favorite. Part of that was based on the fact that he would be the first southpaw that Briggs had faced as a pro. And part of it was based on the belief that Shannon simply wasn't in shape.

Once a slender heavyweight, Briggs has become a large bulky man. He started his career at 205 pounds and weighed 227 for his signature victory over George Foreman. But in Atlantic City, he tipped the scales at 273 pounds, giving credence to the view that he hadn't trained much and that neither his head nor his heart were into fighting. The assumption was that Ibragimov would stay on Shannon's chest all night long, throw punches with abandon, and force Briggs to fight at a fast pace. Shannon, the theory went, wouldn't be able to do that for more than a few rounds. So unless Sultan got caught with something big early, it would be his fight.

"People can think anything they want," Briggs said one day before the fight. "What's going to happen is going to happen. I don't live in fear. I've been in this business a long time. I've persevered; I've prevailed; I'm still here."

On the night of June 2, Briggs entered his dressing room at Boardwalk Hall at precisely nine o'clock. Trainer Yoel Judah and several other camp members were with him. Don King, bejeweled and wearing his trademark red-white-and-blue "Only In America" jacket, followed.

The room was overly air-conditioned and uncomfortably cold. Shannon's first words upon entering were, "Can someone make it a little warmer in here?" Over the next two hours, the temperature never changed.

Shannon sat on a folding metal chair in the corner. Don King sat beside him, holding a small American flag in each hand.

"The true heavyweight champion of the world," King proclaimed. "Shannon 'The Cannon' Briggs. This show is on the road. You're going to kick ass. There's no stopping us now, brother."

Briggs had brought mood music with him. A mellow voice sounded through the room. Shannon closed his eyes and leaned back in his chair.

"Oh, girl; let me hold you tight . . . Can we make love, baby? Can we make love?"

It was music for sipping wine on the way to a seduction; not what one normally hears when a fighter is in his dressing room readying for combat.

Tempering his persona to the mood, King sat quietly.

At 9:20, Shannon rose from his chair, took a pair of silver trunks from his gym bag, and put them on. Then he moved to the mirror and studied his image before taking a second pair of trunks (black with white-and-gold trim) from the bag and holding them over his lower body.

Silver.

Black.

Silver.

Black.

He repeated the process several times.

"Which ones look better?" he asked at last.

King had a look on his face that said, "I thought I'd seen everything in boxing, but I ain't never seen anything like this."

"The silver ones have more shine to them," King offered.

"You won the title wearing the black ones," Scott Hirsch (Briggs's manager) noted.

"Then go with the black ones," King said.

Shannon solicited several more opinions before opting for black. Then he chose black shoes rather than white. That done, he turned to King.

"The room they have me in at Bally's is pitiful. I'm the heavyweight champion of the world, and the treatment I've received is ridiculous."

"You're gonna make them pay for that shit," King assured him.

"Before I beat Liakhovich, everyone was crying that there's no American heavyweight champion. So I beat Liakhovich, and what happens?"

The room was quiet for long stretches of time with only the background music intruding on the silence.

"Touching your lips to mine . . . Every day, every night . . . Baby, baby; making love between the sheets."

Briggs sipped slowly from a container of black coffee. At 9:30, he began doing stretching excercises on the floor.

"I want to feel you. I want to caress you. I want to touch you . . . Don't say goodbye when you know I've got to have your love."

There was quiet conversation around the room.

Shannon interrupted his stretching for a brief cell-phone conversation before resuming his pre-fight preparation. Then he lay down face-first on a towel on the floor for a massage. The dressing room seemed less like the calm before the storm than the calm before more calm.

The massage ended. Shannon's hands were taped.

The music changed to gangsta rap.

"Nigger . . . Motherfucker . . . Big titties . . . Smoking some crack . . . Push me in . . . Seventeen stab wounds . . . Shots in the air . . . Laying him out."

Shannon gloved up, moved to the center of the room, and began working the pads with assistant trainer Carlos Albuerne. There was no fire.

Yoel Judah took Shannon aside.

"Come on, man," Yoel said. "Do what you got to do. He ain't never been hit as hard as you're gonna hit him. I promise you."

Shannon looked down, averting his eyes.

"He can't beat you, man. It's your show. You're gonna catch him. He's going down."

Shannon sat down on the folding metal chair in the corner of the room and stretched out his legs.

"You walk in five minutes," he was told.

Yoel picked up the pads and began working with his fighter.

"Nice . . . There it is . . . Hands are fast, reflexes are sharp . . . Take him to school, baby . . . Beautiful . . . Hands like bricks. Hit him like that and he goes."

But there was no conviction in Yoel's voice.

Shannon stopped punching and sat down on the chair again with a look of resignation on his face. A few minutes later, he left for the ring.

"America, baby," Don King said as they left the dressing room. "Bring it home, brother."

It wasn't much of a fight. Briggs won round one with his jab. But more significantly, midway through the stanza, he whacked Ibragimov with a solid right hand and Sultan took it well. There would be no early knockout.

Thereafter, the bout fell into a pattern that elicited boos from the crowd for most of the night. Briggs threw a lot of stay-away-from-me jabs, while Ibragimov circled and attacked cautiously from time to time. The dance played out in the center of the ring. Absent an early knockout, Shannon's plan was to conserve energy through a strategy similar to a basketball team that runs down the clock before shooting because, the more scoring there is, the more its chances fade. Ibragimov's surprising lack of aggression fed into Briggs's need to shorten the fight. But it didn't matter.

Shannon was strangely passive. He simply didn't throw punches, and a fighter has to throw punches to win. Sultan dictated when punches were exchanged (which wasn't often) and landed the more telling blows. This observer scored it 117–112 for Ibragimov. The judges reached a similar verdict.

Briggs lost badly. Not in the sense that he was beaten up or knocked out. Badly in the sense that he never did what a champion is supposed to do when he gets in the ring. Shannon didn't defend the title as much as he gave it up. In the dressing room afterward, he seemed more relieved that the fight was over than hurt by the loss. He also struck an ungracious note, saying, "Ibragimov is a coward; he's a punk. He was running the whole time. He was scared to death."

Then Shannon addressed the matter of his own performance. "I came into the fight wounded," he said. "Three weeks ago, I was diagnosed with pneumonia again. I missed the last three weeks of training and, before that, there were forest fires in Florida so I couldn't run because the air was bad. If it wasn't for that, my timing and stamina would have been better and I could have pressed him. But there were no bullets in my gun."

"Do you hear what I'm saying?" Briggs continued. "I fought with pneumonia. I wasn't happy about it, but what could I do? I've got two kids to feed. I had to fight because it was like, 'If you don't fight now, you'll be stripped of the title and you'll never fight on television again.' In football, if you're hurt and can't play, you still get paid. In basketball, if you're hurt and can't play, you still get paid. In boxing, you don't get paid if you don't fight. It's an ugly business, but at least I made some money tonight."

That, of course, raises the question, "How does a fighter with pneumonia pass a pre-fight physical?"

On May 24, 2007, Briggs was examined in Florida by Dr. Alan Fields, who told this writer on June 5, "I didn't conduct a full pulminary examination, but his lungs were clear and I saw no clinical evidence of pneumonia."

Fields's report was forwarded to the WBO and the New Jersey State Athletic Control Board. Nick Lembo of the NJSACB has since said, "Everyone at the agency was fully aware of Mr. Briggs's pre-existing health conditions and the stated reasons for the postponement of the same match-up previously scheduled [for March 10] at Madison Square Garden. Due to the issues involved, the commissioner [Larry Hazzard] specifically assigned ringside physician Dr. Michael Kelly to review all of Briggs's pre-licensing medicals and to conduct both the pre- and post-fight medical exams. Mr. Briggs's lungs were examined both prior to and after the bout. Mr. Briggs was cleared to fight by Dr. Kelly. The NJSACB had no concerns about Briggs's physical ability to compete that night."

There are three possibilities: (1) there's something wrong with the way the New Jersey State Athletic Control Board administers pre-fight physicals; (2) false statements were made and false documents were submitted to the board (in which case, a crime was committed); or (3) Briggs didn't have pneumonia in the weeks leading up to the fight.

On June 5, Larry Hazzard told this writer, "Fighters offer all kinds of excuses after a loss. Either Shannon lied to us or he lied to the media after the fight. I really don't know which it was."

Maybe Hazzard should find out.

Meanwhile, before condemning Briggs, one should keep in mind the thoughts of James Baldwin, who, decades ago, wrote, "Life is far from being as simple as most sportswriters would like to have it."

Boxing is the toughest sport in the world, and Shannon is the one who has to get in the ring and fight. He's the one who traded blows with Lennox Lewis and George Foreman and was punched countless times by men trained in the art of hurting. There are those who say that he failed to live up to his potential as a fighter; that he went from young to old without ever having had a prime. But Shannon is content with where his life is today.

"I feel like I've been successful in boxing," Briggs said after his loss to Ibragimov. "I didn't achieve the status of a Mike Tyson or a Lennox Lewis, but I'm happy with what I achieved. Coming from where I came from, homeless in Brooklyn, sleeping in shelters, everything I did was an accomplishment. How many kids come from where I did and break the cycle? People who've been comfortable all their life and were given everything when they were young think it's easy to break away from a bad situation. They say stupid things like, 'Just go out and work hard.' But most people who come from where I came from wind up doing what their parents did and living like their parents lived. I live in a million-dollar home in a gated community in Florida. I've got one son in private school and another son who will be there when he's old enough to go. I don't care what anyone else says. I made good; I'm proud of what I've accomplished. And I was the lineal heavyweight champion of the world whether people like it or not."

After several unsatisfying championship fights, boxing put its best foot forward with Miguel Cotto versus Zab Judah.

Bob Arum Mans the Ramparts with Cotto–Judah

The first fight that Bob Arum promoted was Muhammad Ali versus George Chuvalo in 1966. Arum is seventy-five years old now. He and Don King are self-described "dinosaurs of the sport." But while King has seen his influence fade in recent years, Arum's remains constant. His current roster of fighters includes Manny Pacquiao, Antonio Margarito, Kelly Pavlik, Erik Morales, José Luis Castillo, Humberto Soto, Kid Diamond, Jorge Arce, Julio César Chávez Jr., Hasim Rahman, and Miguel Cotto.

Arum constructs his arguments and states his positions with precise logic. To hear him tell it, morality and the good of boxing are always on his side. He speaks with total sincerity and conviction in his voice. When he says that X is "a great, great fighter" and Y versus Z is "a great, great matchup," he sounds as though he believes it's true. When he is aggrieved, the pain of the moment is etched on his face. He's smart and, at times, ruthless. Like all successful boxing promoters, he's obsessed with his trade. How else does one explain a seventy-five-year-old man flying 15,000 miles so he can slog through the Philippines and campaign for Manny Pacquiao in a congressional race against Darlene Antonino Custodio?

Having fulfilled his commitment to democracy in the Pacific rim, Arum returned last week to a more familiar role. On June 9, he promoted Miguel Cotto against Zab Judah at Madison Square Garden. In many ways, that fight meant more to the future of boxing than last month's encounter between Oscar De La Hoya and Floyd Mayweather Jr. In his golden years, Arum has become a standard bearer for the sweet science.

This was the third consecutive year in which Arum promoted a Cotto fight at the Garden on the eve of the Puerto Rican Day Parade. But this time, the competition for media attention, television viewers, and on-site fans was less formidable than in the past.

In 2005, Cotto versus Mohamad Abdulaev was up against Mike Tyson's farewell battle with Kevin McBride. Then, in 2006, Arum matched Cotto against Paulie Malignaggi, only to learn that HBO was planning a pay-per-view telecast of Bernard Hopkins versus Antonio Tarver from Atlantic City on the same night.

Arum was livid. First, he aimed his fire at Hopkins. "Last year before the Puerto Rican Day Parade," Arum proclaimed, "Cotto fought Abdulaev and it was such a success that we reserved Madison Square Garden for this year. Bernard Hopkins—and you know how Hopkins feels about Puerto Ricans; he defaced the flag while he was in Puerto Rico—tried to get Madison Square Garden for the same date this year, knowing we had it reserved. Can you imagine that? This moron wants to reserve Madison Square Garden the night before the Puerto Rican Day Parade to fight Tarver. Is that fucking moronic? Fortunately we had a hold on it."

Then Roberto Arum turned his attention to HBO and declared, "I've never encountered a situation where people you were loyal to and have done business with for years would do something like that. Instead of working with promoters like they've done in the past, they've become promoters themselves. They make the fights, just like promoters, and pay fighters. HBO wants to eliminate Don King and Bob Arum. HBO wants a monopoly, and they aren't getting it."

"We're not playing around here," Arum continued. "We're going to blow the other guys out of the water. This will be a road map for other promoters and show people in boxing that there's an alternative to HBO. We're going to sell out Madison Square Garden and beat their asses on pay-per-view. I don't give a shit how much money Time Warner has; we'll beat them."

Arum marketed Cotto–Malignaggi as boxing's version of *West Side Story*, playing excerpts from *When You're A Jet* at the kick-off press conference. He also brought in heavy artilliary in the form of a multi-ethnic ten-bout undercard featuring John Duddy, Julio César Chévez Jr., Kevin Kelley, Juan Manuel López, and a Notre Dame football player named Tommy Zbikowski, who was making his pro debut. George Foreman was hired to serve as a color commentator for the telecast.

Cotto–Malignaggi drew 14,000 fans to the Garden. But HBO's power was evident in the world of pay-per-view. Tarver–Hopkins did 330,000 buys, while Cotto–Malignaggi scored 60,000.

This year, Arum's Puerto Rican festival was an HBO-PPV telecast and the promoter had a new target. Arum spent years developing Oscar De La Hoya, only to see his prime attraction jump ship and start his own promotional company. Worse, Oscar has been successful in leveraging his popularity to gain an advantage with HBO. Rubbing salt into the wound, in addition to promoting thirty-nine of De La Hoya's first forty-two pro fights, Arum promoted thirty-five of Mayweather's first thirty-seven. But when Oscar and

Floyd met earlier this year in the largest-grossing fight of all time, Arum was on the sidelines.

One was tempted to feel a bit sorry for Arum when De La Hoya–Mayweather rolled around. "Any moron can take two superstars that someone else has developed and put them together," he said. "Boxing needs promoters who develop fighters. We're very proud that we developed both guys and we really believe that, without us, this fight wouldn't happen; so I think that's a real feather in our cap. Are we saddened because we're not promoting it? Sure, we'd have loved to promote the fight, but you can't have everything."

Meanwhile, a firefight was erupting between Arum and Golden Boy CEO Richard Schaefer. Referring to a suitcase filled with $250,000 in cash that Golden Boy had given to Manny Pacquiao in an effort to sign the fighter, Arum declared, "These people will do anything to achieve their purposes. Now, I don't know if there's anything illegal in giving a suitcase full of twenty-dollar bills that total $250,000 to somebody. I wouldn't do it. That's not the way I do business."

Then, when Golden Boy failed in its effort to get a court order that would have halted the April 14 championship bout between Pacquiao and Jorge Solis, Arum proclaimed, "It's a disgrace that, with all of the money he makes from fighting, De La Hoya would spend so much time and money trying to stop fighters from fighting. He is supposed to promote fights, not prohibit them."

In sum, boxing had a new mega-fight entitled, "The World Awaits Arum–Schaefer."

"In Golden Boy, I'm dealing with a Swiss banker with that mentality," Arum told Steve Kim of Maxboxing. "Remember, Swiss bankers come from a long line of people who acted in extraordinary ways that most people don't. I'll never forget the Swiss bankers during the second World War, what they did to my people. Leopards don't change their spots."

"Arum is Arum," Schaefer responded. "It's unfortunate that he says these kinds of things. But they call him 'the snake,' and this is not just a name you get. You have to earn it. If somebody is called a snake, you know what that means. I'd rather be a Swiss banker than a snake."

Meanwhile, there was a fight to be fought at Madison Square Garden on June 9.

To his adoring fans, Miguel Cotto is one of them. Félix Trinidad was the boy next door turned matinee idol; the man their sisters dream of marrying. Cotto is the guy they work side by side with on the job and the man their sisters actually marry.

Cotto is stoic, quiet, and a very good fighter. "The guy is vicious," says Paulie Malignaggi, who absorbed a brutal beating in going the distance against Miguel in June 2006. "Every round, he lets you know you're in there with him. He hits hard. He's always in your face. If he's not hitting you clean, he's hitting you low, butting you, throwing you around, being physical."

Judah talked a good game in the days leading up to the fight. "I'm not just from Brooklyn," he advised the media. "I'm New York City; I'm worldwide.

Miguel Cotto is a local fighter. If you step outside the Latino community, Miguel Cotto is a nobody."

Then, after naming Cotto "the robot," Zab decreed, "When you match a great fighter against a robot, there's going to be a malfunction. Cotto has no jab. He has no right hand. All he does is throw hooks, and he has to plant his feet to throw."

Judah's partisans felt that he had the speed and southpaw style to outbox Cotto and a punch that was good enough to test Miguel's chin. But the other side of the coin was that Zab hadn't won in more than two years and was burdened with a history of imploding in big fights. His last appearance at Madison Square Garden had resulted in an embarrassing loss to Carlos Baldomir. Then he'd gone to Las Vegas, where he lost a decision to Floyd Mayweather Jr. Zab had the tools to make things interesting, but the assumption was that, once Cotto hit him a few times, he'd revert to form.

"Don't think that Paulie Malignaggi going twelve rounds with Cotto means that Judah will do it," Arum cautioned. "Malignaggi didn't give Cotto problems. Making weight gave Cotto problems. At 140 pounds, Miguel was losing muscle to make weight. Now he's at 147."

On fight night, the Garden was sold out for boxing for the first time since Holyfield–Lewis I in 1999. Brooklyn might have been "in the house," but Brooklyn was hard to find. As the fighters made their way to the ring, there were prolonged boos for Judah and a sustained roar for Cotto. This wasn't a Las Vegas crowd. These were fight fans, loud and passionate. They had come for a fight, not an event.

Cotto was a 3-to-1 betting favorite, but Judah didn't go quietly. The one predictable thing about Zab is that he will be unpredictable. This shaped up as possibly the final crossroads bout in his career, and he fought like it. "He hit me pretty good," Cotto admitted afterward. "He had me in trouble two, maybe three, times."

It was a brutal bloody dramatic war. In round one, Judah played matador to Cotto's bull before landing a sizzling left uppercut followed by a sharp straight left that wobbled Miguel. Cotto steadied himself and, moments later, fired the first of several notable low blows that he landed during the fight. That earned a warning from referee Arthur Mercante Jr. and was reminiscent of the manner in which Félix Trinidad (Miguel's esteemed countryman) went low on Fernando Vargas when he was buzzed. "As soon as I hit Cotto with some good shots, he went low on me," Zab would say afterward.

Round two saw Judah shake Cotto again with another sharp left. Then, in round three, Cotto scored (in real terms, if not on the judges' scorecards) with another low blow. This one had Zab rolling on the canvas in agony. Mercante took a point away from Miguel, but the damage was done. Zab's punches lost a bit of their sting thereafter, and Cotto's bodywork began to take its toll.

Cotto has an aggressive crowd-pleasing style. His opponents know what's coming, but knowing and being able to do something about it are separate matters. For the rest of the night, Miguel moved relentlessly forward, throwing sledgehammer blows. He was bleeding from the mouth and from a cut above his eye. But inexorably, he broke Judah down. As the fight wore on, Zab tried to pick his spots, but the spots became fewer as the battle wore on. Miguel was simply too strong for him.

By the late rounds, Judah was getting beaten up. His body had become a punching bag for a brutal puncher. Cotto's hooks opened an ugly gash above Zab's right eye, which was so badly swollen that Judah could no longer see the left hand coming. Near the end of round nine, he took a knee to regain his composure. Mercante could have stopped the fight then, but he allowed it to continue. Just before the bell, Zab landed a hard desperation left that temporarily halted the onslaught. But that simply delayed the inevitable.

The beating resumed. Twenty seconds into round eleven, a right hand put Judah down again. He rose; the assault continued; and Mercante stopped the fight. All three judges had Cotto ahead 97–91 at the time of the stoppage. He outlanded Judah in every round except the first (when Zab enjoyed a 16-to-15 edge). Overall, the punches landed as tabulated by CompuBox, favored Miguel by a 292-to-132 margin.

There was a lot of anger in Judah's dressing room after the fight, much of it voiced loudly by cornerman Tommy Smalls. Each camp had been cautioned by the New York State Athletic Commission before the fight with regard to fouls and, in particular, low blows. Zab understood that, coming into the bout he had two strikes against him (his knockout loss at the hands of Kostya Tszyu, when he attacked referee Jay Nady for stopping the fight; and his participation last year in an ugly mid-fight riot that began with his flagrantly fouling Floyd Mayweather). Both of those incidents had resulted in suspensions. A third such incident could have ended his career. He also knew that the passionate sell-out crowd of 20,658 had the potential for violence if things inside the ring got ugly.

"The low blows took everything out of Zab," Smalls shouted. "If Zab did that to Cotto, there would have been a riot. If it was Zab that threw the low blows, he would have been disqualified. All the referee was worried about was the crowd and boxing getting a bad name if he stopped the fight, so he let Cotto get away with it. Cotto should have been disqualified."

"What's done is done," Yoel Judah (Zab's father and trainer) said.

"It ain't done," Smalls countered. "After the low blows, Zab couldn't move like he usually does. He was a dead man walking."

Ron Scott Stevens (chairman of the New York State Athletic Commission) came into the dressing room to check on Zab's condition.

Smalls became more heated.

Stevens listened to Smalls's grievances, congratulated Zab on a good fight, and thanked Zab and Yoel for conducting themselves in a professional manner.

That got Smalls started again.

A knock on the door interrupted the shouting. Miguel Cotto, all alone, bloodied, still in his trucks, not wearing a robe, entered the dressing room.

There were some ugly looks from Judah's entourage.

Zab rose, walked over to Cotto, and embraced his conqueror.

"I am sorry for the low blows," Cotto said in halting English. "It was not on purpose. This was my hardest fight ever. You are a great fighter."

"You're a great fighter too," Zab told him.

Looking at the fight in retrospect, and contrary to conventional wisdom, it now seems that Zab's best chance of winning might have been a firefight early. He showed that he had the power to hurt Cotto. And against Miguel, it's possible that the best defense is a good offense.

Meanwhile, history tells us that Cotto's opponents tire from the punishment they absorb as a fight goes on, and so does Judah. So while the low blows might have been a factor, they probably weren't dispositive of the outcome. Either way, one thing is clear. A fighter can't go into the ring against Cotto simply trying to survive. If he does, Miguel will track him down, beat him up, and knock him out.

Cotto–Judah was Miguel's coming-out party; the biggest fight of his career before the biggest audience of his career against his toughest opponent to date. There's a difference between being a superstar and being a great fighter. Cotto might be on his way to becoming both. It's not who he beats but how the beating is done that's so impressive. It will take a very good fighter to defeat him; maybe a great one.

The best fight in boxing now would be Cotto against Floyd Mayweather Jr. Put it in Madison Square Garden on the eve of the 2008 Puerto Rican Day Parade and it would be the largest-grossing Garden fight ever. But Cotto is precisely the kind of boxer that Floyd doesn't want to fight; a determined, wilfull warrior who punches hard, takes everything that's thrown at him, and keeps coming until he imposes his will on his opponent. More likely, when Floyd returns to the ring, it will be against a lesser foe.

That's a shame because sports have to be entertaining to succeed. And boxing hasn't been entertaining enough lately. But on June 9, fans at Madison Square Garden caught a glimpse of why boxing is great. When Miguel Cotto and Zab Judah stepped into the ring, their opponents were history and each other. For one night at least, the Garden and boxing were young again.

At age forty-two, Bernard Hopkins was still one of the best fighters and most compelling personalities in boxing.

Bernard Hopkins: He's Baaack!

Glory came late for Bernard Hopkins.

Bernard's first pro fight was at age twenty-three for a purse of $400. He lost, sat out for sixteen months, returned to the ring in 1990, and was defeated only once over the next fifteen years. In 1995, he captured the IBF middleweight crown with a seventh-round knockout of Segundo Mercado. Ultimately, he made twenty consecutive title defenses. But it wasn't until he beat Félix Trinidad in a 2001 title-unification bout at Madison Square Garden that he achieved superstar status.

Most fighters fade badly after age thirty-five. Looking at some of boxing's greatest middleweight champions; Sugar Ray Robinson was 37–15–4 after his thirty-fifth birthday. Marvin Hagler and Carlos Monzón were retired at thirty-five. Hopkins has had thirteen fights since he turned thirty-five and lost only twice; each time by a razor-thin margin to Jermain Taylor. During that time, he has beaten Trinidad, Oscar De La Hoya (his glitziest victory), and Antonio Tarver (a legacy-defining triumph).

Indeed, one can make a credible argument that, at age forty-one (his age on June 10, 2006, when he beat Tarver), Hopkins was the best over-forty fighter ever. Archie Moore had thirty fights after age forty, but didn't beat any elite opponents during that span. George Foreman, at age forty-five, triumphed over Michael Moorer but his other post-forty victories were unremarkable. Hopkins, at forty-one, was in the top five on everyone's pound-for-pound list. He even had a flashy new nickname ("B-Hop") to go with his old moniker ("The Executioner").

Hopkins retired from boxing the night he beat Tarver. "There's nothing else to do," he told a post-fight press conference. "I'm done." That was in keeping with a promise he'd made to his mother, who had died of cancer several years earlier. "My mom knew Joe Frazier," Bernard further explained. "She saw what happened to Joe. And from a mother's love, she didn't want me to wind up like that, so I promised her that I'd retire before my forty-first birthday. I missed it by a few months, that's all."

But Hopkins grew bored with retirement; and before long, he was planning a return to the ring. His first proposed target was Oleg Maskaev, who'd captured the WBC heavyweight crown with a twelfth-round knockout of Hasim Rahman in August 2006.

"I'm serious," Hopkins said two months after Rahman–Maskaev. "Bernard Hopkins fighting a heavyweight would be shocking at first. But when people think about it, it's not that crazy. The heavyweight division is not in good shape in America or in good shape period. I need to save the reputation of heavyweight boxing in America so Joe Louis can rest in his grave, so Jersey Joe Walcott and Floyd Patterson can rest easy. I'm the last hope for the American heavyweights, and I believe the American people would support that. We are being dominated by other countries, and I don't like it."

"I won't go in the ring to take a fight I can't win," Hopkins continued. "I got a blueprint on fighting Maskaev. I've watched him fight. I've sparred with guys 190, maybe 200 pounds. I've never been hit by a 235-pound heavyweight with 10-ounce gloves. I would be taking a huge risk. People will either see a train wreck or see Bernard Hopkins pull off history again. But people will take me real seriously once they realize I'm hiring Mackie Shilstone again to help me prepare myself safely and correctly. I'll be 205 by April, and I'll look even better at 205 than I did at 175 against Tarver."

Shilstone, of course, worked with Hopkins for his fight against Tarver and also with light-heavyweight champions Michael Spinks and Roy Jones Jr. prior to their successful challenges against Larry Holmes and John Ruiz.

As for the pledge that he'd made to his mother, Bernard declared, "I know I made a strong personal promise to my mom. She's up there listening, and I'm asking her and God for forgiveness. I was thirty-four years old at the time I made that promise. How was I to know that I'd be at my peak in my forties? Now what has happened is, my four sisters and my wife have replaced my mother and they've given me their express approval to come back."

On October 18, Richard Schaefer (the CEO of Golden Boy, which promotes Hopkins) acknowledged, "Bernard is really serious about it. He gave me the instructions to seriously explore if the fight can be made. I have had conversations with Dennis Rappaport [Maskaev's promoter] about the fight being held in the spring. They are open to it."

On November 25, Hopkins formally unretired. "Still got the fire; still got the legs," he proclaimed. "If the opportunity lays out to be fair on my side, you'll see the most historic, the most anticipated, the most courageous thing that anybody in boxing will ever witness. The only thing that will get Bernard Hopkins back to the ring is to fight for the heavyweight championship of the world. That's the only risk that will motivate me to train as hard as I always did; to go in there with the mentality of upsetting the world, upsetting the critics, and cementing my name furthermore in boxing history for all times."

Hopkins fighting against an elite heavyweight would have been compelling drama. Alas, it never happened; so Bernard turned his attention to Roy Jones, who had defeated him on a twelve-round decision in 1993.

The loss to Jones still rankles Hopkins, largely because he knows that he fought Roy the wrong way. He tried to box cleverly, when he should have gone into the trenches, mauled, brawled, and done everything possible to rough up Jones.

A lot of people didn't want to see Jones–Hopkins II happen. Bernard is better technically now than he was when he fought Roy. Jones isn't. Bernard is close to being as gifted physically now as he was then. His legs aren't the same and he's a touch slower, but he's just as strong if not stronger. Jones, by contrast, isn't close to what he was physically in 1993. He's slower, his reflexes aren't the same, and his chin seems to have been rewired. Hopkins 2007 might beat Hopkins 1993. Jones 1993 knocks out Jones 2007. For some observers of the boxing scene, the appropriate tagline for a Jones–Hopkins rematch was, "Jones–Hopkins II: Better never than late."

Not to worry. Jones took exception to the financial terms that were offered to him and turned the fight down with the advisory: "Bernard Hopkins uses De La Hoya as the front man to fuck you. He's cute, but I don't do dudes."

So Hopkins turned to Winky Wright. They will meet in the ring on July 21, 2007, in Las Vegas at Mandalay Bay.

"Winky Wright has never been knocked out in his entire career," Bernard said at the kick-off press conference in Las Vegas. "But he ran the light without his seat belt on when he signed for this fight, and there's a truck coming. Winky thinks he's better than me. I know I'm better than him. I'll beat him and beat him until that drop of water where you didn't fix the ceiling tears the floor up."

"I know how to win," Wright responded. "I'm gonna kill the boogeyman. People don't have to be scared no more. The boogeyman will be gone."

As is usually the case at his press conferences, Hopkins had the last word. "I can't look back on my record years from now and see that a guy named 'Winky' beat me," he said.

Not everyone sees Bernard's comeback the way he would like them to. "Hopkins is like most other boxers," Stephen A. Smith wrote in the *Philadelphia Inquirer*. "He just wants you to believe otherwise. He's a champion who can't let go. A pugilist fueled by dollars more than by his legacy. A man whose word evidently is not as strong as his ego, hunger, or business acumen, since he plans to fight long after he promised his mother he would be done."

But Hopkins has an answer for his critics. "This isn't a Holyfield situation," he says. "In boxing, you're only as good as your last fight. My last fight was against Tarver. Based on June 10, 2006, do you think I should retire?"

Why is he still fighting? Obviously, money is a factor. When a man has shopped at Costco for most of his life, it's hard to turn down millions of dollars for one more fight, and then another. But there are other considerations as well.

"I'm not fighting because I need the money," Hopkins says. "I'm fighting because I can. I'm the one who has to be satisfied with my decisions, good and bad. I like hitting people without getting locked up. This is therapy for me." Then he adds, "The best thing about being a fighter is that you're in control."

As for what kind of fight Hopkins–Wright will be; the naysayers have been out in full force. Bob Arum (who has no promotional stake in the bout) calls it "a businessman's dance" and explains, "By that, I mean a fight where you have two guys and neither one wants to get hurt and both of them leave the ring looking the same as when they came in."

Teddy Atlas says, "There's a good chance it's not going to be one of your more scintillating fights. Their styles call for them to cover up, counter, stay out of danger, take what the other guy gives them, and not necessarily force the issue. Do they care about changing to make the fight more fan-friendly? I don't think so."

Angelo Dundee calls it "a chess match" and adds, "I don't think they're going to try to please anybody. If you're expecting blood and guts, it ain't gonna happen."

But Hopkins–Wright is a competitive fight between two superb boxers. And it's a meaningful fight for each man in terms of his legacy.

People talk about Bernard's twenty consecutive title defenses and his having been being undefeated in twenty-six consecutive fights over a twelve-year period. But Winky hasn't lost in thirteen fights over the past seven-and-a-half years. That's one reason why he opened as a 6-to-5 betting favorite over Bernard. And the odds haven't shifted since then.

"We're going to force this fight," says Dan Birmingham (who has trained Wright since Winky's amateur days). "We're going to set a fast, hard pace. You look at Winky's past fights; he's landed punches every five to ten seconds on every opponent, and Bernard's not going to be any exception. We're coming right at him. We're going to start this fight hard and we're going to finish this fight hard right up until the last second. We're going to make Bernard fight. And if they think they're going to wear us down, then I'm glad they're thinking that way because it's not going to happen. I guarantee it."

"If you look at my last couple of fights," Wright adds, "I'm always coming forward. With Jermain Taylor, I came forward. Ike Quartey, I came forward. Trinidad, came forward. I don't go for the knockout but I can punch. You don't see fighters just running in on me. If I couldn't punch, they'd come right up to me. But I can hit, I got a great defense, I'm a smart fighter, and I come to win. It's going to be a fight like he never fought. He never fought anyone like me."

Give Hopkins credit for going in tough. He's at a point in his career where he has the luxury of fighting who he wants to fight. Yet he fought back-to-back bouts against Jermain Taylor; then took on Antonio Tarver; and now he's facing Wright.

"Tarver was a puncher," Hopkins notes. "He was a scary kind of fighter, but Winky brings his own set of problems to the table. Winky can box. People don't jump up and down to fight Winky Wright."

Not many people stand in line to fight Hopkins either.

Bernard has been a champion for so long because he always trains like a challenger. He doesn't just prepare well during the weeks or months leading up to a fight. He has lived a Spartan lifestyle for almost two decades. He is as disciplined as any fighter ever.

"I watch tapes of a guy before I fight him," Hopkins says. "I've watched tapes of Winky going back to the amateurs. I want to know everything there is to know about my enemy. This is war."

Hopkins prepared for the Tarver fight with Naazim Richardson as his head trainer and John David Jackson as the number-one assistant. Earlier this year, Richardson suffered a stroke and Bernard turned to Freddie Roach for guidance.

As for how Hopkins–Wright will evolve, Bernard says, "There is no puzzle in a boxing ring that I can't solve. This fight is based on who can figure out the puzzle and make the other guy do what he don't want to do. Winky is like a turtle. He likes to go into his shell, but I've seen every style and fought every style. I know everything that Winky has, and I also know that Winky don't have as many weapons in his arsenal as I do. I'm going to get the turtle to stick his head out of his shell and then I'm going to knock it off. I'm undefeated against southpaws; ten and oh with nine knockouts. There's nothing Winky can do that will surprise me. Winky's going to get hit more in this fight than he's been hit in any fight in his life. I'm gonna punish him and then I'll knock him out."

Hopkins elaborated upon that theme during a July 11 conference call. "Winky has the ability to absorb a lot of punishment," Bernard told the media. "That's where you'll see a reincarnation of Bernard Hopkins and William Joppy. His face will change from round one to round two to round three or whenever his corner and the referee feels that he's had enough. Remember what you all said. 'Winky Wright has the best defense in boxing. No one can figure it out. His elbows is low; he keeps his hands up. He has those jabs, one hundred a round.' Remember you all said that, and then look at his face when the fight is over."

Pat Burns, who trained Jermain Taylor for his two fights against Hopkins, believes that Bernard has to fight more aggressively than he has lately in order to prevail.

"To beat Winky," Burns says, "you have to back him up. You cannot let Winky Wright come forward. Usually, Bernard fights hard for about sixty seconds a round. To beat Winky, he'll have to raise that to seventy-five or eighty."

Roach is an offensive-minded trainer. The fact that Hopkins decided to work with him might be an indication that he agrees with Burns's logic. In that vein, Freddie says, "The pace will be set by Bernard. I'd like to see him pick it up a bit and start a little sooner than he usually does. Hopefully, the body shots will get to Winky and take a toll late in the fight. Winky's defense is good but it's not unbreakable."

Both Hopkins and Wright are exceedingly difficult to play catch-up against, so the early rounds will be particularly important. Winky doesn't have one-punch knockout power, so Bernard can take more risks than he usually does.

Hopkins's big edge in the match-up might be his size. The contract weight is 170 pounds. At six-foot-one, he's three inches taller than Wright. His most recent fight was at 175 pounds. By contrast, Winky has never fought above 160 and his last fight was against Ike Quartey (who began his career at 140 pounds and now fights at 154).

"Do you know what it took with this body for me to make 160 pounds all those years?" Hopkins asks rhetorically. "I went through torture for thirteen years to make 160 pounds. I've got a new body now, and it's like driving a new car."

Still, if weight is Bernard's edge, age might be Winky's advantage.

Boxing fans have come to accept the proposition that Hopkins is ageless. He isn't. The sweet science is the most physically demanding of all sports. And by the time Bernard steps into the ring on July 21, he will have been out of combat for 407 days. At some point, he simply won't be able to perform like a great fighter anymore. The question is when.

"Everybody has their time end," Hopkins acknowledges. "I'm not a robot. I got aches and pains like everybody else. Boxing is a young man's sport; and in any sport, even golf, forty-two is old. I don't know how long it's going to last."

"Michael Jordan went to Washington and, all of a sudden, young guys were slamming on him," Bernard continues. "Allen Iverson almost broke Michael's ankles on a crossover. That hasn't happened to me yet; but if I stay around long enough, it will. There comes a time for every fighter when he thinks he can do it, but then he gets in the ring and his body tells him that he's wrong. You can win a fight and still know from the way your body feels that it's time to retire. My body will tell me when it's time to go. But I've never been cut. I've never been beaten up. It's twelve years since I was stunned. There's some miles on this car but it's still in good shape. I'm in this game at age forty-two because I can still do it. And if anyone thinks different, prove it to me in the ring that I'm wrong."

Bernard Hopkins and I have had our differences over the years (as referenced in some of my earlier books). So I was pleased and honored that he invited me into his dressing room for the hours before Hopkins–Wright.

Bernard Hopkins: History in the Making

Egos are big in boxing and few people in the sweet science have a bigger ego than Bernard Hopkins. The fighter himself says, "I admit that your ears can get tired listening to Bernard Hopkins."

Hopkins is a writer's fighter. He's quotable and charismatic with marvelous ring skills to match his persona. He's also an exceedingly complex man with personal potential that has yet to be fully tapped. He doesn't like being wrong, and rarely admits it when he is. He can be smart and foolish, diplomatic and brusque, funny and mean, charming and cruel. At times, he's wise.

In Bernard's world, relationships are often tenuous. Allies like longtime trainer Bouie Fisher and promoter Lou DiBella (who was instrumental in Bernard's rise to stardom) are cast aside. Some people marvel at how Hopkins makes pacts with the devil (e.g., Don King and Bob Arum), breaks them, and comes out ahead. DiBella voices a different view and queries, "How can Bernard Hopkins make a pact with the devil? He is the devil." But in the next sentence, the promoter acknowledes, "There are a lot of very appealing things about Bernard as a person. That's why, when he turned on me and revealed that other side of his character, it hurt me so much."

Love him or hate him (and there's reason for both), Hopkins deserves respect for what he has accomplished. There have been many controversies in his life, some of them ugly; but he has kept his name free of scandal. When he was released from prison at age twenty-three, he had meager vocational skills and little margin for error, in the ring or out of it. Then he lost his first pro fight.

"That was a gut-shot," Bernard says. "I had to make it in boxing to get to where I wanted to go in life. There was no plan B. But I never begged, I never pleaded, I never lay down. And it all worked out for me."

Boxing is about who executes best in the fractions of a second when an opening is there. The outcome of a fight is determined by which fighter does what has to be done in those fleeting slivers of time. Forget about the costume mask and executioner's hood that Hopkins often wears to the ring. He executes, that's the key.

"Bernard knows the art of boxing," says Freddie Roach, who stepped in to train Hopkins when Naazim Richardson suffered a stroke on March 29 of this year. "He studies it; he knows this game well. He thinks. He sets things up. He doesn't make mistakes. You should watch him shadowbox. His feet are always under him; his balance is perfect; his chin is always down. He's not your usual fighter, that's for sure."

"There are times when I've been in Bernard's corner during a fight," says Richardson. "I've seen something and said to myself, 'When Bernard gets back to the corner, I want to tell him this.' And before the round ends, he's made that adjustment."

But the key to Hopkins's success is his work ethic. A lot of fighters maintain discipline while they're on the way up. Some keep it for a few years after they become a champion. What makes Bernard special is that he has kept his discipline for almost twenty years.

"Bernard gives more of himself than any fighter I've ever known," says Richardson. "Most fighters, if they tried to do what Bernard does, they'd break. There are very few human beings who can give what Bernard gives, mentally or physically. He's extreme in a lot of what he does. Sometimes you have to tell him to back off and slow down. There are times when something isn't working right and he'll just work it harder instead of trying a different approach. But I've never seen a fighter get up mentally fight after fight like Bernard does. Each time he steps in the ring, it's like his first championship fight. Boxing is as hard as everyone thinks it is, harder; and Bernard does it right. Every trainer who ever lived would like to work with a fighter like Bernard Hopkins."

"A lot of people talk a good fight; I back it up," says Hopkins. "I have a problem with losing. I don't take that well. Patience is the key to winning a fight. You have to wait for the right time to make things happen. There's patience, discipline, and it helps to have luck. We never know how the dice roll. There are no guarantees in boxing. You can train right and live right and still roll snake eyes when you get in the ring. But I promised myself a long time ago that, every fight I have, I'm giving myself every chance possible to win."

Hopkins loves the sweet science and thinks long and hard about his place in boxing history. His proudest achievement is his string of twenty consecutive middleweight title defenses. He enjoys contemplating what might have happened had he faced off against the ring legends of another time. Keep in mind, the middleweights of old weighed-in on the day of a fight; not thirty hours before the opening bell as is the custom today. But that doesn't keep Bernard from visualizing what might have been.

"Sugar Ray Robinson at 147 pounds was close to perfect," Hopkins posits. "But at middleweight, he was beatable. I would have fought Ray Robinson in close and not given him room to do his thing. He'd make me pay a physical price. But at middleweight, I think I'd wear him down and win. Me and Marvin Hagler would have been a war. We'd both be in the hospital afterward with straws in our mouth. We'd destroy each other. I wouldn't run from Marvin. My game plan would be: rough him up, box, rough him up, box. You wouldn't use judges for that fight. You'd go by the doctors' reports. Whichever one of us is damaged less gets the win. Carlos Monzon? I could lose that fight. Monzon was tall, rangy, did everything right. I see myself losing that fight more than winning it. I ain't saying I'm number one, but I'm one of the best middleweights of all time. My legacy is what it is. If you want to be great, then beat Bernard Hopkins."

On July 21 at the Mandalay Bay Hotel and Casino in Las Vegas, Winky Wright tried to do just that.

It had been two years since Hopkins came to the oasis in the Nevada desert to fight Jermain Taylor in what he'd assumed would be a satisfying finale to his long and illustrious ring career. He would beat Taylor, perhaps fight an encore against a lesser opponent as a grace note, and then retire; or so it was thought.

Taylor won a controversial split decision to hand Hopkins his first defeat in twelve years. Five months later, there was a rematch and Jermain triumphed again. Thereafter, Bernard went up in weight and seized the light-heavyweight crown with a dominant performance over Antonio Tarver. That victory, at age forty-one, redefined his legacy.

Boxing needs competitive fights between elite fighters. Hopkins–Wright was that kind of match-up. Both men were in the top five on virtually everyone's pound-for-pound list. Neither man had ever been knocked out. Their encounter was for the *Ring Magazine* light-heavyweight championship belt, which was a bit disingenuous since the bout contract required them to weigh in at 170 pounds or less rather than 175 (a concession to Wright who hadn't fought previously above 160). But as Bernard observed, "One of the great things about fighting for the *Ring* belt is that there are no sanctioning fees."

Much of the pre-fight reporting voiced the view that Hopkins–Wright would be a "boring" fight. That was unfair to the combatants, both of whom are genuine ring craftsmen. Yes, Bernard and Winky are known for defense. But if Roger Clemens and Randy Johnson faced off against one another next month and each man reached back to recapture his prime, no true baseball fan would complain about a 1–0 pitchers' duel. It was exhilarating to watch Pittsburgh's "steel curtain" defense and Minnesota's "purple people eaters" perform on the football field years ago. Good defense isn't necessarily bad. Hopkins dismissed the criticism with the observation, "The guys who write about this being a boring fight never took a punch. Maybe they took a punch or two in the playground, but not a real punch."

Meanwhile, the match-up represented a special opportunity for Wright, who (despite two victories over Shane Mosley and another over Félix Trinidad) was still looking for his signature win. Winky has always been the "other guy" in big-money fights. He was the other guy against Fernando Vargas. He was the other guy against Mosley (who was later devalued as "too small") and Trinidad (demeaned as "used goods" because of his loss to Hopkins). He was the B-side in the marketing of Taylor–Wright. Against Hopkins, Wright was once again the other guy.

Age matters in boxing, and Bernard's forty-two years were seen as a handicap. Although, as Bernard pointed out, "Winky is thirty-five; he ain't no spring chicken either." As for the 170-pound weight limit, Hopkins noted, "People are saying, 'Oh, Bernard is too big.' They aren't saying, 'Bernard agreed to take five pounds off from what's his best weight now so this fight could happen.' "

Freddie Roach was confident in the days leading up to the fight. Prior to the start of training, he'd confided, "Bernard probably knows more about boxing than I do, but I might know a few things that he doesn't. The hard part will be getting to know each other because we don't have much time. But Bernard is a hard worker and I'm pretty straightforward, so I don't anticipate any problems."

As fight night approached, Roach (who has struggled to get fighters like James Toney in shape) said with pleasure, "I'd heard that Bernard works hard, and he does. I'd heard he was disciplined, and he is. It's nice not to worry about your guy going home and eating the wrong meal and staying out late partying. Bernard makes that part of the job easy."

As for strategy, Roach declared, "If Winky comes out aggressive, Bernard will go with him. He might think he wants to push Bernard because of Bernard's age. But when the fight starts, he'll think something different. The Fernando Vargas fight exposed Winky a bit. They say it was a bad decision; but no matter how you look at it, it was close and Winky left himself vulnerable to the body during exchanges. And I saw some things in Winky's fights against Shane Mosley. Shane just wasn't big enough to take advantage of them."

"Long layoffs are never good for fighters," Roach acknowledged, referring to Hopkins's 407-day absence from the ring. "It's hard to fight once a year and be sharp. But we've done extra sparring to cover that and gone ten rounds a couple of times. Everything has been working well in the gym."

"People will be shocked at how dominant I am in this fight," Hopkins added. "Winky Wright can't beat Bernard Hopkins just on defense. We got a thing in boxing called offense. To win a fight, you got to throw punches and do damage with them. Winky Wright has two bullets in his gun; his defense and his jab. Winky can only do two things. I'm an all-around fighter."

Meanwhile, the psychological warfare between the fighters was ratcheting up.

Wright is the antithesis of Hopkins. His public persona is level and easy-going. He doesn't stir passions. He just quietly does his job.

Still, by virtue of their trade, any two fighters in the ring have more in common with each other than with virtually anyone else in the arena. And there are other similarities between Winky and Bernard, including the fact that each of them enters the ring as a confident fighter.

In the weeks leading up to the fight, Hopkins engaged in his usual "executioner" rhetoric. "When I go in the ring, I try to hurt my opponent real bad," he said. "I beat guys up before I knock them out. It's like foreplay before the orgasm. When Winky looks across the ring and sees a bald-headed guy with that penitentiary look staring at him, and everybody else in his corner is going down the stairs, he's gonna wish he wasn't there. I know when fear is there; I read fear well. Winky is scared."

But Wright wasn't scared. He meant it when he said, "Bernard is talking a lot of trash, and I want to shut his mouth." Then, during a July 10 conference call with the media, Winky labeled Hopkins a dirty fighter.

"Bernard's always going to be a dirty fighter," Wright declared. "Bernard's a tough fighter, he's awkward, and he does a lot of dirty things. The way he uses his head, the way he hits you on the cup and hits you on the leg. It's definitely things he does on purpose; and he's been fighting for so long, he knows when to do it and when the referee is on the other side. That's how he fights. He's just a dirty fighter."

"What am I going to do?" Hopkins said in response. "Argue and plead that I'm not? I've been called worse names than 'dirty.' I take it as a compliment. I'm going to kick his ass whether I'm a dirty fighter, a clean fighter, a nice fighter. It's not his job to worry about nothing but fighting. That's why we have a referee. People have watched me for years. If you think I'm dirty, then I think you should throw in a tape of Rocky Marciano or Benny Briscoe. Go back to the '40s and '50s when they was fighting, real fighting. If Winky feels that I'm doing something, he has the right to defend himself by any means necessary. I think he's just trying to put people on notice for him to start crying when things don't go his way. Winky is starting to realize the reality of his fate, and he's trying to put the message out there so he can get some help. Boxing is boxing. No fight is clean."

Then came an ugly confrontation.

The weigh-in is the last public ritual before a big fight. In recent years, big-fight weigh-ins in Las Vegas have been open to the public and held in the arena where the fight will occur. They bring fans into the casino and are covered on television (which engenders pay-per-view buys).

Fighters tend to be irritable in the hours before a weigh-in. They're thirsty, they're hungry, and they have a fight coming up. Moreover, a big-fight weigh-in is very different from the press conferences that precede it. The two combatants strip almost naked to face each other and their physical condition is gauged. Psychologically, it's a taste of the ring.

On Friday afternoon at 2:30, Hopkins and Wright climbed nine stairs to an eight-by-sixteen-foot stage in the Garden Arena to weigh in. Bernard is a master of weigh-in intimidation. Many observers felt that Antonio Tarver was beaten the day before he and Hopkins fought when the fighters faced each other at the scale. Conversely, Bernard's inability to intimidate Jermain Taylor at a weigh-in confrontation prior to their first fight was seen by some as a significant moment.

Standing on the platform, Hopkins tucked his elbows against his ribs, raised his fists to his face, and mocked Wright's defensive style. That was followed by a few awkward jabs that drew laughs from the crowd. Each man weighed in at 170 pounds. The fighters were brought together for a stare-down. Then things got out of hand.

There were too many people on the platform. Each fighter had been told that he could be accompanied by his trainer and one security guard, but both camps had exceeded that number. Add in Nevada State Athletic Commission officials, Golden Boy Promotions personnel, an ESPN camera crew, and a boy from the Make-A-Wish Foundation, and the situation was ripe for disaster.

Being in a fighter's entourage at a big fight is a heady experience. You're with The Man. Sometimes, part of The Man's machismo rubs off on you in your own mind, albeit not in anyone else's.

Wright's entourage was jawing at Hopkins. "That escalated everything," Freddie Roach said later. "They were staring down and talking like they were the ones who'd be fighting on Saturday night."

"Too bad you can't fight for him," Hopkins told them.

"They don't have to," Winky countered. "I'll fight for myself."

Then Hopkins crossed over the line that separates ritual from chaos. He reached out and, with an open hand, shoved Wright hard in the face. Wright shoved back. Suddenly, punches were flying. Before order was restored, Roach was pushed sideways, hit his ribs against the edge of the stage, and careened to the concrete floor four feet below.

After the incident, the Nevada State Athletic Commission announced that it would withhold 10 percent of Bernard's purse pending a disciplinary hearing in August. A bigger concern within the Hopkins camp was how the incident might affect referee Robert Byrd's conduct of the fight.

After the weigh-in, theories abounded as to why Hopkins did what he'd done. Bernard implied the next day that it had been a calculated move to build pay-per-view buys, but that's nonsense. There was too much danger inherent in the situation. An innocent bystander could have been seriously injured. If either fighter had fallen from the platform, the fight could have been cancelled.

A more likely explanation lies in the fact that, throughout the build-up to the fight, Hopkins had been jawing at Wright and Winky had just laughed at him. He wasn't intimidated, and that was getting to Bernard. So when

Bernard started jawing at the weigh-in and Winky laughed again, Bernard went to the next level for a psychological edge, if not to intimidate Winky then to motivate himself.

"Bernard comes from a world where he can't escape that mentality," Naazim Richardson said afterward.

Why did Hopkins shove Wright in the face?

Because he wanted to.

At 5:55 on Saturday night, wearing blue jeans and a black-and-gold hooded shirt with a navy-blue doo-rag on his head, Hopkins entered dressing room 4 at the MGM Grand Garden Arena. A rush of "smart" money had raised the odds to 9-to-5 in Wright's favor. It was 9-to-2 that the fight would go the distance.

Bernard sat in a cushioned chair, put his feet up on a folding chair in front of him, and smiled. "I slept all afternoon," he said. "Weighed myself in the hotel right before I left; 184 pounds tonight."

For most of the next two hours, Hopkins chatted amiably with those around him. He was remarkably relaxed with a kind word for everyone who was part of his team.

Naazim Richardson has worked with Bernard since 1997. He'd been hospitalized for five weeks after his stroke but made a remarkable recovery. His speech is now good and he's moving well, although there's still some weakness on his left side. His presence was a reminder that the human brain is fragile.

"How you feel, Naazim?"

"Blessed to be here with my warrior."

Bernard turned to cutman Leon Tabbs.

"Leon, my man. I ain't needed you yet, but it's good to know you're here."

"I'm ready, champ."

The dialogue continued with others.

"How's your wife? How's your kids?"

"That's the way Bernard is," Richardson said. "The only time I felt tension in the locker-room was before Bernard fought Robert Allen the last time. We needed that one for the fight with Oscar to happen, and Bernard was worried that something might go wrong."

There was a fifty-inch flat-screen television at the far end of the room. Michael Katsidis could be seen going to the ring for his undercard fight against Czar Amonsot. Katsidis was wearing an elaborate Greek-warrior helmet with an imposing protective mask.

"Look at that mask," Richardson chortled. "He's got you beat, champ."

Hopkins smiled.

Katsidis versus Amonsot began. Soon, Roach and most of the others in the room were watching the fight, which was fast becoming a brutal, bloody brawl. Roach and Hopkins had discussed how Bernard likes things done in the dressing room before a fight. Freddie was following protocol by leaving the fighter on his own.

Meanwhile, Roach had his own problems. He'd suffered a torn muscle over his rib cage when pushed from the stage during the weigh-in fracas the previous afternoon. There was an ugly welt on his left side. Mario Chavez had broken one of Freddie's ribs in a 1981 fight that Roach won. "This feels similar," the trainer said. "It's killing me."

Hopkins took off his jeans and shoes and pulled on a pair of royal-blue boxing trunks. Then he sat down again and stretched out his legs. Richardson covered his chest and legs with towels.

Bernard leaned back and closed his eyes.

"That's a time when all sorts of whispers cross my mind," he said later. "So I shut out the world and think about my mom."

No one talked. The only voices heard were those of Bob Sheridan and Dave Bontempo on the international television feed. Bernard opened his eyes periodically to watch the action on the screen unfold.

There wasn't a lot of intensity in the air. Everything was methodical, measured, and calm. Bernard took a sip from a bottle of water. "No sense using up energy now," he said. "I can turn it on and off. Watch me when the time comes."

At seven o'clock, assistant trainer John David Jackson went next door to watch Wright's hands being wrapped.

Roach began taping Hopkins's hands.

"Winky's a part-time boxer now," Bernard said. "And those part-time boxers are soft. Body shots early."

Katsidis–Amonsot ended and the semi-final bout between Oscar Larios and Jorge Linares began.

At 7:20, the taping was done. Bernard lay down on a towel on the floor and began a series of stretching exercises; his first physical activity since entering the dressing room.

Referee Robert Byrd came in and gave his pre-fight instructions. There was no mention of the previous day's shoving incident. After Byrd left, Hopkins stretched some more and began shadow-boxing.

At 7:45, Bernard gloved up and began working the pads with Roach. "Somebody cut a towel and put it over my head," he said after five minutes of work. "I'm sweating like a motherfucker."

At eight o'clock, the pad-work stopped and the room fell silent. There was a prayer in Arabic, ending with "Allahu Akbar" [God is great].

More pad-work with Roach.

"How much time?" Hopkins asked. "What are we working with?"

Richardson looked at the television monitor. "Ninth round," he answered.

"Naazim," Bernard said, still hitting the pads. "They couldn't keep you in no bed."

"This ain't your first time down this path," Richardson responded. "Just be you, soldier. Nobody ever made you fight at their pace. You control."

Linares stopped Larios in the tenth round.

Hopkins finished hitting the pads with Roach, sat down on a folding metal chair, and stretched his legs out on the floor. Then he opened his mouth, and, with his tongue, pushed out a bridge of false teeth.

"It's all mental," he said. "That's what great fighters are made of. But the psychological stuff means nothing if you can't fight."

Hopkins stood up. Now there was a street-alley sneer on his lips. His eyes were mean.

The Executioner was ready to kill.

It was a better fight that the critics said it would be. This wasn't two aging guys hanging around for one last payday. It was two extremely talented professional boxers coming to win.

In the early going, they traded rounds. Wright showed his jab, and Hopkins was Hopkins. He boxed and mauled, taking what was given to him and more. He looked older than the last time he stepped into the ring. Then again, he was. And regardless of age, Bernard still has a nasty right-hand lead that scores when an opponent stands still for a fraction of a second in front of him.

Eight seconds into round three, a clash of heads opened a hideous gash on Wright's left eyelid. It was ruled unintentional; but Bernard's head movement, more than Winky's, was the cause. Thereafter, Hopkins compounded the handicap by rubbing his head and gloves against the cut from time to time, not to mention punching at it. On several occasions, Robert Byrd warned Bernard about holding and using his head on the inside. But he never took a point away and ignored the occasional low blow.

The first six rounds saw a lot of action with Wright forcing the pace. Then the action slowed. After eight stanzas, one could have made an argument that "B-Hop" was "B-hind." But as is usually the case, the final rounds belonged to Bernard. This writer scored it 115–113 for Hopkins. The judges gave it to him by a 117–111, 117–111, 116–112 margin.

"Winky comes to fight," Bernard acknowledged in his dressing room after the fight as Leon Tabbs held an ice pack to the swelling around his left eye. "Winky can be dead tired and he still does what he does. Winky don't go away when things get tough, and Winky is strong."

As for what happens next, one assumes that Hopkins will fight again.

"This is an addictive sport," says Freddie Roach. "It's hard to give it up. I know, I was there. I loved the crowd, but what I missed most after I retired was the pat on the back and someone saying, 'Good fight.' It's sad when it's over. But forty-two is just a number. I was washed up at twenty-seven. Age in boxing comes from how many wars you've been in, and Bernard hasn't taken any beatings. The way he looks now, he should be able to fight at least a few times more."

It's remarkable to watch a fighter add to his legacy at age forty-two rather than chip away at it. At age forty-two, with fifty-three fights and nineteen years of boxing behind him, a boxer isn't supposed to perform like Hopkins. And there are no telltale signs of damage outside the ring. Bernard talks as fast and verbalizes as well as he ever did.

"My plan is one fight at a time," Hopkins says. "Time beats every athlete, and Father Time will hit me some day. The time will come when I can't control my destiny as a fighter anymore, but that time isn't here yet. We all know the fighters who stay in the game too long. It's not a secret. But I'm not showing signs like Evander Holyfield or Arturo Gatti or some others we can all name. I ain't some fool in denial about a career that's over. Nobody is embarrassed about Bernard Hopkins getting in the ring."

"For each fight now, it has to be historically right," Hopkins continues. "It has to be financially right and it has to motivate me. There's no harm in making money, but that's not the priority for me anymore. I'm doing this to add to my legacy and because I enjoy it. I'm in the position now that Roy Jones was in six, seven years ago in terms of choosing my opponents. Look at who Roy fought then and look at who I'm fighting now."

The future for a forty-two-year-old athlete is usually bleak, but Bernard Hopkins is on his own timetable. "Love me or hate me; they will never be another one like me," he says in closing. "Not many people have the same spirit that Bernard Hopkins has. Enjoy me while I'm here. Don't rush me away until it's my time to go. You'll miss me when I'm gone."

Taylor–Pavlik: "And the NEW Middleweight Champion of the World . . ."

For most of the world, a prize fight is a sporting event, entertainment, a show. For a fighter, each bout carries the potential to be a crucial turning point in his life.

Kelly Pavlik is a fighter, a self-described "skinny white kid from Ohio." He has a thin muscular body and knows one way to fight: going forward, punching. In high school, he worked odd jobs to get the money to go to amateur tournaments. More often than he cares to remember, he was busing tables in a Youngstown restaurant when his high school classmates came in for something to eat after a school dance.

On September 29, years of sacrifice paid off for Pavlik, when he dethroned Jermain Taylor at Boardwalk Hall in Atlantic City to become middleweight champion of the world.

Pavlik was born on April 4, 1982. His father, Mike, was a steelworker and now works as an insurance agent for American International Group. His mother, Debbie, is a cook at Hardee's. The family has Slovak, Sicilian, Irish, and German roots.

Kelly lived at home with his parents until autumn 2006. He now lives in Boardman (a Youngstown suburb) with Samantha Kocanjer and their sixteen-month-old daughter, Sydney.

When Pavlik was nine, he took up combat sports. At first, he experimented with martial arts. "But it was dull," he says. "There was no contact; so after a while, I wanted to try boxing. My parents were against it. I had to fight tooth and nail to get them to let me do it. Finally, they gave in and my mom took me to the gym."

The gym was the Southside Boxing Club; a converted pizza joint where a Youngstown native named Jack Loew taught children to box. "I loved it from the start," Kelly remembers. "When coach finally let me fight, I went to war with everybody in the gym."

Pavlik's first amateur fight came at age nine in a Golden Gloves competition between Youngstown and Steubenville. His opponent was eleven-year-old Anthony Batisella (the Ohio State Fair Junior Olympic Champion and a "veteran" with thirty amateur fights to his credit). Kelly won a three-round decision. Thereafter, he kept improving. "I was tall and awkward," he remembers. "At age nine, I already wore size twelve shoes. I couldn't do the Ali shuffle because I kept tripping over my feet. But I loved boxing. In other sports, you have teammates who help carry the load. The best thing about being a fighter is, when you win, you know you did it."

Over the next eight years, Pavlik compiled an amateur record of eighty-nine wins against nine losses. He was never knocked down or given a standing-eight count. He also played high school baseball (he was a catcher) and football (running back and cornerback). "But I didn't have the size or speed to make it in football," he says. "And in baseball, no matter how good you are, it's almost impossible to make it to the top level. I was good in boxing and I was winning, so I figured why not get serious about it."

"I really didn't think he'd turn pro," Mike Pavlik says of his son. "His mother and I thought he'd tire of it, and that would have made us happy. Now, as a father, there are times when I just sit there and smile; I'm so proud. But there's also a terror and fear in seeing your son in combat. And make no mistake about it; boxing is combat."

Pavlik turned pro in 2000 with Cameron Dunkin and his father as co-managers. Top Rank (his promoter) was grooming him for stardom and put him in showcase bouts on the undercard of De La Hoya–Vargas and De La Hoya–Hopkins. But a fighter's career moves slowly in the early going, and Kelly was further hampered by tendon problems in his right hand. To supplement his income, he washed dishes and took other jobs. Until the start of this year, he did occasional landscape work for $10 an hour to help make ends meet.

Then, on May 19, 2007, Pavlik's life changed. He knocked out Edison Miranda in seven rounds. That performance silenced a lot of doubters. Suddenly, Kelly was no longer a protected white kid. He was the mandatory challenger to middleweight king Jermain Taylor and, in the eyes of his fans, "heir apparent" to the middleweight throne.

Meanwhile, Taylor was struggling. Jermain won the undisputed middleweight championship on July 16, 2005, with a twelve-round decision over Bernard Hopkins. Five months later, he duplicated that feat and seemed poised for superstardom.

Taylor is skilled in the ring, handsome, and likeable with a gift for charming people. "I'm sorry I'm late," he told reporters at the kick-off press conference for his 2006 fight against Winky Wright. "I was chasing my daughter around. I had to take her to day care, and she was tough to catch." Then he observed, "This is weird. I'm used to being up here arguing with Bernard Hopkins. Winky came over and shook my hand. I didn't know what to do."

But by then, Taylor had done something self-destructive. After his second victory over Hopkins, he'd allowed himself to be separated from one of the mainstays of his success as a fighter. Pat Burns (who had trained Jermain from his first pro fight) was at odds with Ozell Nelson (the "father figure" in Jermain's life). At Nelson's urging, Burns was dismissed and Emanuel Steward was brought in to work with Jermain.

When Burns was removed, Taylor lost the boxing voice that he trusted most. His subsequent performances reflected Pat's absence. Against Wright, Jermain fought without his usual fire and salvaged a draw. That was followed by lackluster victories over Kassim Ouma and Cory Spinks.

There's a time-honored maxim in boxing: "If a fighter isn't getting better, he's getting worse." With each succeeding fight after Burns's departure, Jermain's performance declined.

The Taylor camp responded by noting that Wright, Ouma, and Spinks were all former champions and southpaws, which made them difficult to fight. But after a while, the whining about opponents' styles wore thin. Wright, Ouma, and Spinks were also smaller men who had come up from 154 pounds to face Jermain. And the Spinks fight was particularly troubling. Against a smaller light-punching foe, Taylor had seemed to be out of shape and a bit gun-shy.

"Jermain has a lot of skills," Naazim Richardson (who works with Bernard Hopkins) said after Taylor–Spinks. "But mentally, he wasn't ready to be champion."

"At one time, you had ten guys in the middleweight division who could have been the champion," opined Don Turner (who trained Evander Holyfield and Larry Holmes). "Now the champion can't even be a champion."

Taylor wasn't particularly bothered by criticism from the boxing community. "Let 'em talk," he said. But he was stung by criticism from the media in his home state of Arkansas; some of it cruel. One radio talk-show host in Little Rock went so far as to tell his audience, "We have Jermain Taylor with us today." Then he introduced a cohort who imitated Jermain's stutter.

In sum, Taylor was falling short of his fans' expectations and, more importantly, his hopes for himself. It seemed as though the joy had gone out of fighting for him. His next career move was both perilous and obvious. He signed to fight Pavlik.

People wanted to see how good Jermain still was and how good Kelly could be. Taylor–Pavlik would be a fight between the middleweight champion of the world and a hard-punching, undefeated legitimate number-one contender. With one good win, Jermain could wipe away the residue of three disappointing performances and begin the process of restoring the lustre that had worn off his crown.

"It took longer than I thought it would," Pavlik said when the contract was signed. "Longer to get on HBO, longer to be in the top five, longer to make good money. Seven years is a long time."

When serious pre-fight training for Taylor–Pavlik began, Jermain went to the Poconos, in Pennsylvania, where he worked for eight weeks with Emanuel Steward, Ozell Nelson, and Joey Gamache. Pavlik trained in Youngstown, maintaining the same routine with the same people that he'd been with from the start.

Youngstown has gotten old. The city has a proud boxing tradition, having sired former champions Ray Mancini, Jeff Lampkin, and Harry Arroyo. But it was hit hard by the economic downturn of the 1970s and never recovered. Steel mills closed and factories shut down. Unemployment is still high.

"I like training at home," Pavlik says. "Everything I need is there. The gym, the Iron Man Warehouse (where he does much of his conditioning work). I can walk out the door and go running. My whole family is nearby. Everything is the way I want it to be for me to get ready to fight."

Pavlik's training was overseen by Jack Loew, the only trainer that Kelly has ever had. Loew is also the owner and sole employee of a company called The Driveway Kings. He seals asphalt driveways for a living. One week before Taylor–Pavlik, he was sealing driveways in the morning before going to the gym.

As might be expected, there have been whispers about Loew . . . "He's an amateur . . . He doesn't know how things are done in the bigtime . . . Kelly needs a professional trainer."

But Mike Pavlik, who fervently guards his son's interests, said shortly before the big fight, "Jack Loew knows boxing. I'm not worried about that. And he understands Kelly very well, which is just as important."

Loew, for his part, says, "Kelly has stuck with me and I've stuck with him through some rough times. I might not be good for someone else, but I'm good for Kelly."

After Taylor–Pavlik was scheduled, the fighters were respectful of one another. "Kelly Pavlik is a fighter just like me," Taylor said. "He comes to fight; no running, no holding." Pavlik responded in kind, saying, "Jermain is a great fighter. He's the world champion for a reason. He's tough, he's big, and he's fast for his size. I'm looking forward to the challenge of being in the ring with him."

Then things changed. Emanuel Steward began trash-talking, which isn't his style.

"Pavlik is pretty much a media creation," Steward declared. "Kelly had a good performance against Edison Miranda. But Miranda isn't all that good and, against Kelly, he had a problem making weight. There is absolutely no way Kelly Pavlik is operating on the same level that Jermain is on right now, mentally or physically. He's a basic right-handed fighter. Jermain will control him with his jab and knock him out in about three rounds."

That was followed by another Steward declaration: "Kelly Pavlik has never been in with a fighter on Jermain's level. Kelly is a Versus fighter. Jermain is an HBO fighter. The smaller guys that Jermain fought were world champions. Kelly has fought a bunch of B-list smaller guys. This will be like jumping from junior high school to college for Kelly. Jermain Taylor will knock out Kelly Pavlik. It will be a tough fight for one round at most."

Thereafter, Emanuel went into overdrive, proclaiming, "In all the years I've been training fighters, I've never had a fighter in better shape mentally or physically than Jermain is now. I'll be honest with you. Even if I was Marvin Hagler or Sugar Ray Robinson, I wouldn't want to be fighting this Jermain Taylor."

And Ozell Nelson put in his two cents, saying, "This fight is going to be easy pickings. They better have Pavlik ready, because the way Jermain sees it, he's going to break something off in Pavlik."

Even Taylor strayed from form, declaring, "I plan on beating Kelly down. I'm supposed to say that he's a great fighter. But he's not. He's slow. He doesn't have a lot of head movement. The only thing I see good that he does is that he's a strong fighter. Other than that, nothing. I'm going to whup him easily."

One gets the sense that, if Taylor and Pavlik were neighbors, they'd be in each other's home from time to time. One can imagine them sitting on the sofa, side by side, watching Ohio State play Arkansas in football. Their personalities seem to be compatible.

Pavlik is gracious and soft-spoken. "I'm pretty low-key," he says. "I don't care about flashiness. I like being at home or hanging around my parents' house. I play softball and a little golf." Taylor is also immensely likeable. "I try to keep a level head about all the attention I receive and never forget where I came from," he told the BBC earlier this year.

But by its trash-talking, Team Taylor was casting its fighter as the heavy.

"Jermain is running his mouth, saying he's going to break my face," Pavlik said in response to the taunts. "I hope he comes to do that because he's going to have to make it a fight to do that."

In truth, an intelligent case could be made for victory by either fighter. Taylor's partisans were buoyed by the fact that Jermain had faced off against present or former world champions seven times and survived three fights against Bernard Hopkins and Winky Wright. He'd never been on the canvas as an amateur or a pro.

Jermain would have an edge in hand-speed over his opponent. Add to that the fact that Pavlik doesn't move his head enough and tends to bring his left hand back low after throwing his jab. Against Miranda, Kelly had showed he could take a punch. But could he take jab after jab and combinations?

Taylor had fought through adversity. He'd suffered a bad scalp wound against Bernard Hopkins. His left eye had been shut by Winky Wright. Each time, he'd emerged with the crown. His will is strong. He had gone twelve rounds seven times. By contrast, Pavlik had gone nine rounds once. Kelly had never heard the ring announcer say, "round ten . . . round eleven . . . round twelve." By the time round ten rolled around against Jermain, Pavlik would have thrown a lot of punches. And word was that he was struggling to make weight. If the fight went long, rounds ten through twelve could be harder than Kelly anticipated. Taylor might even stop him late.

But the case for a Pavlik victory was equally strong. Pavlik has a solid chin and power in both hands. He was expected to hit Taylor harder than Jermain had ever been hit. "Kelly sees a hole in the dike, and he's going to break through it with a sledgehammer," Loew said. "The longer this fight goes, the worse it will be physically for Jermain."

"Jermain is a great fighter, but I see him declining," Pavlik added. "I don't know if it's the money he's made or changing trainers or something else, but he seems to have slipped. It's been a long time since he fought a natural 160-pounder who can hit, so we'll see what happens when I'm firing away. We'll see how he adapts when I'm throwing seventy or eighty punches a round with power on each shot. A lot of things can happen during a fight. Some of them are good, and some of them are bad. But they think I'm just a slow white kid, and I've got a few surprises for them."

And then there were the intangibles, which seemed to weigh in Pavlik's favor. Kelly was peaking mentally, while behind the bravado, Jermain seemed to have lost some of his belief in himself. Kelly appeared to be more comfortable than Jermain with who he is and where he is in his life right now.

"On their recent performances, I'll go with Pavlik," Joe Calzaghe observed. "Their skills are about equal. But boxing is a hungry sport, and Pavlik is a hungry fighter. Taylor looks as though he has lost the hunger for boxing."

"Jermain is capable of beating Kelly," Naazim Richardson offered. "But I think he'll overreact to some of the negative things that have been said about him and fight a brave fight instead of a fight that gives him the best chance to win."

That was Pat Burns's concern. "If Jermain goes into the ring with the attitude that he can simply out-punch Kelly or out-tough Kelly, he's making a mistake," Burns said several days before the fight. "That would be giving up his edge in skills and playing into Kelly's hands. There's no secret to what Kelly does. He'll come right at Jermain and pressure him from the start. Jermain isn't a one-punch knockout artist. He hits line-drive singles and doubles, not home runs. If Jermain wins, it will be by chopping the tree down punch by punch. Kelly won't fall with one blow."

"I'd tell Jermain to box Kelly early," Burns continued. "Don't bang with him. Stay outside; pepper him with jabs. If Kelly gets inside, tie him up. Kelly is big and Kelly is strong, but Jermain can break him down with the jab and take control later in the fight. That's what should happen if Jermain is in shape and has a good fight plan. But what I'm afraid will happen is that Jermain won't be in great shape and he'll abandon his jab. Believe it or not, Kelly might start to out-jab him. And when Jermain drops his left hand, which he does no matter how many times you tell him not to, Kelly will land some big right hands over the top."

Meanwhile, more than one observer was moved to note that Taylor–Pavlik seemed eerily similar to the first fight between Taylor and Bernard Hopkins.

Only now, Pavlik was the challenger stepping up in class and Jermain was the big-time fighter speaking disdainfully about how he'd crush the favorite son of Youngstown, Ohio. He was talking down to Kelly the same way that Hopkins had talked down to him.

At a pre-fight press conference for Hopkins–Taylor I, Bernard had declared, "Jermain has the talent to take my place one day. One day. But not now; not against me." At the final pre-fight press conference for Taylor–Pavlik, Jermain spoke virtually the same words about his opponent. And the Pavlik camp was getting angry.

"The people around Taylor can't get any more arrogant than what they are," Mike Pavlik said.

And Jack Loew declared, "I'm tired of hearing how great Emanuel Steward is. I've never disrespected Emanuel Steward, but he's disrespecting me. I like Jermain; he's good for the sport. But I don't think Jermain is a great fighter, and I think all this talking that Steward is doing is nothing but trying to build his fighter's confidence. Jermain makes as many mistakes as Kelly does; sometimes more. If Jermain stands and trades with Kelly, Kelly will knock him out early."

One day before the fight, the boardwalk in Atlantic City was a sea of scarlet, grey, and white (Ohio State football colors). Ohio had embraced Pavlik. *The Youngstown Vindicator* (Kelly's hometown newspaper) featured a separate index labeled "Pavlik Coverage" on the main page of its website. It was above the section for Ohio State football, even though the Buckeyes were undefeated through four weeks of the season. General Motors announced that it would shut down the late shift at its plant in Lordstown (near Youngstown) on Saturday night because so many of its workers planned to stay home and watch the fight.

The fighters weighed in on Friday evening at six o'clock. Five thousand Pavlik supporters had journeyed from Ohio to Atlantic City, and a substantial number of them were in the Palladium Ballroom at Caesars to witness the ritual.

Prior to the Spinks fight, Taylor had experienced trouble making weight. Thirty hours before the weigh-in for that encounter, he'd tipped the scales at 169 pounds.

"This is my last fight at 160," Jermain said after signing to face Pavlik. "I've been fighting at 160 since I turned pro. With my body frame, it's too difficult and it's not healthy to make 160." But a revised training regimen had put Taylor on track to make weight for Taylor–Pavlik. On Thursday morning, he weighed 163. The final pounds would be lost through routine drying out.

Pavlik, by contrast, was struggling to make weight. At six-feet-two-inches, he's tall for a middleweight. His face is drawn with hollows around his eyes in the best of circumstances, and the rigors of reaching 160 were preying upon him. On Thursday afternoon at 4:30, he was on the roof terrace at Bally's, wearing a rubber suit, hitting the pads with Jack Loew. From there, he'd gone to the steam room, which he visited again at nine o'clock on Thursday night and also on Friday morning. As late as 4:00 P.M. on Friday (two hours before the weigh-in), he was checking his weight on the official scale at Caesars.

"Making 160 is harder now than it used to be," Kelly acknowledged. "I don't have the same bounce in my legs that I did before. It's the last few pounds that drain a fighter. They're the ones that hurt."

Taylor weighed in at 159 pounds; Pavlik at 159.5. Then the fighters posed side by side, and Jermain flexed his biceps. They looked like mountains.

"I'm not impressed," said Michael Cox (a Youngstown Police Department patrolman, who's Kelly's friend and would serve as the third man in Pavlik's corner on fight night). "You punch with your body, not your biceps. Look at Jermain. He's got biceps, but the rest of him is less developed than it was before."

After the weigh-in, Pavlik began the process of replenishing his body with a dinner of steak and pasta. In the preceding weeks, Team Taylor had frequently referenced an encounter between Jermain and Kelly that occurred at the 2000 Olympic trials. Jermain had won a decision in that fight, although, during the build-up to Taylor–Pavlik, he conceded, "To be honest, I don't remember it."

"It was a good fight," Pavlik said, sipping from a bottle of water as he recovered from making weight. "Jermain won. I'm not going to take that away from him. But he was twenty-one years old with a lot of amateur experience, and I was a seventeen-year-old kid. I'm a grown man now."

Meanwhile, Taylor was in a strange place. For his entire career, he'd been the darling of Little Rock, Arkansas. But Little Rock wasn't supporting him for this fight the way Youngstown was supporting Pavlik. For the first time as a pro, Jermain would be entering an arena with the crowd overwhelmingly in favor of his opponent.

Emanuel Steward was playing upon that fact. Five days before the fight, he'd told Chris Givens of the *Arkansas Democrat-Gazette*, "The biggest factor in this fight is Little Rock, Arkansas, and the rejection Jermain got in that town. My advice to Jermain, the way to get even, is to be a winner. I'm going to be honest with you. I've never seen this animosity in a fighter in training before, and this isn't even directed at another fighter. There's so much tension because of the Little Rock situation. I've never had a fighter train with such focus and intensity. You can almost see he's about to explode."

It helps a fighter to have something larger than himself to flow into. When Taylor fought Hopkins, he'd felt as though the entire state of Arkansas was behind him. Now, in an effort to motivate him, he was being told that Arkansas had abandoned him. But that was a misreading of Taylor's psyche. Unlike many fighters, Jermain isn't fueled by anger.

On Saturday night, Kelly Pavlik entered his dressing room in Boardwalk Hall at 8:34. He was wearing a gray warm-up suit with a scarlet stripe and white piping down each leg. Mike Pavlik, Jack Loew, Cameron Duncan,

Michael Cox, John Loew (Jack's son), and Mike Pavlik Jr. (Kelly's oldest brother) were with him. Miguel Diaz, who has worked Kelly's corner since his first pro fight, was already there.

The preliminary fights were underway. In the first bout of the evening, Ray Smith (one of Taylor's sparring partners from Little Rock) had been knocked out by Richard Pierson (a Pavlik sparring partner). Then heavyweight Terry Smith (also from Little Rock) lost a six-round decision to Robert Hawkins.

"I got good news for you," Diaz told Kelly. "Both of Jermain Taylor's guys lost."

The dressing room had seen better days. The industrial carpet was worn and the vinyl-topped rubdown table was scarred with discolored tape covering multiple gashes. But it was luxurious compared to some of Kelly's past surroundings. For early pro fights, he'd dressed in storage rooms and hallways and fought in makeshift arenas like an old flea market with tiles missing from the ceiling.

Lee Samuels (Top Rank's director of publicity) came into the room. "Seven years of hard work pays off tonight," he said.

"Seven years for you guys," Jack Loew told him. "Fifteen years for me and Kelly."

A few minutes later, referee Steve Smoger entered and gave Pavlik his final pre-fight instructions. Dr. Sherry Wulkan of the New Jersey Board of Athletic Control administered a final pre-fight physical. When they were done, Kelly yawned. Then he began text-messaging friends.

"Oklahoma got beat pretty good today," Loew said.

"Texas too," Mike Pavlik added. Then Mike pointed toward the HBO television monitor by the door. "Too bad we can't get Ohio State on that thing."

Kelly stopped text-messaging long enough to pull up some college football scores. "Ohio State is losing to Minnesota," he said.

"What?" his father uttered in disbelief.

Kelly smiled. "Just kidding. The Buckeyes are up 14–0; 7:22 left in the second quarter." He put down his cell phone and stretched out his legs on a folding chair in front of him.

"Who do you like next week; Pacquiao or Barrera?" Cameron Dunkin asked the group at large.

"Pacquiao," Mike Pavlik answered.

Dunkin turned toward Jack Loew. "And you?"

"Barrera."

"Really?" Dunkin said in surprise.

"Three years ago, I'd have said Barrera," Kelly offered. "But the way they are now, I don't see Barrera in the fight."

Larry Merchant came in for a brief pre-fight interview. "I've waited for this for seven years," Pavlik told him. "I just want to get in there and let my hands go. He'll have to keep up with me."

At 9:41, Kelly lay down on the carpet and began a series of stretching exercises. Ten minutes later, he stood up. "Time to put my soldier gear on," he said.

Shoes first. Then his trunks; grey with red, white, and blue trim.

The conversation around the room was casual and low-key; what one might expect to hear in the gym before a sparring session.

Loew began wrapping Kelly's hands. Throughout training, the muscles in the fighter's back had been tighter than he would have liked. Now, as Loew wrapped, Mike Pavlik massaged his son's back and shoulders.

Mike had been a constant presence in Atlantic City. Broad-shouldered with a shaved head, he looks as though he could bench press the Empire State Building. He was enjoying the journey and, at the same time, looking after his son.

The odds had been virtually even in the days leading up to the fight, with the "smart" money on Taylor and the Youngstown money on Pavlik. In the past twenty-four hours, the professional money had come in, making Jermain an 8-to-5 favorite.

That was understandable. Kelly had struggled to make weight. He had a history of tendon problems with his right hand, and his nose had been banged up pretty good in training camp.

Jack Dempsey once observed, "Any nose hurts when it gets hit." Bleeding from the nose cuts off part of a fighter's air supply. And a week earlier, Kelly had come down with a cold. His nose was still running a bit.

Michael Cox checked his cell phone. "Ohio State is winning; 23–7," he said. "Nine minutes left in the third quarter."

At 10:17, the taping was done.

"How are we doing?" Mike Pavlik asked.

"I'm very, very confident," Loew told him. "Nothing to do for this boy anymore but let him fight."

Kelly gloved up and began hitting the pads with his trainer.

"Stay behind the jab," Loew instructed. "Jab, right, jab, right."

Each time, the follow right was a bit off target.

"Stay behind the jab and relax . . . There. That's it. Double jab. Now let it go."

The punches began landing with explosive power.

When the pad-work was done, Kelly alternated between pacing back and forth and shadow-boxing.

Miguel Diaz put Vaseline on Kelly's face.

The fighter hit the pads with Loew one last time.

"That's it . . . Wow . . . Nice and easy . . . Push him back with that big long jab. Double it up . . . There you go. Back him up and you win."

"Two minutes and you walk," Team Pavlik was told.

Kelly stood up and moved toward the door.

There had been no music; no shouting; no one calling out: "What time is it?" Just quiet confidence and calm.

Michael Cox checked his cell phone one last time. "The Buckeyes won; 30-to-7," he announced.

Mike Pavlik put an arm on Kelly's shoulder. All that work, all those years; it comes together now," he told his son. "You were born to be here tonight."

Youngstown was in the house. That was clear as the fighters approached the ring. The crowd made it sound as though the bout was being fought in Ohio. There was a thunderous roar for Pavlik and loud boos for Taylor.

A lot of things are said in the days leading up to a fight. None of them matter once the bell rings.

Taylor came out aggressively in round one, going right after Pavlik. He was quicker than the challenger and his hands were faster. All three judges gave him the round. When the stanza was over, Jack Loew told his charge, "Control the pace. Be patient. Stay behind the jab. It's a basic fight."

Round two began with more of the same. "I was surprised," Pavlik said later. "I thought he'd try to box me more, but he came to fight. He has hand-speed and he can punch."

Definitely, he can punch. Midway through round two, Taylor timed a right hand over a sloppy Pavlik jab. The blow landed high on the challenger's head. Pavlik staggered backward, and the champion followed with a fifteen-punch barrage that put Kelly down.

"I was scared to death," Mike Pavlik admitted later. "That's the worst feeling I've ever had in my life. I wouldn't have cared if the referee had stopped it. To be honest, I was hoping it was over."

"The first thing that went through my mind," Kelly said in his dressing room after the fight, "was, 'Oh, shit.' But I heard the count. I was aware at all times. I told myself, 'Get up, get through this.' "

Pavlik rose at the count of two, but there were eighty-eight seconds left in the round. "I was shaky," he admitted later. "That right hand hurt. I've been knocked down before but there was never a buzz. It had always been a balance thing. This time, there was a tingle and my legs weren't so good. I did what I could to survive. He hit me with some more hard shots, but I got through the round. Some guys quit when they get knocked down, and some get back up."

There comes a time when a fighter has to dig deep within himself by himself. In the corner after round two, Kelly managed a weak smile. "I'm okay," he told Loew. But he was bleeding from the nose and mouth.

"Stay on that double fucking jab," Loew ordered. "There's a lot of time left. You have ten more rounds to do your job."

Then, incredibly, Pavlik won round three. The punches that Taylor had thrown in the second round seemed to have taken more out of the champion than the challenger. Jermain paced himself in the stanza rather than following up on his advantage. Pavlik threw ninety-nine punches over the three-minute period, earning the nod on each judge's scorecard.

The die was cast. Taylor was faster. He was ahead on points throughout the bout. But inexorably, Pavlik was walking him down with non-stop aggression behind a strong double jab. More and more often, the champion found himself having to punch his way out of a corner. When the fight moved inside and one of the challenger's hands was tied up, he fought with the other rather than clinch. He made Jermain fight every second of every round.

"Jermain has a chin," Pavlik acknowledged afterward. "I hit him with some punches, flush, right on the button early, and he didn't budge. But then he started to wear down. In the fifth round, I thought I hurt him a bit against the ropes. But he came back with a right hand that came close to putting me in trouble again, so I reminded myself to be careful. In the seventh round, I hit him with another good right hand and his reaction was different. I saw his shoulders sag. There was that little buckle in his knees, and I knew I had him."

When the right hand that Pavlik was referring to landed, Taylor backed into a corner again. Kelly followed with a barrage of punches. "Jermain went limp," referee Steve Smoger said later. "He was totally gone, helpless."

Smoger stepped between the fighters. Two minutes and fourteen seconds into round seven, Kelly Pavlik was the new middleweight champion of the world.

It was an important night for boxing. Millions of fans saw Taylor–Pavlik because it was on HBO, not pay-per-view. There was lots of action. And Pavlik put on a show reminiscent of Arturo Gatti's never-say-die, blue-collar, ethnic appeal. It's rare that a fighter comes back to win after finding himself in the circumstances that Pavlik found himself in during round two. But Kelly did. Fighting him is starting to look like playing Russian roulette with five bullets in the gun.

"Boxing fans are hungry for a new guy to come around who goes in the ring and takes care of business and doesn't shoot his mouth off in a negative way," Kelly said last month. "When Ali was running his mouth, he had something to say. Too many of the guys today don't say anything worth listening to and they aren't even funny."

Taylor never assumed the role of poster boy for boxing that was envisioned for him when he dethroned Bernard Hopkins. Maybe Pavlik will. But Jermain shouldn't be written off too quickly. His best days as a fighter aren't necessarily behind him. In round two, he was one punch away from beating Pavlik. All three judges had him ahead at the time of the stoppage. And the more Bernard Hopkins wins, the better Taylor's two victories over him look.

Losing is part of boxing. Losing respect is something else. It would be a terrible injustice if Jermain were to lose the respect that he earned in the past with his hard work, courage, and blood.

A contract is already in place for Pavlik–Taylor II to be fought at 166 pounds with a fifty–fifty financial split between the two camps. If and when that fight occurs, the outcome is not a foregone conclusion. However, for Jermain to win, he'll have to get his house in order.

One doesn't have to debate the issue of whether Emanuel Steward is a better trainer than Pat Burns. It's enough to say that Burns was a better trainer for Taylor.

Burns was ousted because Jermain felt more of a personal obligation to Ozell Nelson than he did to Pat. But he had confidence in Burns as a trainer and relied on him emotionally as a fighter. In the ring, neither Steward nor Nelson has been able to fill that void. The chemistry between Jermain and Emanuel simply isn't there, and that might have been the determining factor on September 29. It led to a situation where, deep down, one fighter believed in himself and the other didn't.

Beyond that, it should simply be noted that Jermain Taylor has always been loyal to Arkansas. Now would be a good time for Arkansas to be loyal to Jermain.

A Note on a Related Matter

After referee Steve Smoger gave Kelly Pavlik his instructions in the dressing room prior to Taylor–Pavlik, Mauricio Sulaiman came into the room. Mauricio is the son of WBC president José Sulaimán. In recent years, he has assumed an increasingly active role within the sanctioning body. He is now the WBC's executive secretary and is in charge of the organization's executive office in Mexico City.

In the dressing room, Mauricio approached veteran cornerman Miguel Diaz and told him, "If Kelly wins, I would like his trunks to present as a gift to my father." Diaz relayed the request to Mike Pavlik, who responded, "No way."

After the fight, Mauricio returned to the dressing room and renewed his request.

"Oh, man," Kelly said. "These are my trunks. Next fight, maybe; but not this one. I just won the championship in these trunks. My blood is on them."

More people were drawn into the conversation. One-on-ones followed. Some words were exchanged regarding the discretionary powers of WBC officials and their ability to make things easy or hard on WBC champions. Mauricio Sulaimán left Boardwalk Hall with Kelly Pavlik's bloodstained trunks. In the wee small hours of Sunday morning, he was confronted regarding the matter and the trunks were returned.

"It was a misunderstanding," Mauricio told this writer. "I was led to believe that Kelly wanted the trunks to be presented as a gift to my father because of his respect for my father and the WBC. When it was brought to my attention that Kelly wished to have the trunks back, I arranged quickly to return them."

Federal law states, "No officer or employee of a sanctioning organization may receive any compensation, gift, or benefit, directly or indirectly, from a boxer [other than a sanctioning fee]." Violation of this law is a crime punishable by up to one year in prison and a fine of $20,000.

When a powerful WBC official makes a request such as the one Sulaimán made of Pavlik, there's an inherent coercive factor at work. That's why there's a law against it.

Craig Hamilton (the foremost boxing memorabilia dealer in the United States) estimates that Pavlik's trunks from his championship-winning fight could be worth as much as $25,000. The WBC received a substantial sanctioning fee for Taylor–Pavlik. That should suffice for everyone's purposes.

This isn't the first time that Mauricio Sulaimán has made a request of this nature. One hopes it's the last.

It's the fights that matter; not the belts.

Forget the Belts:
Madison Square Garden—
October 6, 2007

The thrill of heavyweights is in the way they punch. The blows come in slow-motion in comparison to those of smaller fighters. Fans in the nosebleed seats can follow their arc. And they land hard.

On October 6, Don King promoted a night of boxing at Madison Square Garden. When it was over, the crowd had seen three pretty good heavyweight fights.

King initially built his card around a match-up between WBC heavyweight champion Oleg Maskaev and Samuel Peter. Maskaev won his belt with a victory over Hasim Rahman in August 2006 and has ducked all credible challengers since then. The most notable things about Maskaev's record are (1) Rahman is the only world-class heavyweight that he has beaten (Sinan Sam is not a world-class heavyweight), and (2) he has been knocked out five times. But that didn't stop Dennis Rappaport (Maskaev's promoter) from proclaiming, "Oleg's story is 'Cinderella Meets High Hopes.' It's fairy tales can come true when you wish upon a star."

Unfortunately, in an unfairy-tale-like twist, Cinderella turned into a pumpkin before dancing at the ball with Samuel Peter. On September 21, it was announced that Maskaev was suffering from a herniated disc. Thereafter, the WBC named Peter as it's "interim champion" and decreed that Jameel McCline was a worthy challenger. By September 26, Maskaev–Peter had morphed into Peter–McCline.

King had a hard time selling the fight. Neither Peter nor McCline has much of a following in New York; the show was competing with Pacquiao–Barrera II for media attention; the baseball play-offs are in full swing; and LSU was defending its number one ranking against Florida on national television in prime time.

There was a small media blip in support of the card when Madison Square Garden announced that it was retiring the ring it had used since

1925. After eighty-two years, it had become increasingly difficult and expensive to maintain the structure and set it up for fights. MSG senior vice president Joel Fisher called the retirement "bittersweet" and noted that the old ring had hosted more championship fights than any other in boxing history. But he prophesized the start of a new era when a virgin twenty-by-twenty-foot ring (the old one was eighteen-feet-three-inches squared inside the ropes) was pressed into service on October 6.

The Garden was virtually empty at 7:00 P.M. when the first heavyweight match-up of note (Kali Meehan against DaVarryl Williamson) began. Both men can punch a bit, and each has a questionable chin. Beyond that, Meehan has the disturbing habit of announcing his punches. He winds up as if to say, "I'm drawing my arm back now . . . Get ready . . . Here it comes." That enabled Williamson to build a lead through five rounds. Then, two-minutes-fifty-nine-seconds into round six, both guys threw right hands at the same time and Meehan's landed. Williamson collapsed in a heap, struggled to his feet at the count of nine-and-a-half, and staggered back to his corner on spaghetti legs. Inexplicably, referee Earl Brown didn't stop the bout, but the ring doctor did.

By the time Andrew Golota and Kevin McBride entered the ring, the crowd (which was generously announced as 7,102) had increased in size and was buzzing a bit. Both fighters have seen better days, but their downward curves are intersecting in a way that made for an entertaining brawl.

McBride went after Golota at the opening bell and wobbled him several times. Andrew is not known for coming back from adversity. But Kevin was only in shape to fight one round, which is what happens when a fighter likes beer and reports to training camp at 320 pounds before working his way down to 288. Thereafter, the two men pounded away at each other with Golota getting the better of the action. McBride fought courageously. But by round six, he was badly cut around both eyes, was being pounded, and resembled a badly wounded mountain. At the 2:42 mark, referee Arthur Mercante Jr. stopped the action.

The final heavyweight confrontation saw Peter defending his interim belt against McCline. Samuel was a heavy favorite. After all, Jameel had been afforded three previous title opportunities (against Wladimir Klitschko, Chris Byrd, and Nikolai Valuev) and come up empty each time. But in boxing, once the bell for round one rings, yesterday doesn't count.

Peter was the aggressor in round one and for all but the final second of round two. McCline is a well-sculpted 6-feet-6-inches 266 pounds. But he looked anxiety-ridden and almost fragile as Samuel chased him around the ring. Then, just before the bell ending the second stanza, Jameel rammed his shoulder into Peter in the manner of a tight end blocking a linebacker and followed with a right uppercut that put the interim champion down for the first time in his career. It appeared to be a flash knockdown, and Samuel had been so dominant up until that point that two of the three judges only gave the challenger credit for a 10–9 round.

Not so in round three. Early on, another right uppercut staggered Peter and an overhand right deposited him on the canvas. Samuel rose but was badly hurt. Jameel pummeled him some more and floored him again. Now Samuel was in trouble big-time. He didn't know how to hold on; his only defense was his chin (which was starting to look like Waterford crystal), and there were fifty-seven seconds left in the round.

But McCline couldn't finish the job and seemed as tired as Peter by the end of the stanza. When the bell for round four sounded, the challenger went into retreat, gasping for air while the champion advanced (although Samuel was more cautious than before).

By round seven, McCline was moving like it was round twelve, and a fatigued Peter was pushing his punches rather than snapping them. He kept coming, though, while Jameel was in survival mode. McCline landed when he let his hands go, but he only let them go when he had to in order to keep Samuel from getting in too close.

When it was over, Peter had retained his belt with a 115–110, 115–111, 113–112 decision. He showed heart in coming off the floor, but his overall reputation was tarnished. A skilled boxer (if one under the age of thirty-seven can be found in the heavyweight division) might take him to school.

Meanwhile, the WBC now has three heavyweight "champions": regular (Oleg Maskaev), interim (Samuel Peter), and emeritus (Vitali Klitschko). And of course, Wladimir Klitschko, Sultan Ibragimov, and Ruslan Chagaev also hold heavyweight "championship" belts. One can draw an analogy between the fragmentation of the heavyweight crown and the break-up of the Soviet Union into fifteen smaller nations (some powerful and some not). But no matter how one views the situation, it's an embarrassment to boxing.

The idiocy inherent in trumpeting bogus "title" fights is obvious. Today's proliferation of belts deprives boxing of recognizable champions and has the effect of devaluing match-ups that don't have some sort of title denomination attached to them. Not every football, baseball, and basketball game is a play-off contest. Most aren't. But fans still buy tickets and turn on their television sets to watch mid-season games in those sports.

The lesson of October 6 is simple. Few spectators cared that Peter–McCline was for an interim WBC title; that Golota–McBride was for an IBF North American belt; or that Meehan–Williamson was for an NABO bauble. What mattered was that, in an age when some heavyweight "title-fight" participants seem to show up for the money without making an all-out effort to win, three entertaining heavyweight fights were contested. And three fighters who were in trouble came back from adversity to triumph.

So forget the belts and stop paying the exorbitant sanctioning fees that are prerequisites to fighting for them.

Cotto–Mosley:
Youth Will Be Served

Some of boxing's most memorable battles have been contested in the courtroom, not in the ring. In June 2007, a Swiss banker, a lawyer, and a media-savvy superstar were locked in legal combat. Then mediator Daniel Weinstein intervened.

"Once the mediator broke our logjam," Bob Arum later proclaimed, "the animosity just melted away. It had a cathartic effect, where you rid yourself of any bad feelings you've harbored for years." Richard Schaefer (now an American banker, having been granted U.S. citizenship) and Oscar De La Hoya (the most golden of fighters) seemed equally pleased with the discontinuance of litigation.

Not everyone swooned over the settlement. Kenneth Bouhairie called it "three Richie Riches deciding to play nice in the sandbox" for their own financial gain. But for boxing to thrive, the best have to fight the best in the ring, not out of it. And the rapprochement between Top Rank and Golden Boy was an important step in that direction.

On November 10, the truce between boxing's two most powerful promoters paid its greatest dividend to date when Miguel Cotto and Shane Mosley faced off against one another at Madison Square Garden. For hardcore boxing fans, it was the most anticipated fight of the year.

Mosley is a gracious man who embodies the best traditions of the sweet science. There was a time when he stood beside Roy Jones Jr. at the top of boxing's pound-for-pound rankings. He's not there anymore but still battles with the ambition and purpose of a younger fighter on the rise.

Shane has always been willing to go in tough. In his youth, speed and power were his greatest assets. Then he moved up in weight, slowed a bit, and his power failed to increase in tandem with his size. "Welterweight is my best weight now," he said recently. "I was at my worst at 154. People say I'm not the same fighter I used to be; and at 154, they're right."

"When I started my rise," Mosley continued, "my thing was, 'I can't lose. I have to make a living from this, and no one can beat me.' Then you're on top and you cross over a barrier where you're not working out as much as you should because you're only fighting twice a year and the fire goes out a bit. I've been up and down a little, but I'm still a force to be reckoned with. At this point, I don't have to prove anything to anybody anymore. I'm just proving it to myself."

Cotto, by contrast, is a fighter whose greatest days are presumed to lie ahead.

Jake LaMotta once said, "The first thing you gotta do if you want to be a fighter is fight." Cotto fights. He isn't a one-punch knockout artist. He's more like a wrecking ball that demolishes buildings, blow by thudding blow. The left hook to the body is his money punch, but his arsenal is more varied than many people realize. "Everybody looks fresh in the first round against Cotto," says cutman, Miguel Diaz. "Then he beats them up."

Cotto is all business in the ring and seems to be that way out of it too. While other fighters are out bragging, he's in the gym working. "Miguel doesn't say a lot in English," notes promoter Bob Arum. "But he's not very verbose in Spanish either."

Meanwhile, Cotto observes, "Every boxer is going to get hit. Everyone is going to get hurt sometime during a fight. It's just a question of what are you going to do with it. Each time I fight, I try to do my best and a little bit more. With hard work, I always reach my goals."

As Cotto–Mosley approached, the stakes were high. A win for Shane would further define his legacy and put him in line for yet another multi-million-dollar payday. A Cotto triumph would lift Miguel from the status of a star in the Hispanic community to the verge of being a mainstream superstar.

Mosley partisans pointed to the fact that Shane had fought elite opponents throughout his career and been knocked down only once as an amateur or pro. Cotto, by contrast, had faced softer competition and been rocked by DeMarcus Corley, Ricardo Torres, and Zab Judah.

Jack Mosley (Shane's father and trainer) expressed confidence, declaring, "Cotto hasn't faced anybody like Shane, period. Shane is just too powerful and too fast for Cotto." Jack then went a bit overboard and proclaimed, "Cotto is worried sick about fighting Shane. You can look in his eyes and tell. He knows he's not as strong as Shane. He knows he's not as fast as Shane. And Shane hits just as hard, if not harder. I don't know what Bob Arum was thinking when he said, 'We'll fight Shane.' "

Shane was more understated but equally confident, saying, "Cotto is going to be tough; he's going to be strong; but I'm just too fast. If I'm moving around, giving him little angles here and there, it's going to mess him up. He's not going to be able to throw his shots the way he wants to. A lot of Cotto's fights, he beat guys by his will to win. Mentally, he breaks guys down and they fold in the later rounds. But I think I'm the best at this weight and I have to beat Cotto to prove it. Miguel is a great fighter, but so am I."

Team Cotto, of course, had a different view of the proceedings. It acknowledged that Shane would be the toughest fighter Miguel had faced and that Shane had fought the tougher competition. But unlike Cotto (who is undefeated), Mosely had lost four times. He had never faced an opponent who brutalizes foes the way Miguel does. And Cotto is a better fighter at 147 pounds than he was at 140. "Miguel is peaking now," Arum said. "He's stronger now than he was before. At 140 pounds, we were depriving him of muscle and power."

Also, Cotto's backers were encouraged by the issue of age. The numbers were self-evident. Shane Mosley, age thirty-six. Miguel Cotto, age twenty-seven.

"They're thinking that Shane's age is going to be a factor," Jack Mosley said, seeking to downplay the nine-year differential. "He's too old; he isn't going to be able to sustain. That's what they're hoping, but they're wrong."

Jack might have added that at thirty-six, Shane was the same age that Bernard Hopkins was when he beat another Puerto Rican idol (twenty-eight-year-old Félix Trinidad) at Madison Square Garden in 2001. But in boxing, when an aging star meets a young fighter on the rise, the younger man usually wins. Shane himself sounded an ominous note when he acknowledged, "Before Oscar fought me the first time, he'd never fought anyone as fast as he was. I was too fast for Oscar the first time. The second fight was closer because I was slower, so he was just as fast as I was."

Bottom line: Cotto was a 6-to-5 favorite in a fight that, on paper, looked to be everything a fight should be. "Maybe Mosley is the ultimate stepping-stone," Eric Raskin wrote. "Or maybe Sugar Shane is too good to be anybody's stepping-stone. Nobody knows for sure, which is why Mosley–Cotto has Fight-of-the-Year buzz."

When fight night arrived, there were 17,135 fans in Madison Square Garden hoping to enter a time warp and experience championship boxing the way it used to be. Their wish was fulfilled.

Cotto–Mosley was tense drama fought at a high level of skill between two brave warriors. Round one was largely tactical with each man evincing respect for the other. Cotto actually out-jabbed Mosley, which was a bad omen for Shane. Then the action heated up, with Mosley landing the cleaner, harder blows for several rounds, but Cotto landing more of them.

Mosley tried to fight with Cotto. "I love to stand and trade," Shane has said. "But that's not what I do best." Miguel absorbed everything that Mosley threw and kept coming forward, seeking to impose his will. By round six, Shane appeared to be slowing down, even losing form. He was missing by more, and there was less sting on his punches when they landed. Each man was pushing himself as hard as he could. But Cotto seemed impervious to pain and fatigue.

In round seven, Mosley changed tactics. For the next two stanzas, he boxed (or ran, depending on one's point of view). His offense seemed motivated by a desire to keep Cotto off him rather than to inflict damage. He did his best to avoid exchanges.

Then, in round nine, the fight turned. Shane came out aggressively, and Cotto became the counter-puncher in the face of Mosley's assault. Now Miguel was fighting more defensively than ever before as a pro. Round ten was more of the same. Cotto was the fighter seeking to avoid exchanges. A rally in round eleven gave Miguel a much needed point on the judges' scorecards. Shane had the edge in round twelve.

It was a remarkable display of will by both men. Each fighter landed 248 punches. The decision was fair and unanimous in Cotto's favor: 116–113, 115–113, 115–113. In a just world, Miguel will now receive pound-for-pound consideration.

As for what comes next; it should first be noted that these are heady times for Top Rank. Over the past six weeks, its fighters have won three major fights.

On September 29, Kelly Pavlik dethroned Jermain Taylor to become middleweight champion of the world. Next, on October 6, Manny Pacquiao won a twelve-round decision over Marco Antonio Barrera to solidify his standing as a superstar. Now Cotto has beaten Mosley. And the victories are all the sweeter because, although Arum snagged Pacquiao late in the fighter's career, Pavlik and Cotto have been with Top Rank since their first pro bout.

"We build fighters at Top Rank," Arum says. "We build them step by step so, by the time they fight for a title, the fans know who they are and they're ready to win. It takes time. The process moves slowly and can be frustrating for the fighters. But if a fighter is patient and does his job in the ring, that patience pays off in the end."

Cotto's plans are on hold pending two variables. First, he must wait for the outcome of the December 8 mega-event between Floyd Mayweather Jr. and Ricky Hatton. And second, like a lot of people in boxing, he's waiting to see what Oscar De La Hoya wants to do.

The current plan is for De La Hoya to fight in Las Vegas or Los Angeles on May 3, 2008. The presumption is that, if Hatton beats the odds and topples Mayweather, De La Hoya–Hatton will follow. If Ricky loses to Floyd, the best fight for boxing would be Cotto against either Oscar or Mayweather.

"Mayweather will never fight Cotto," says Arum. "Cotto would run him out of the ring, and Floyd knows it. There's no chance that Floyd will take the fight."

As for Cotto against De La Hoya, Oscar has said in the past that he won't fight Miguel. "I promised my wife that I wouldn't fight any Puerto Ricans," he told ESPN.com in August. "So I don't think so. The fight would be great. We would stand toe-to-toe. But I can't do it. It's not because I would be afraid of Cotto or not want to fight. It's out of respect for Millie. She sincerely asked me not to fight Puerto Rican fighters, so I have to respect that."

But De La Hoya is a money guy. De La Hoya versus Cotto would be HUGE. And there have been other instances when Oscar said he'd never fight a particular opponent (e.g., Floyd Mayweather Jr. and Fernando Vargas) and later changed his mind. Thus, it's not beyond the realm of possibility that De La Hoya–Cotto will happen if "the Puerto Rican people plead with Millie" to allow it.

"If it takes something extra to make it happen," Arum says helpfully, "I'll have Cotto apply for Israeli citizenship."

But whatever comes next, Cotto is moving into territory occupied by José Torres, Carlos Ortiz, Wilfredo Benítez, and Wilfredo Gómez in the collective Puerto Rican heart. Is he as popular as Félix Trinidad? Not yet. But he's as good a fighter.

"It's two different stories, me and Félix," Cotto said several days before he fought Mosley. "The comparison with Trinidad is good; it's a compliment. But people know we are different. My personality; I can't do anything with that. I'm a shyer person than Tito. That's my way. I'm not Tito. I'm Miguel Cotto."

That's good enough.

"Miguel is a great young man," says Arum. "He has a great personality. I don't want him to be a phony. I don't want him to be what he isn't. Besides, if Miguel were more outgoing, he might not be as good a body puncher."

Vinny Maddalone: "When the Candle Burns Out, I'll Walk Away"

Vinny Maddalone is a club fighter with the heart of a champion. Boxrec.com lists him as the 217th-ranked heavyweight in the world. His records stands at twenty-eight wins and four losses with nineteen knockouts. There was a fifth loss, but the verdict was changed to "no contest" after his opponent tested positive for marijuana.

Maddalone's fights have the look of a slugfest from a 1940s movie. There's nothing subtle about the way he fights. He comes straight forward. He throws punches. He gets hit. Then he throws more punches. "Vinny could be dead," says matchmaker Ron Katz, "and he'd still keep coming forward, throwing punches."

Boxing is a backstabbing world, but Maddalone is popular in boxing circles and well liked by other fighters. He's friendly and outgoing with a ready smile and fights his heart out every time he steps between the ropes.

"In the ring," says IBF 140-pound champion Paulie Malignaggi, "Vinny is one of the toughest SOBs you'll ever meet. Outside it, he's a big teddy bear. He's always smiling. He's a big-hearted guy with a word of encouragement for everyone he meets. When I see him fighting, it's like, 'Whoah! What got into him tonight?' "

If boxing was fun, everyone would do it. It's a hurting business. But boxing is a joy in Maddalone's life. He loves to train; he loves to fight. He's always willing to pay the price, no matter how expensive it is. "I might not win every time," he acknowledges. "But I never quit."

"If you were going to war," says promoter Lou DiBella, "Vinny is one of the guys you'd want fighting beside you. He's the guy who would risk his own life to pick you up and carry you out if you got hit."

Maddalone was born in Queens (one New York City's five boroughs). He's the youngest of three brothers. His father died when Vinny was seven. His mother worked in a school cafeteria and never remarried.

"I didn't have a father figure in my life," Vinny says, reflecting back on his childhood. "My mother was my mother and my father. If I could have my father back for a couple of hours now, I'd want to talk boxing with him. I don't remember him well, but I know he liked boxing. And I'd tell him what a great job mom did with the three of us; how she looked after us so we'd grow up to be the kind of people he wanted us to be. One of the reasons I'm boxing now is, I'd love to be able to give my mother a better life for everything she gave to me."

Maddalone graduated from Holy Cross High School in 1992 and Pfeiffer University in North Carolina in 1996. He put boxing gloves on for the first time when he was in college.

"I was in a convenience store and saw a sign for a toughman contest," he remembers. "I was a fight fan and I was in pretty good shape, so I figured, 'Let me try this.' I went in for the physical on a Friday night. It was like, 'Touch your toes. Okay, you're good to fight. Go in back and glove up.' So I'm in back. I'm an eighteen-year-old kid and the other guys are grown men; truck-drivers, construction workers, 280 pounds. I felt like a soldier going to war."

"There were three one-minute rounds," Vinny continues. "First fight, this big guy came right at me; but after forty seconds, he was dead tired. Second round, I went back at him and knocked him out. It was the best feeling I'd ever had; the highlight of my life. I can't put into words how great it felt. The next night, I went back, fought three more guys—knockout, decision, knockout—and won the tournament. They gave me a thousand dollars. My friends and I bought a couple of kegs of beer, went back to campus, and celebrated."

But Maddalone wasn't thinking about a career in boxing. Baseball was his first love. He was good enough in college that, after graduation, he pitched for two seasons with the Adirondack Lumberjacks (a minor league team in the independent Northeast League). Dave LaPoint, who had pitched in the major leagues for twelve seasons, was his manager. On one occasion, Vinny matched skills on the mound against former Boston Red Sox hurler Dennis "Oil Can" Boyd.

"They tried me as a starter and middle-reliever," Maddalone recalls. "But temperamentally, I was a closer, and that's how they used me most of the time. I had an eighty-nine-mile-an-hour fastball. Five miles more and maybe I'd have made it to the major leagues. But I didn't have that little extra. Near the end of the '97 season, I got tendonitis in my shoulder and they released me."

Then Maddalone turned to boxing. The night he won the toughman contest, the owner of a gym near Pfeiffer University had been one of the fans in attendance. After the fights, he invited Vinny to his gym and taught him some fundamentals.

"There are similarities between pitching and boxing," Vinny says. "When you're pitching, you can't just go fastball, fastball, fastball. You have to hit the corners and think. It's the same way with boxing. You have to think and place your punches. The biggest difference is, when you're pitching, you initiate the action. And in boxing, the other guy does that too. Also, in baseball, someone is trying to hit a home run off you. In boxing, someone is trying to punch your face."

Following his release by the Lumberjacks, Maddalone decided to dedicate himself to boxing. He turned pro in 1999, and with virtually no amateur background, won his first fifteen fights. The record was deceiving.

No fighter travels an easy road; but in some respects, Vinny's was less difficult than most. He was a ticket-seller, so his promoter (Joe DeGuardia, who has built Star Boxing into a force to be reckoned with) put him in fights that he was expected to win. The word was, "Don't match Vinny against guys who can punch because he's going to get hit a lot. Don't put him in with guys who can stick and move because he might not catch up to them."

Vinny was aware of his limitations, but that didn't keep him from enjoying the ride. "The early fights I had in Yonkers were fantastic," he says. "It was such a great feeling to know that so many people were there for me and to hear them cheering."

The first bump in the road came in 2002, when Vinny lost a six-round decision to Al Cole. He rebounded with six consecutive victories, which brought his record to 21-and-1. Then he was stopped in the tenth round by Brian Minto in a fight marked by the only knockdown he has suffered as a pro. That was followed by three more wins, and a fight on ESPN2 against Shannon Miller.

"The best I ever felt after a fight was when I fought Shannon Miller," Maddalone recalls. "He was 11-and-0. I knocked him down twice in the first round and stopped him in five. At that point, I figured, finally, I'm on my way. Then I lost again to Minto."

The die was cast. Vinny was sturdy and durable. He fought with the stubborn determination of a snowplow clearing twelve inches of snow on a wintery day. He would take whatever punches an opponent threw and come back for more. If he fought Godzilla, he'd go toe-to-toe with him. But given his propensity for getting hit and cut, if he fought Bambi, he'd win but wind up looking like he'd fought Godzilla.

As 2007 began, Maddalone's record was 27-and-3. He had never been matched against a world-class fighter. Meanwhile, the power brokers behind Evander Holyfield were trying to rehabilitate their man for a world title fight. Vinny was a building block in that process. On March 17, he entered the ring in Corpus Christi, Texas, to face the former champion. For the first time in his career, Vinny was "the opponent."

"I grew up watching Evander," he says. "His fights against Qawi, Bowe, and Tyson were incredible. And I met him once at a WBA convention after I'd been fighting for a year or two. He posed for a picture with me. But when the opportunity to fight Evander came, there was no doubt in my mind. Right away, I said 'definitely.' "

Vinny likes to talk in the dressing room before a fight. It calms his nerves. "That's the worst part of the game," he says. "A million things are going through my mind. Any guy who says he's not nervous before a fight is lying. When I'm getting my hands wrapped, my stomach is turning. I've had a lot of fights now; and in the dressing room, they all feel like the first. I tell myself again and again, 'Throw punches; stay focused. Throw punches; stay focused.' It wasn't any different before Evander. All I was thinking about was staying focused and putting my fist through his face. When we got in the ring, I said to myself, 'Hey, that's Evander.' But it was no big thing. Then the bell rang and the fighter in me took over."

Holyfield–Maddalone was a bloody one-sided war. Midway through round one, a clash of heads opened up an ugly gash on Vinny's forehead. "I could have told the doctor, 'I can't see,' " he says. "They would have called it a 'no contest' and I would have walked out with my paycheck. But what would that prove? In my mind, this was my fight for the heavyweight championship of the world."

In round two, Maddalone went right at Holyfield, trying to pressure the former champion and turn the contest into a brawl. "I took some shots, but I was okay," he recalls. "Evander is a sharp puncher, but he's not a big puncher. Every punch you take hurts. But when you're in a fight, you don't feel the pain. It's tougher for the people that care about you that are watching."

In round three, Holyfield intensified his assault. Vinny stayed on his feet, but was bleeding profusely and getting pummeled. "Evander caught me with some good shots," he acknowledges. With twelve seconds left in the round, Al Certo (who trained Maddalone for the fight) jumped onto the ring apron and stopped the beating. "I was upset," Vinny says. "It was like, 'This is the biggest fight of my life. How could you do that to me?' But Al was looking after me; I know that. He did what he thought was right."

Maddalone's moment in the spotlight of big-time boxing was gone. The reach for the brass ring had come up short. "I can never accept losing," Vinny says. "But it happens sometimes and I have to deal with it. Without a doubt, I'm glad I fought Evander. The only thing is, I wish I'd won. And if I had to lose, I would have liked to go out on my own terms."

Seven months passed before Maddalone entered the ring again. When he did, the opponent was Jason Barnett. The fight (an eight-rounder at the Manhattan Center in New York on October 18) was made for Vinny to win. All but one of Barnett's bouts had been in Florida. He had nine wins and five losses against undistinguished foes.

Maddalone entered the arena to the theme music from *Rocky* and the roar of the crowd, which was solidly behind him. The bell rang and Barnett began throwing jabs, landing with ease. Vinny plodded methodically forward, telegraphing his blows. Barnett was too quick for him. Vinny's face reddened and began to puff up. The fight was one minute old. A flurry of punches punctuated by a right hand opened a nasty cut beneath Maddalone's left eye and sent him reeling backward just before the bell.

"All my fights; I get hit in the first round," Vinny said afterward. "Maybe I stumbled back a bit, but I wasn't hurt. That was a wake-up call."

And the cut?

"I know going into every fight that I'll probably get cut. If I get cut, it's Danny's [cutman Danny Milano's] job to stop it."

Round two began with more of the same. Then Vinny fired a left hook that appeared to land below the belt followed by an overhand right that put Barnett down. Referee Eddie Cotton called it a knockdown. Barnett rose and began working his jab again. He couldn't miss, but the knockdown made it a 10–8 round for Maddalone.

Round three: Barnett was still jabbing. Vinny kept coming forward, winging punches, pounding away, hitting anything he could hit. "I take their best shots and keep coming," he said later. "It wears the other guy down, physically and mentally."

Round four: More jabs from Barnett. Another cut opened; this one above Vinny's left eye. Blood streamed down his cheek, staining both fighters' trunks. But Barnett was tiring. He could outbox Vinny; he could never out-tough him. Vinny had begun the process of chopping him down.

Round five: Barnett was losing form. Vinny kept coming forward. A lot of his blows went low and to Barnett's kidneys. Vinny isn't a dirty fighter. But he hasn't mastered the art of pinpoint accuracy and often throws punches without being certain where they'll go. The referee seemed oblivious to the fouls.

Round six: Vinnie now had control of the fight. The biggest danger he faced was the possibility of a stoppage by the ring doctor because of the cuts above and below his left eye. The low blows and kidney punches continued. Then, strangely, Cotton took two points away from Barnett; one for what he called a head-butt and the other for pushing his glove in Vinny's face.

In round seven, the scorecards became academic. Barnett raked the laces of his glove against Vinny's cut and Cotton disqualified him. It was an unsatisfying ending to a good fight. Vinny didn't need the referee's help. He was winning on his own. And more to the point, Cotton had called the fight one way. Vinny was given carte blanche to do what he wanted, while Barnett had been held to a stricter standard of conduct.

"Who wants a DQ?" Vinny said afterward. "I wish the ref had let it go. I'd have won a unanimous decision or knocked him out."

So where does Maddalone go from here? The cuts he suffered against Barnett put him on a sixty-day suspension list. Eventually, they'll heal and he'll be in the ring again. He hopes to step up in class once more and, this time, get lucky against a name fighter. Or maybe it won't be luck. Maybe this will be the night that Vinny puts it all together and lands the big punch and gets the "W." Then maybe he'd get a shot at one of the belts, and who knows?

"There are four titles out there," Vinny says. "I'd like a shot at one of them. Maybe it will come, maybe it won't. I'm not the most skilled guy in the world. I'm not gonna tell you I'm Muhammad Ali or Lennox Lewis. I get hit with too many punches. I don't move my head enough, and I let the other guy get off on me. I say, 'Okay, your turn now; then it's my turn and we'll see what happens.' I make every fight a war. But I work hard; I want it more than most guys. Anyone who comes to see me fight gets their money's worth. And I'm more than just tough. I'm more than just heart. I've got some skills. Guys sit on the couch and watch a fight on TV and say things like, 'This guy's a bum.' They have no idea what fighting is like."

"There's millions of people out there who have dreams and never try to fulfill them," Vinny says, putting his career in perspective. "I'm pursuing my dream. I'm thirty-three years old. I feel good; I'm still learning. Right now, I'm doing what I love to do. There's a burning desire inside me to fight. When the candle burns out, I'll walk away from boxing."

The Sunday Times *in London commissioned this article to run the week before Floyd Mayweather versus Ricky Hatton.*

The American Perception of British Fighters

There will be a lot at stake when Ricky Hatton fights Floyd Mayweather Jr. in Las Vegas on December 8. Mayweather's "pound-for-pound" crown and various sanctioning-body belts will be on the line. But more significantly, an entire historical era could be laid to rest.

England is the cradle of modern boxing. But for most of the past century, the American public has looked down its collective nose at British fighters. If Hatton beats Mayweather, it will be among the biggest wins ever for a British boxer.

In the first two decades of the twentieth century, British fighters campaigned successfully in the United States. Featherweight Jem Driscoll came to New York in 1908, and the following year, outboxed the legendary Abe Attell. Freddy Welsh won the world lightweight crown in 1914 and fought more than 100 times in America, emerging victorious against the likes of Ad Wolgast and Benny Leonard. Ted "Kid" Lewis fought the middle years of his 279-bout career in the colonies and seized the welterweight crown from Jack Britton in 1915. Lewis and Britton fought each other twenty times, including six world title fights that were evenly divided between them. Flyweight champion Jimmy Wilde ventured to the United States for the final years of his career.

The turning point in America's perception of British fighters came in 1927, when British, European, and Empire heavyweight champion Phil Scott came to New York and was knocked out in one round by Knute Hansen. Thereafter, Scott became known in the United States as "Phainting Phil" because of his penchant for faking fouls to win via disqualification. Then, in 1935, a heavily-hyped heavyweight named Jack Doyle came to America from Ireland, fought Buddy Baer at Madison Square Garden, and was knocked down seven times before the action was halted in the first round.

Scott and Doyle gave birth to the maxim, "British heavyweights are horizontal heavyweights." Thereafter, Tommy Farr lost a fifteen-round decision to Joe Louis. (Years later, Farr would say, "Every time I hear the name Joe Louis, my nose starts to bleed.") And Don Cockell was demolished by Rocky Marciano.

There were moments of triumph for British boxers. Jack "Kid" Berg won the junior-welterweight title in London in 1930, but lost it to Tony Canzoneri in Chicago a year later. Benny Lynch reigned as flyweight champion from 1935 through 1938, but fought exclusively in the United Kingdom. Freddie Mills toppled Gus Lesnevich in London for the light-heavyweight crown in 1948, but was dethroned by Joey Maxim in his first defense against an American. Randy Turpin defeated the great Sugar Ray Robinson in 1951, also in London, but was knocked out two months later in a rematch in New York. Terry Downes beat middleweight champion Paul Pender in London in 1961, but lost an immediate rematch in Boston.

The pattern was obvious. Even the best British boxers failed when they came to the United States. And all the while, the British heavyweights kept losing. Muhammad Ali beat four of them.

Henry Cooper was a good fighter whose skin betrayed him. He had all the courage in the world and fourteen losses. Ali stopped him twice; both times on cuts. Sir Henry (as he is now known) later explained what it's like to be behind in a fight against an opponent who's outboxing you: "You keep telling yourself, 'I'll do it in the next round; I'll do it in the next round.' And the next round never seems to come. If you care about winning—and all real fighters do—it's the worst feeling in the world."

Cooper's words were an allegory for decades of British heavyweight boxing. Brian London fueled the stereotype, losing to Ali in three rounds (and Floyd Patterson in eleven). Joe Bugner went the distance with "The Greatest" twice, but wasn't competitive either time. "Bugner," Hugh McIlvanney wrote, "is built like a Greek statue but with fewer moves." Richard Dunn confirmed all the negative clichés about British heavyweights, losing to Ali after being knocked down five times.

To the public at large, boxing is defined by the heavyweight division. Thus, when Americans thought of British fighters, they thought of British heavyweights. And British heavyweights were considered "lovable losers with glass chins" who fought standing straight upright until, inevitably, they were knocked down.

And so it went through Frank Bruno, who nicely fit the mold. "Bruno," American sportswriter Jim Murray declared, "has a chin of pure Waterford crystal. The biggest danger in fighting Bruno is that you might get hit by flying glass. He has been on more canvases than Rembrandt."

There were moments of triumph for British boxers in other weight divisions. Lightweight champion Ken Buchanan was a superb fighter. But the lasting image that Americans had of him was his 1972 loss at Madison Square Garden to Roberto Durán.

John Conteh enjoyed a pretty good run, winning the light-heavyweight crown by decision over Jorge Ahumada in 1974. But after three successful defenses, he was stripped of the title and then lost to Mate Parlov.

John Stracey had the good fortune to lift the welterweight championship from a dissipated José Nápoles in 1975, but lost six months later to Carlos Palomino.

Alan Minter captured the middleweight crown from Vito Antuofermo in 1980, but was defeated the same year by Marvin Hagler.

Jim Watt won lightweight honors in 1979 and defended his belt successfully against U.S. Olympic gold-medalist Howard Davis Jr. But Watt was dethroned by Alexis Argüello in 1981.

More significantly, one is hard-pressed to think of a British fighter who came to the United States and won a major fight in the fifty years preceding 1986. That was the year in which Lloyd Honeyghan journeyed to Atlantic City and stopped Donald Curry in six rounds. Curry was the undisputed welterweight champion at the time and near the top of most pound-for-pound lists. It was a breakthrough victory on American soil for an English fighter against an American star. But Curry had been plagued by lifestyle issues. And one year later, Honeyghan lost to Jorge Vaca.

In sum, as far as Americans were concerned, Great Britain had a great boxing tradition but not the fighters. And as boxing historian Craig Hamilton notes, "Americans think they're superior to everyone anyway. The only way to eradicate that perception is to beat it out of them."

Then Lennox Lewis arrived on the scene.

The 1990s were a time of revival for British boxing. With a multiplicity of sanctioning organizations coming into existence, Nigel Benn and Chris Eubank both won middleweight and super-middleweight titles. Naseem Hamed stirred interest in the featherweight division before imploding against Marco Antonio Barrera. But Lennox changed everything.

Lewis was born in England and spent his adolescent years in Canada, where he learned to box. He represented Canada in the 1984 and 1988 Olympics, winning a gold medal in the super-heavyweight division at the 1988 games. When he turned pro, he chose to campaign out of England.

"I had dual citizenship," Lennox recalls, "and an appreciation for the history of British boxing. There wasn't much boxing in Canada, so it was natural for me to return to my British roots. It bothered me at first, the way Americans talked about British fighters. All I heard was, 'British heavyweights are horizontal heavyweights.' They didn't respect me or my craft. But I have to admit, there was some truth to what the Americans were saying. British boxers have always had a lot of heart. British boxers would always get in great shape and tough it out. But very often, there was a lack of skill because of the way British boxers trained. I had the great advantage of being exposed to different training techniques when I was in Canada and, later, in the United States. I had all types of boxers coming at me, in sparring and in fights. That was the key to learning my craft."

Lewis won his first world title in 1993, when he decisioned Tony Tucker. Three fights later, shockingly, he was knocked out by Oliver McCall. He reclaimed the crown from McCall, consolidated the various heavyweight belts, and was the dominant heavyweight in the world. "Lennox Lewis is in danger of giving British heavyweights a good name," Jerry Izenberg (America's premier sportswriter) wrote. Then, in 2001, Lennox was knocked out by Hasim Rahman.

"I wouldn't have become as good as I was unless I had those losses," Lewis says. "The losses give you character to become a true champion. It proves you're a true champion; to suffer a loss, realize your mistake, adjust, and come back to win."

Lewis avenged his loss to Rahman with a fourth-round knockout to regain the heavyweight crown. But one hurdle to full recognition by the American people remained.

"American fans are tough," Lennox says. "You can't prove it to them by beating someone else. To be fully accepted by the American public, you have to go to America and beat the best American fighters. I did that; and eventually, people started saying, 'Hey, he's good.' But there was one more guy out there; the terror, Mike Tyson. Even when Tyson was young, I felt I could beat him. Yes, he looked great, but who was he looking great against? By the time I fought him, Tyson hadn't done much of anything for years. I knew it was going to be a mismatch, but the American people didn't know it."

On June 8, 2002, Lewis hammered Tyson into the canvas like an oversized hammer smashes nails into a pine board. Finally, he had achieved universal recognition as the best heavyweight in the world.

"Tyson is still a big talking point with a lot of people," Lennox says with a smile. "They're always coming up to me and asking, 'How's Mike? What's going on with Mike?' I doubt very much that they ask him, 'How's Lennox? What's going on with Lennox?'"

Lewis broke the dike. Others followed in his wake, although there's debate in America as to how much British boxing has really changed.

"The British have always produced decent fighters," says promoter Bob Arum. "But they haven't gotten better lately. The American fighters have gotten worse. We're not producing good fighters in the United States anymore. You can see that by how we're doing in the Olympics. And the absence of good American fighters has created a void that fighters from other countries are filling."

"If you look at boxing over the decades," adds Billy Graham (who has trained Ricky Hatton from The Hitman's first pro fight), "we've generally done better than most countries. And considering how much smaller we are than the United States, we've done reasonably well in that comparison too. But no matter how you look at it, for the American public to accept you, they've got to see you do it against one of their own in the flesh."

British fighters now have a solid foothold in the cruiserweight division. Last month, David Haye knocked out Jean-Marc Mormeck to win the WBA and WBC cruiserweight titles, while Enzo Maccarinelli successfully defended the WBO crown. Clinton Woods holds the IBF light-heavyweight belt, although most observers rate him behind Bernard Hopkins and Chad Dawson in that division. Junior Witter and Gavin Rees have each claimed a 140-pound title, but are generally rated behind Hatton and IBF champion Paulie Malignaggi.

Meanwhile, the two premier British fighters today are Hatton and Joe Calzaghe.

Calzaghe is undefeated in forty-four fights and is boxing's longest-reigning current champion, having held one or more versions of the super-middleweight crown for ten years. His signature victories have been against Jeff Lacy and Mikkel Kessler. Calzaghe didn't just beat Lacy. He won every minute of every round in their March 4, 2006, confrontation. He was also clearly superior to Kessler, whom he decisioned on November 3, 2007.

But Calzaghe has fought outside of the United Kingdom only twice in his pro career. His victories over Lacy (in Manchester) and Kessler (in Cardiff) were both on British soil. Most of his opponents have been second-tier fighters. And he has yet to defeat an elite American boxer.

As brilliant as Calzaghe might be, he hasn't convinced the skeptics in America. And he won't win them over by fighting Clinton Woods (the IBF light-heavyweight belt-holder from Sheffield) in his next fight. Calzaghe himself says, "A fighter secures his legacy by winning difficult fights against tough opponents." If Joe wants to be fully accepted by the American public, he should journey to the United States and fight the top-ranked light-heavyweight in the world, Bernard Hopkins.

That would be similar to the path Ricky Hatton is following. Thirty-six of Hatton's first forty fights were in England. In 2005, he gained acclaim for an eleventh-round stoppage of Kostya Tszyu. But Hatton had never beaten a top American fighter. And as Lennox Lewis observes, "Just because a fight is a big event in England doesn't mean that it will impress people in the United States. It's essential to a fighter's legacy that he fight the best and beat the best in America."

Last year, Hatton journeyed to America. In victories over Luis Collazo, Juan Urango, and José Luis Castillo, he garnered respect as a tough gutsy fighter. Now he's facing the ultimate challenge: the man regarded by many as the world's best "pound-for-pound" fighter, Floyd Mayweather Jr. Hatton will enter the ring as a clear underdog on Saturday night. But as Lewis notes, "You fight differently when you have an entire country behind you."

If Hatton beats Mayweather, it will eliminate the last vestiges of prejudice in the United States against British fighters. Indeed, Robert Waterman (who was once Hatton's co-promoter) goes further and says, "If Ricky beats Floyd, the shoe will be on the other foot. The Americans will have to worry about how we perceive their fighters."

Sometimes dreams and reality coincide. And sometimes, they don't.

Ricky Hatton in Las Vegas: Dreams versus Reality

"Every so often," essayist Arthur Krystal writes, "two men arise with differently cast minds representing different constituencies, who capture the attention of people not normally disposed to view a fight. Perhaps each battler embodies the interested spectator's own hopes of how the world works."

On December 8, Floyd Mayweather Jr. and Ricky Hatton met in the last big fight of 2007. The differences between them and their constituencies were self-evident.

Mayweather looks like a sleek high-powered precision fighting machine unscathed by the ravages of his trade. Undefeated in thirty-nine fights, he's boxing's reigning pound-for-pound king and brings to mind the words of Tommy Loughran, who proclaimed, "They have to hit me to hurt me, and they can't hit me."

Tim Keown of *ESPN the Magazine* calls Mayweather, "the most cartoonishly self-absorbed boxer in the world." Once known as "Pretty Boy Floyd," the fighter now refers to himself as "Money Mayweather." That sobriquet is founded on Floyd's victory over Oscar De La Hoya earlier this year in a fight that engendered 2.4 million pay-per-view buys for a domestic gross of $134 million. "Money Mayweather" now fantasizes about "the Mayweather brand" and the future of Mayweather Promotions, which he hopes will become a Fortune 500 company. "Skills pay the bills," he says.

Mayweather has been trying to reinvent himself lately, or at least change his image from that of a serial abuser of women to a good family man and charitable benefactor. He also sought to enter the mainstream of American culture earlier this year with an appearance on *Dancing with the Stars*. "You got twenty million people watching *Dancing with the Stars*," Floyd explained. "My goal is to make some of them boxing fans and Floyd Mayweather Jr. fans so they'll buy my fights. That's the businessman in me."

Thereafter, Mayweather's image took a hit when a profanity-laced video featuring MF (Money Floyd) surfaced on YouTube. It wasn't the image that Mayweather was seeking to create on *Dancing with the Stars*.

Hatton, by contrast, has pale skin that accentuates every bump and bruise on his face. His fighting heart is visible in the scars around his eyes. Prior to meeting Mayweather, he was undefeated in 43 fights and had staked a claim to being boxing's best 140-pound fighter (7 pounds beneath the contract weight for his challenge against Floyd).

Mayweather tells everyone what a great guy he is. Hatton shows them. Ray Hatton (Ricky's father) has a memory of his son that's instructive. "As a boy," Ray recalls, "Richard liked to play on the slide in the playground. He always waited his turn with the other children; he never jumped the queue. But he never let anybody cut in line ahead of him either. It was a mistake to try that."

Ricky dropped out of school at age fifteen and worked briefly as a fitter and salesman at a small carpet shop owned by his parents. "He was terrible at both jobs," his mother, Carol, remembers. "But he was good at sports. We would have preferred Richard to be a footballer. But it was his choice and he chose boxing."

Hatton has spent his entire life in Manchester, England, and the city holds him dear to its collective heart. Most ordinary people want to be treated like stars. Ricky is a star who wants to be treated like ordinary people. His parent's house is visible from the backyard of his own. His six-year-old son, Campbell, goes to the same local school that Ricky went to as a boy. He has a self-effacing sense of humor and turns onlookers into fans wherever he goes.

"Before I fought Kostya Tszyu," Ricky recalls, "I was doing roadwork and the police stopped me to find out why someone was running down the road at two o'clock in the morning. Then they recognized me and one of them said, 'My God, it's Ricky Hatton.' I told him, 'Of course, it's Ricky Hatton. What other dickhead would be out running at two o'clock in the morning?'"

Unlike Mayweather, who seems to consider himself the center of the universe, Hatton regards himself as one person in a larger community. For Floyd, the trappings of success are bling, wads of cash, and multiple cars. For Ricky, the joy of success comes from experiencing it with family and friends. About the only negative thing that anyone in Manchester says about him comes from longtime friend Paul Speak, who acknowledges, "Ricky is not a morning person. If you go around his house in the morning, he's very grumpy."

"I think people watch me because I'm an exciting fighter," Hatton says. "But I think they watch me too because they look on me as a mate. I get a huge rush when fans say how much they love me. But I don't expect people to roll out a red carpet for me when I walk down the street. I'm just a normal kid doing very well at what he does. My life is my family and friends and boxing. I like my food. I'll go to the pub for a few pints and to throw darts. There's two things you'll always get from me; an honest effort in the ring and an honest answer out of it. And I'm very lucky. There's nothing I want for in life."

Mayweather and Hatton first crossed paths in Las Vegas at the December 2005 rematch between Jermain Taylor and Bernard Hopkins. "We sat in the same row," Ricky recalls. "Floyd was a few seats further down, so he had to walk past me to get to his seat. I stood up and, out of respect, said, 'Hi Floyd, how are you doing?' and went to shake his hand. He wouldn't shake my hand, and he muttered something on the lines of, 'Let's get it on; I'll knock you out.'"

Once Mayweather–Hatton was actually signed, the kick-off press conference was held in the skating rink at Rockefeller Center, which was a signal that this would be another big Golden-Boy-promoted event. "Floyd is the best," Ricky told the assembled media. "That's why I want to fight him. It would be easy for me to stay in the comfort zone in my own weight division in my own backyard in England. But I fancy the challenge."

Thereafter, as the media tour progressed, the differing personalities of the combatants became clear.

Floyd was Floyd. "Ricky took this fight because he's getting older and losing his edge," Mayweather said. "Look at how scarred up his face is and how beat up he is. He knew he was going to lose soon. That's why he wants to fight me. If you lose to the best, there's little shame; but if you lose to a nobody, you're washed up. Ricky Hatton should be appreciative just to be sharing the ring with me."

Hatton, in turn, responded to Mayweather's jibes with a mix of insight and humor:

- "I think Floyd is a very insecure man. That's why he surrounds himself with five or six bodyguards, and they always seem to be 'yes' men. He always needs people whispering in his ear, 'You're the man; you're number one; you're going to do this and you're going to do that.' If you believe you're the best, you don't need anybody reminding you or reassuring you. If I talked to Billy [trainer Billy Graham] and Paul [Paul Speak] and Kerry [nutritionist and conditioning coach Kerry Kayes] the way Floyd talks to his people, giving orders, snapping my fingers at them, they'd tell me to fuck off."
- "Floyd's life is a lot like his fights; all show, no substance. With Floyd, it's all about what his watch is and what jewelry he's wearing. His watch is bigger than my world title belt. He makes a Christmas tree look gritty. What man gets up on stage and goes on about his suit and his rings and his watches? Financially, I've done fantastically well. I have a nice home, two good cars, and I can go on holiday whenever I want. But I don't flash my money. I think to do that belittles people."

- "I was never someone to get right in your face, try and intimidate you like that. I knew it was coming. 'I'm going to beat you like a bitch, butt-fuck you.' Basic stuff like that. It was nonsense, really. I found it quite amusing. Floyd's not exactly intimidating-looking with his nice suits and his bling. He doesn't make me want to run down the street to get away."
- "Floyd has his way and I have my way. I don't take it personally because he says the same things about his opponent every time he fights. Besides, nothing that either of us says matters. It's only about what happens when we fight. But where do you draw the line between selling tickets and looking for an edge and disrespecting the sport? What's the point of being the best fighter in the world if everyone thinks you're a dickhead?"

At the final stop on the media tour (a September 21 press conference in Manchester), Hatton told Mayweather. "All week, you've bad-mouthed Ricky Hatton. But none of it has worked, and it's a waste of time trying to upset me and my fans. Floyd, you're pissing in the wind."

At the same stop, Mayweather began stroking Ricky's leg, and Hatton responded, "Stop trying to feel my dick, Floyd. All week, you've been talking about kicking my ass and now you're feeling my dick. I'm getting worried about you. People ask me whether I've missed my six–year–old son, Campbell. I have in many ways. But to be honest, I've spent the whole week [on the media tour] with this fucking six-year-old next to me, so nothing has changed there."

There was also a moment of pathos later when Hatton discussed Mayweather's much-publicized split with his father. "Even after all the abuse and the disrespect Floyd has shown me," Ricky said, "I can't help but feel sorry for him. He never had a childhood, never had time to grow up. I knew Floyd had differences with his dad and that things were frosty. Now it seems the relationship is over completely. To my mind, that's a crying shame and something that would be unbearable. I couldn't imagine being at war with my dad. If for some reason, Heaven forbid, I fell out with my dad or something happened to him, I'd hang up my gloves. I can't imagine boxing, or life, without him."

As for the fight, Mayweather was a clear favorite. Age wasn't a factor. Floyd is thirty; Ricky is twenty-nine. But weight was. This would be Hatton's second fight at 147 pounds. In the first (against Luis Collazo in May 2006), he eked out a decision but faded late. Collazo had him in trouble in the final round.

Also, Hatton has a penchant for gaining as much as forty pounds between fights. "When you play darts," he says "it's required that you have a few pints and something to eat afterward. I don't lie about it. People ask, 'Do you like to have a drink of alcohol?' Yes, I love to. 'Do you like fast foods?' Yes. 'Do you put weight on?' Yes."

But as Mayweather observed, "You don't see me at a pub drinking beer. You don't ever see me twenty or thirty pounds outside my weight. I fight at 147; I walk around at 147. That's wear and tear on the body; gaining that much weight and losing that much weight."

And more significantly, Mayweather is one of the most gifted fighters on the planet. Thus, Hatton would be giving away size, speed, and skill.

In the weeks leading up to the fight, Mayweather proclaimed, "Hatton is one-dimensional. He comes forward in straight lines. He's easy to read and easy to predict. I can adapt to any style of fighter, but the come-forward style is made for me to show my full range of boxing skills. I'm the better fighter; I'm the better-conditioned fighter; I'm the smarter fighter. Ricky Hatton has never fought anyone like me. He's the best fighter in England. I'm the best fighter in the world."

Roger Mayweather (Floyd's uncle and trainer) was equally condescending and confident. "Hatton can put on all the pressure he wants," Uncle Roger said. "Can he outbox Floyd? Do he have more skill than Floyd? The only thing he can do is pressure Floyd. But other than that, he can't do shit. He ain't nothing but a high-profile club fighter."

On a more objective note, middleweight champion Kelly Pavlik voiced the view, "Hatton is a pressure fighter. He has the style to beat Mayweather but not the punch. When Hatton gets into position to do damage, he can't do the job with one punch. He wears his opponents down, but he won't hit Mayweather enough to do that."

And boxing maven Don Elbaum opined, "Hatton has a good chance to beat Mayweather until the bell rings."

Still, Hatton's partisans were optimistic. Ricky has an effective mauling style (some call it "the Greco–Roman school of boxing"). And if Mayweather chose to fight off the ropes (which he'd done against De La Hoya), it would improve Ricky's chances.

"I think Floyd Mayweather is an absolutely fantastic fighter," Hatton's trainer, Billy Graham, said. "Defensively, he's breathtaking. His hands are unbelievably fast. I've got no argument to say that he shouldn't be regarded as the best pound-for-pound fighter on the planet. Ricky hasn't fought anybody quite like Floyd, because there is nobody like Floyd. But Ricky has fought similar fighters; people with fast hands, boxers, movers. And I don't think Floyd has ever faced a more skillful pressure fighter in his life than Ricky because there's not a more skillful pressure fighter on the planet."

"I know Ricky Hatton better than anyone," Graham continued. "I know what he's got. Ricky Hatton is a special fighter. If you can't see that, you don't know what you're looking at. He's blessed with fantastic peripheral vision, fantastic balance, and fantastic reflexes with amazing strength and ferocity. He works hard; he's a learner; and his boxing brain is incredible. Floyd is fantastic at what he does. And Floyd can punch. I keep reminding Ricky not to get careless and forget that. But Ricky has the perfect style to beat him."

Hatton, of course, was in accord. "I've studied the tapes," Ricky said. "Floyd is very very good at what he does. He's got fantastic hand speed. He's got a wonderful defense, and he likes to take the steam out of his opponents by making them miss. He's a very versatile fighter. He can pretty much do everything. He has so many tricks; you have to deny him the time and space to do his thing."

"But it's very pleasing for me that the fight where Floyd was at his least comfortable was the first fight against José Luis Castillo, who was able to bully him to the ropes a lot. I don't think Castillo is physically as strong as me, as quick as me, or has footwork as good as me. I move in very, very quickly on my opponents and stick to them like glue. I've got the style to give Floyd absolute nightmares. His hand speed will concern me if I'm on the outside, but it won't bother me when I'm on his chest. I will constantly be in his face and give him no chance to rest."

"One thing that Floyd hasn't bargained on," Hatton continued, "is how clever I am. That's going to be the key, really. I don't think Mayweather realizes I'm as good as I am. He just sees the obvious. Strong kid with a big heart who keeps coming forward. But there's a lot more to me than that. There's a lot of thought to what I do; if you watch carefully how quick I move in on my opponents, how I change the angles. It's only when fighters actually get in there with me that they realize there's a method to the madness."

"I'm an underdog, and I understand that. Very few people are picking me to beat him, which suits me fine because I know what an oh sweet victory that's going to be when I do it. If boxing history has told us anything, it's how many upsets there's been. You don't have to fight at a distance to be a talented fighter. I'm not going to beat Floyd at his game. I'm going to beat him at mine. My heart will explode before I leave him alone for one second. Anyone who says I haven't got a chance against Floyd Mayweather; I honestly don't think they know what they're talking about."

And there was one more factor to be considered. The Hatton camp wanted (and needed) a referee who would let Ricky fight on the inside and not prematurely separate the combatants.

"I'm expecting to get a fair shake in America," Billy Graham said. "That's all we want. Anyone who says Ricky holds on the inside is talking rubbish. The last thing Ricky wants to do when he gets inside is stop the action and have the referee break the fighters apart. What Ricky does on the inside—and it's perfectly legal—is he tries to rearrange the position of his opponent's arms to create avenues for his punches. So let's have a good referee who's going to let the two best fighters on the planet fight. Let the fans see what they've paid for."

There was a buzz in Las Vegas during fight week. An estimated 18,000 Hatton fans flew in from England, bringing energy to the strip that hadn't been seen since De La Hoya versus Trinidad in 1999. "I thought I was in Manchester when I got here," Hatton quipped.

A majority of the Brits didn't have fight tickets and wound up watching the action at closed-circuit locations around the city. During their stay, they made the owners of beer distributorships very happy. And one had to go back twenty-seven years to Muhammad Ali against Larry Holmes to find a fight where the expert opinion and betting odds were so divergent. The consensus in the boxing community was that Mayweather deserved to be a 4-to-1 favorite. *The Associated Press* declared, "From a technical standpoint, Mayweather's superior size, reach, and defensive skills make the fight a mismatch." But British hearts were moving the line, which would close at slightly less than 2-to-1 in Floyd's favor.

The final pre-fight press conference went pretty much as expected. "I'm not going to say that I'm in the best shape of my life," Mayweather advised the media, "because I'm always in great shape."

Hatton injected a note of levity into the proceedings, when he declared, "I'm just a big, fat over-protected Englishman who hasn't fought anyone." Then he added, "I feel the confidence building with each day. There's no doubt in my mind what the outcome of this fight is going to be."

"It's a nice position to be in," Graham said that night. "Fully believing you're going to win when almost no one thinks you have a chance."

Graham was in a philosophical mood. A former fighter, he had fourteen pro bouts as a junior-middleweight, winning twelve and losing two. He retired at age twenty-two.

"I had ten fights in my first year," Billy reminisced. "That was too much. I had great balance, fast reflexes, fast hands. But to be honest, I had a chip on my shoulder and never applied myself the way I should have. If I was training the young me, I wouldn't have put up with me. I'm a better trainer than I was a fighter."

Graham is deaf in his left ear and has the wear and tear of fifty-two years of hard living on his body along with twenty-one tattoos. Ed Caesar of *The Times* has described him as a bartender's closing-time nightmare with the kind of face one sees hanging from Notre Dame. Billy and Ricky have been together on a handshake agreement for fourteen years. "We're just two local lads from the housing estates in Manchester that have done very, very well," Graham says. "If boxing had ended for me five years ago, we'd still be mates."

Now Graham was tired. "The attention is flattering but I'm exhausted," he said. "Every step you take, someone wants a picture, a handshake, an autograph. There are all these interviews. Everyone wants to buy you a drink. There's no chance to retreat into yourself. My brain's tired; I'm getting stale. And if a trainer feels that way, there's a danger that the mood will rub off on his fighter."

"I'll be getting out of boxing soon," Graham continued. "People don't believe me when I say it. I've been in boxing my entire life. But it can't possibly be any better for me than what I've had with Ricky. Taking him from a very young man to where he is today has been a joy in my life. My knees are gone. There are times when I need a shot of lidocaine to work the pads. There's no sense in making a lot of money and living long if you can't enjoy it. When Ricky leaves boxing, I think that will be it for me."

Then Graham's thoughts turned to the fight ahead. "Floyd walks around like fucking Apollo Creed," he said. "But Ricky isn't fazed by reputations. There's no fear; no intimidation. If Floyd wins, it will be because he's the better fighter. I think I'll just stay in my room tonight; read a book or something. No fight tapes; no talking with boxing people. Just relax and think a bit."

On Friday, each fighter's camp was readying for battle. The weigh-in (which was open to the public) was scheduled for 2:30 P.M. in the MGM Grand Garden Arena. The Brits started lining up for admission shortly after five o'clock in the morning.

Ultimately, 6,000 fans (virtually all of them passionately pro-Hatton) jammed their way into the open portion of the arena. They roared for all things British (appearances by Lennox Lewis and Joe Calzaghe) and booed Bernard Hopkins as vociferously as he'd been booed in Puerto Rico prior to fighting Félix Trinidad.

They also sang. "God Save the Queen" received some play. Indeed, one half-expected Queen Elizabeth to make an appearance in the media center. But the Ricky Hatton theme song was the composition of choice. Said to have been written so that even drunk people can remember the words, it combines the tune from "Winter Wonderland" with lyrics as follows:

There's only one Ricky Hatton
One Ricky Hatton
Walking along
Singing a song
Walking in a Hatton Wonderland

By one count, it was sung seventy-three times before Hatton weighed in at 145 pounds and Mayweather at 147. "If the fight is as good as the weigh-in, it will be great," Hatton said afterward.

Mayweather wasn't intimidated by the crowd, but he could have been forgiven if he were a bit jealous over the affection that it lavished on his opponent.

On Saturday night, Hatton entered dressing room 4 at the MGM Grand Garden Arena at 5:45 P.M. An eight-and-one-half-by-eleven-inch piece of paper taped to the door read, "Blue Corner—Ricky Hatton." Beneath that, someone had scrawled in a blue marker pen, "Ready by 7:55 P.M."

The dressing room was hot and stuffy. A British flag was taped to the wall. A large, blue, plastic tub filled with ice and several dozen bottles of water stood by the door. Three pint bottles of Guinness had been thrown into the mix.

Minutes earlier, Ricky's brother (Matthew) had completed an eight-round fight against Frankie Santos of Puerto Rico. He had yet to return to the dressing room.

"Matthew won," Ricky was told.

"Knockout or decision?"

"80–72, 80–72, 79–73."

Ricky smiled. "That's a good start on the evening."

Matthew and his cornermen (Billy Graham, Kerry Keyes, and cutman Mick Williamson; all of whom would also work Ricky's fight) came through the door. "We got that one out of the way," Graham said. "One down and one to go."

Ricky fingered a rolled-up piece of tape and shot it toward a garbage can in the manner of a basketball point guard. The tape missed its target. "Not my sport," he said. He walked over, picked the tape off the floor, and dropped it in the trash.

A SKY-TV crew came in to conduct a brief interview for British television. They were followed by Larry Merchant of HBO. "Just leave me alone and let me do what I have to do," Hatton said to no one in particular after the television crews were gone. "I'm trying to make sense when I talk, but my mind's not on doing interviews now."

Then Hatton set about connecting the wires on an audio system he'd brought with him and positioned the speakers where he wanted them. For a moment, he looked like a young man moving into a new apartment.

At 6:35, music began to blare. For the next two hours, it would be very loud in the dressing room. Except for the time spent having his hands taped, Ricky would be on his feet, constantly moving like a hyperactive child, pacing and shadow-boxing with increasing intensity to the music.

A television monitor at the far end of the room showed Edner Cherry knocking out Wes Ferguson with a picture-perfect left hook in the first pay-per-view bout of the evening. "I wouldn't mind landing one of them in a bit," Hatton offered. "Please give me one of them tonight."

Graham looked across the room at cutman Mick Williamson and said quietly, "I'm afraid we're going to need him tonight. I'm a realist. I think Ricky will win, but he gets cut. He gets bad cuts; and Floyd throws those fast slashing punches."

As time passed, Sugar Ray Leonard, Shane Mosley, and Marco Antonio Barrera entered to wish Ricky luck. The music kept changing, from rap to acid rock to something akin to an Irish jig. At seven o'clock, Hatton changed tracks again and the raspy voice of Mick Jagger was heard.

"I can't get no satisfaction . . ."

Ricky picked up the pace of his shadow-boxing and sang aloud.

"I can't get no satisfaction . . . Cause I try and I try and I try and I try."

Soon everyone in the room was singing.

"I can't get no . . . I can't get no . . . When I'm drivin' in my car, and that man comes on the radio . . ."

Floyd Mayweather's image appeared on the television monitor.

"I'm coming for you, fucker," Ricky growled.

David Beckham entered the room. He and Hatton met earlier in the year and have been text-messaging back and forth ever since. "I can't believe that someone like David Beckham texts me," Ricky said several months ago. The fighter had attended a Los Angeles Galaxy soccer game as Beckham's guest. Now the favor was being returned.

Beckham stood by the door, maintaining a distance; one world-class athlete respecting the mental preparation required of another. At 7:15, for the first time in ninety minutes, Hatton sat and Billy Graham began taping his hands. Only then did Beckham walk over and clasp Ricky on the shoulder.

Recording star Tom Jones (who would sing "God Save the Queen" later in the evening) entered. Ricky looked up. "Is Elvis coming too?" he queried.

At 7:24, referee Joe Cortez came into the room to give Hatton his final pre-fight instructions. In June of this year, Cortez had refereed Ricky's fight against José Luis Castillo without incident. Now Cortez ran through the usual litany and closed with, "Any questions?"

"Ricky is an inside fighter," Graham said. "He fights clean but he's an aggressive fighter."

"I'll let the fight take its course," Cortez promised.

The referee left. Graham finished taping Hatton's hands. David Beckham and Tom Jones slipped out the door. Kerry Kayes helped Ricky on with his trunks; teal-and-silver with black trim and black fringe.

The television monitor showed Jeff Lacy and Peter Manfredo facing off for round one in the final preliminary bout of the evening. It was expected to be a short fight. Hatton gloved up and began working the pads with Graham.

Eight o'clock. Lacy and Manfredo were in round five.

Ricky paced a bit . . . There was more pad-work with Graham.

8:12 . . . Lacy and Manfredo began round eight.

8:20 . . . Aggravation was etched on Ricky's face. He had expected to be in the ring by now.

At 8:23, Lacy–Manfredo ended. In the main arena, Tom Jones sang "God Save the Queen" followed by Tyrese's rendition of "The Star-Spangled Banner."

Finally, Team Hatton left the dressing room. As Ricky came into view of the crowd, there were thunderous cheers.

The fighters were introduced and the bell for round one sounded.

As expected, Hatton moved forward from the start, with Mayweather potshotting from the outside. The crowd roared with every blow that Ricky landed, but Floyd's hands were exponentially faster. Mayweather's speed was a problem for Ricky. And the conduct of referee Joe Cortez made the challenge more daunting.

To get inside, Hatton had to navigate his way past Mayweather's fists and also Floyd's left elbow. Once inside, he was frequently fouled. Mayweather was allowed to go low; hold; and use his head, forearms, and elbows as offensive weapons. Often, Ricky maneuvered into position to work effectively and Cortez broke the fighters even though Hatton was still punching. By breaking them prematurely again and again, the referee denied Ricky the chance to impose his physical strength and forced him to fight much of the battle at long range. That, in turn, exposed him to Floyd's potshots as he tried to work his way back in again.

In the first round, Cortez broke the fighters eleven times; many of them when one or both men had an arm free and was punching. From there, it got worse; thirteen times in round two and fourteen in round three.

A live underdog waits for the moment when the favorite makes a mistake that will undermine his superiority. In Mayweather–Hatton, it never came. In round three, Floyd opened an ugly gash above Ricky's right eye. Still, Hatton persevered. In round five, he did his best work of the night, winning the stanza on the cards of all three judges. Significantly, Cortez broke the fighters only four times in round five.

Round six began with another Hatton offensive. Then, fifty seconds into the stanza, Mayweather appeared to turn his back as a defensive maneuver with his head going through the ropes. Ricky threw a punch and missed, and Cortez took a point away from Hatton. "When the referee took a point away, I lost my composure a bit," Ricky said afterward. "I thought I was doing all right. I was two rounds down probably, but coming on nicely. Then the point got taken away, and I felt it wasn't going to be a level playing field. So I began trying to force things and took more risks and left myself open more than I should have."

Thereafter, Mayweather ran the table. In round eight, he began putting his punches together, landing hard, clean shots to the head and body. Round nine was more of the same. But Hatton kept coming and his fans' ardor never dimmed. The crowd sang "there's only one Ricky Hatton" again and again with a fervor that increased as their hero's troubles grew, as though they were trying to will him to victory.

In round ten, Mayweather closed the show. Hatton launched a left hook from too far away. And as Ricky's arm went in motion, Floyd countered with a highlight-reel blow. Rather than wait for the punch to miss, he threw second and landed first with a lightning left hook of his own. Hatton never saw the punch coming. He went down and got up, but he knew he'd been hit. Then Mayweather landed several more blows, and Cortez appropriately stopped the fight.

Six thousand miles is a long way to travel for a broken heart.

In the dressing room after the fight, Hatton sat on a chair and bowed his head. The damage done to his face by Mayweather's fists was accentuated by several cold sores above his upper lip.

Carol Hatton walked over to her son, leaned down, and hugged him. "You did us proud," she said. Ray and Matthew Hatton joined them.

"I really thought I was going to win," Ricky told them.

Ray Leonard came in to offer condolences. Billy Graham stood off to the side. After the fight, the trainer had approached Roger Mayweather, offered his hand, and said, "Congratulations."

"I told you he was going to get fucking whupped," Roger responded.

Now, in the dressing room, Graham shook his head. "It's hard to be gracious in defeat," he said. "It's easy to be gracious when you win, but even that was too much for Roger. I'd rather train Ricky Hatton than Floyd Mayweather Jr., and I'd rather be Billy Graham than Roger Mayweather." Billy took a deep breath. "I still think Ricky can beat Floyd. But he didn't; so that's it, isn't it? And I give Floyd credit. He finished the fight. He brought the curtain down, didn't he?"

A security guard opened the door. "Brad Pitt and Angelina Jolie would like to come in. Is it all right?"

Before Ricky could answer, the women in the room, who now included Jennifer Dooley (Ricky's girlfriend) and Jenna Coyne (Matthew's fiancée) in addition to Ricky's mother, answered in the affirmative.

The celebrity couple entered. Brad Pitt walked over to the fighter. "There's still only one Ricky Hatton," he said.

Ray Leonard went in search of a photographer who would take a photo of him with Pitt and Jolie.

Eventually the well-wishers filtered out and Ricky was left with his core team. "The referee did me no favors tonight," he said, reflecting on the previous hour. "I can't complain about Floyd. It's a rough business. You do what you can get away with, and Floyd was good on the inside. I'm not exactly Mother Teresa in the ring myself. If I can get a sly one in there, I'll do it. But the referee let Floyd foul the living daylights out of me. And when I was in position to do damage, he forced me out to long range again. Let's be honest. The referee was poor tonight."

Then Hatton lay down on the rubdown table, motionless with his hands crossed across his chest. Dr. Frank Ryan closed the wound above his right eye with one deep stitch on the inside and seven on the outside. One could only begin to imagine the echoes that were reverberating in Ricky's mind. The three bottles of Guinness lay in the ice, untouched.

So . . . What is one to make of Mayweather–Hatton?

The first thing to say is that Mayweather is a superbly gifted fighter. With a different referee, most likely he still have been too skilled, too big, and too fast for Hatton. But the fight would have unfolded differently.

After the bout, Cortez declared, "I know in my heart that I was honest and fair to both fighters. I went home satisfied and proud." But former champions Barry McGuigan and Jim Watt have since respectively labeled the referee's conduct of the fight "disgraceful" and "deplorable."

Cortez is fond of closing his instructions in the ring with the words, "Remember, guys; I'm fair but I'm firm." He has even legally trademarked the phrase.

"Fair but firm" is a nice concept. But on the night of December 8, Cortez wasn't. Let's be charitable and say that the usually capable referee had a bad night. Let's also acknowledge that no other major sport has officials who bring their own arbitrary interpretation of the rules to their job to the degree that boxing does.

Hatton says he wants to fight again. There's more boxing left in him, but he would be well-served by returning to 140 pounds.

Evaluating Mayweather's future requires a look at the past. This has been quite a year for Floyd with victories over De La Hoya and Hatton (both of which were featured on HBO's 24/7) and an appearance on *Dancing with the Stars*.

Roger Mayweather tells anyone who will listen that Floyd and Sugar Ray Robinson are the two greatest fighters who ever lived, although he concedes that Henry Armstrong runs a close third. Leonard Ellerbe (Mayweather's friend and business representative) says, "Floyd's operating on a level all by himself. He's competing by himself. These other fighters out there aren't even challenging Floyd. If Floyd wanted to, he could win the middleweight title."

Mayweather has amassed an impressive body of work. He's an excellent fighter who would have been competitive with the best in any era. Against Hatton, he unveiled another tool in his arsenal by demonstrating that he can fight tough on the inside. But to prove that he ranks among the legends of the sport, he'll have to seek out greater challenges.

Here, a look at the career of Sugar Ray Leonard is instructive. Leonard turned pro after winning a gold medal at the 1976 Olympics. He had his share of early triumphs, including a tenth-round knockout of Floyd Mayweather Sr. Then he stopped Wilfred Benítez for the 147-pound crown. Mayweather has significant victories against Diego Corrales, José Luis Castillo, Zab Judah, Ricky Hatton, and Oscar De La Hoya. But there's nothing on Floyd's resumé to match the later inquisitors that Leonard had.

As Leonard's career progressed, he made the incomparable Roberto Duran say "no mas." He came from behind to score a dramatic fourteenth-round knockout over Thomas Hearns in one of boxing's most memorable dramas. And he moved up in weight to score a split-decision triumph over Marvelous Marvin Hagler. Before Mayweather is canonized, let him fight Miguel Cotto (as a parallel to Duran); then Paul Williams (Thomas Hearns but with a lesser punch). And if he beats those two, he should look for an opponent who approximates Hagler.

Pound-for-pound isn't about being undefeated or how many belts a fighter has. Pound-for-pound is about beating the best.

If Mayweather wants to electrify the boxing world and prove his greatness, he'll fight Cotto next. Miguel is a bigger, stronger version of Hatton. One can imagine a scenario in which Floyd dances rings around Cotto, frustrates him, and potshots him to pieces. But one can also envision a scenario in which Cotto tracks Floyd down and beats him up. Cotto is the most dangerous opponent out there for Mayweather. A fighter isn't pound-for-pound if he's ducking his biggest challenge.

This article gave me the opportunity to write in depth about Jack Dempsey; something that I'd never done before.

Jack Dempsey Revisited

September 22 will mark the eightieth anniversary of the famous "long count" fight between Jack Dempsey and Gene Tunney. The two men are remembered as adjoining links in history's chain of heavyweight champions. But Dempsey was more than just another champion. He was one of the most charismatic fighters in ring history and the bridge between boxing's old and modern eras.

Boxing's most popular heavyweight champions have reflected the age in which they reigned. Joe Louis was perfectly juxtaposed with the trials of the Great Depression and World War II. Rocky Marciano mirrored the simple optimism of the 1950s. Muhammad Ali was inextricably intertwined with the turmoil of the 1960s. Mike Tyson embodied the excess and wanton greed of the late 1980s.

Jack Dempsey personified the "Roaring '20s." It was a time when Red Grange was synonymous with college football, Bill Tilden epitomized tennis, and Bobby Jones dominated golf. Even a horse got into the act with Man O' War winning twenty of twenty-one races entered. But two giants bestrode it all: Dempsey and Babe Ruth.

In the ring, Dempsey attacked with unrelenting ferocity. Ruth swung for the fences every time he stepped to the plate. Dempsey fought like Ruth played baseball, and Ruth played baseball like Dempsey fought. Millions of Americans thrilled to their exploits as they led the way to a previously unimaginable commercialization of sports.

At decade's end, Ruth signed a contract that paid him $80,000 a year. When asked if it was appropriate for him to make more money than the president of the United States, The Babe famously replied, "Why not? I had a better year than he did." Dempsey, by then, had made ten times the president's annual salary for one night's work.

The 1920s are thought of as a "Golden Age of Sports," but they were also a golden age of sportswriting. Grantland Rice, Damon Runyan, Ring Lardner, Heywood Broun, Hype Igoe, and Westbrook Pegler were among the many who contributed to the Dempsey legend. Thus, it's surprising how few books are devoted in their entirety to him.

Jack Dempsey by Randy Roberts (published in 1979) remains the most reliable repository of information about the fighter. Dempsey himself contributed to four autobiographical works. The other biographies (and there aren't many) are, for the most part, hagiographies that contain nuggets of information but also recount incidents that seem less real than apocryphal.

William Harrison Dempsey (the fighter's original name) was born in Manassa, Colorado, on June 24, 1895. His parents were Irish, although both had Cherokee blood. A great-great-grandmother on his father's side of the family (Rachel Solomon) was Jewish.

The life expectancy for a white male born in the United States in 1895 was forty-seven years. For a child born into poverty in the American West, it was considerably less. The Dempseys were poor. "I had only one toy; a spinning top that my father whittled out of wood," the fighter later recalled. "I didn't know any other toys existed." Of eleven children born to Hyrum and Celia Dempsey, two died in infancy, one died of tuberculosis at a young age, one committed suicide after shooting his wife, and another was stabbed to death.

Dempsey was schooled through eighth grade. At age sixteen, he left home. Roberts observes, "Pictures from this period show William Dempsey as a beetle-browed dark-haired youth with dirty hands and long taut muscles on a large-boned but thin frame. One's attention, however, is immediately focused on his face. The nose, broken in several places, the expressionless mouth, and the cold, haunting eyes suggest a childhood that had been less than kind. The reasons for leaving home are written everywhere on that hungry face."

For five years beginning in 1911, Dempsey was a wandering man. "There was no romance in the life," Roberts writes. "He lived in mining camps and hobo jungles, rode the rods, and more than once begged for food. What separated him was his willingness, even eagerness, to work. He accepted any type of employment from washing dishes, cutting lawns, and scrubbing floors to the harder work of coal mining, digging ditches, and picking fruit."

Dempsey later elaborated upon that theme. "On the banks of the railroad tracks," he recalled, "generally near a freshwater stream, hobos, tramps, and others who had fallen on hard times would gather, bundled up in layers of old clothing and newspaper, warming themselves and whatever food they pooled over a fire. As long as you threw a donation in the pot, you were welcome to eat. Moving was part of the business of survival. When all the peaches had been picked in one town, we'd hear that the beets were coming in a hundred miles away. Or the sheriff might drop a gentle hint; something like, 'Get out of here, bum.' I was a dishwasher and a miner; I dug ditches, punched cattle, and shined shoes. I went hungry for days rather than steal. I begged for any kind of job to earn a flop and a meal."

As for riding the rods (the two narrow steel beams on the underside of a train car), Dempsey remembered, "Sometimes it got real cold under the train. You'd be hanging on with your eyes shut to avoid the hot blinding cinders and trying to keep warm at the same time. It wasn't easy, especially when exhaustion set in. When that happened, I would ties my hands and feet to the train's lower rungs. You have to be desperate to gamble like that. But if you weren't desperate, you wouldn't be on the rods."

"Sure, I was a hobo," Dempsey said, summing up. "But I was never a bum."

Dempsey had always loved to fight. "At the age of eleven," he later recalled, "I was preparing to be a prizefighter." From that time on, he'd bathed his face and hands in beef brine to toughen them up and chewed resin from pine trees in the belief that it would strengthen his jaw.

It was during his wandering period that Dempsey began fighting as a source of income. "From the time Dempsey left home," Roberts writes, "he fought to earn money whenever he could. He battled in barrooms, mining camps, wherever men gathered. Sometimes he was beaten; for in the world of miners, cowboys, railroad workers, and lumberjacks, there was frequently someone who could maul a 130-pound sixteen-year-old. But he was at ease amidst violence. He wanted desperately to leave the world of poverty. He was certainly not afraid of being hurt or of injuring other men."

Dempsey estimated that, fighting under the name "Kid Blackie," he had a hundred fights in Colorado, Utah, and Nevada between 1911 and mid-1914. "There were days when fighting only got me a buck or two," he recalled. "I was knocked down plenty. I wanted to stay down; I couldn't. I had to collect that two dollars for winning or go hungry. I had one fight when I was knocked down eleven times before I got up to win. I had to get up. I was a hungry fighter. When you haven't eaten for two days, you'll understand."

It was also during this time that Dempsey developed the fighting style that would serve him well throughout his ring career. He moved forward, chin tucked in, throwing punches from the opening bell with all-out aggression with both hands. Every punch had the power to hurt his opponent. If he was knocked down, he got up and started punching again. As Paul Gallico later wrote, "He recognized no deadlines on the body of his opponent and asked for none to be enforced upon his." He hit low and on the break. Ray Arcel put things in perspective saying, "Dempsey was a saloon fighter. With Dempsey, every part of your body was a legal target. And when he hit you, you stayed hit."

Dempsey himself would acknowledge, "Many said I was ruthless in the ring. How I'd stand over a fellow who was down and clout him as he tried to rise; how I would get behind an opponent staggering to his feet and flatten him with a sucker punch as he turned to face me. I did all those things and more, and I did them well. I learned those tricks from men who flattened me as I struggled for footing or threw brain-shaking sucker rights as I turned groggily to face them. It was part of the rules through many of my ring years. I could hit and I had fast hands. I took them out as quick as I could. Anytime a man is in front of you, regardless of who he is, he's always got a chance. You may get your eye cut; you may break your hand; you may get your jaw broken. So the main thing is, the sooner the safer."

Dempsey's first recorded bouts as a professional were in Colorado and Utah in 1914. Then he dropped the name "Kid Blackie" and became known as "Jack" Dempsey in tribute to the great nineteenth-century middleweight who had fought under that name. In 1916, he journeyed to New York but was unable to earn enough fighting to cover his expenses. In old age, he would reminisce, "Only later did I realize that New York never wants you. It's only you that wants New York." After three months in the big city, he rode the rods back west.

Then Maxine Cates entered his life. "I love women," Dempsey said decades later. "An awful lot of women have been kind and generous and magnificent company. I spent some time [in Salt Lake City] with the girls along Commercial Street. They were, let's say, named for the street. We got along well."

Cates played piano in a saloon on Commercial Street in addition to performing other tasks. She and Dempsey were married on October 9, 1916. He was twenty-one; she was thirty-six. "I knew about girls," Dempsey said later. "I didn't know about women."

Once they were married, Dempsey traveled and fought while Maxine continued to do what she did best. They saw each other occasionally and he sent her money from time to time. In February 1919, they were divorced. She died five years later in a dance-hall fire in Juárez, Mexico.

Meanwhile, Dempsey's ring career took a quantum leap forward in 1917, when he fell under the managerial guidance of John Leo McKernan (better known as "Doc Kearns").

Kearns knew the boxing business, was well connected, and came to his task unencumbered by ethical considerations of any kind. By 1919, thanks to good matchmaking, better publicity, and his fighter's skills, he'd built Dempsey into an attraction of modest renown.

But boxing in the early decades of the twentieth century was at low tide. The sport hadn't produced a popular heavyweight champion since James Jeffries retired in 1904. Moral "reformers" (who enjoyed the upper hand in American life) regarded the sweet science as sinful, and their efforts to abolish the sport had gathered steam as the hated Jack Johnson emerged as champion in 1908 and continued his reign.

Finally, on April 5, 1915, Jess Willard defeated Johnson in Havana, Cuba. A new champion was poised for stardom. After winning the title, Willard was paid $10,000 for a two-week theatrical engagement in New York. Then he went on tour with Buffalo Bill's Wild West Show. Unfortunately, what he didn't do in the ensuing years was fight. Instead, he took the championship into semi-retirement, defending it only once in four years.

In 1919, George Lewis "Tex" Rickard (America's premier boxing promoter) lured Willard back into the ring with a $100,000 guarantee to fight an opponent of the promoter's choosing. Rickard wanted a challenger who could beat Willard and would be a marketable champion. Kearns talked him into designating Dempsey. New York, New Jersey, Texas, and Nevada refused to host the bout because of anti-boxing sentiment. Ultimately, Willard–Dempsey settled in Toledo, Ohio. It was the first major outdoor prizefight held in the United States since James Jeffries had come out of retirement to be battered by Jack Johnson on July 4, 1910 (exactly nine years earlier).

The pre-fight build-up to Willard–Dempsey marked the first time that the public was charged to watch a boxer train. Willard charged fifty cents for admission to his workouts; Dempsey, a quarter. On the day of the fight, the challenger weighed in at 187 pounds; the champion at 245.

The match was contested in a temporary arena constructed from unpolished pine boards replete with splinters and oozing sap. The temperature was over 100 degrees. "You always think you're going to win," Dempsey said later. "That's one thing a fighter must have. Otherwise, there isn't any use fighting." But in the minutes before the bout began, there were doubts.

"Willard kept me waiting," Dempsey recalled. "That can be torture when you're keyed up. Then he came into the ring like a moving mountain, dropped his robe, turned his back on me, and held his arms up to the crowd. I thought I was going to get sick to my stomach. He was in terrific shape. The muscles stood out on his back. The way he was holding up his arms made his fists seem twice as high in the air as I was tall. I looked at all six-feet-six of him and said to myself, 'This guy is liable to kill me.' "

Then the bell rang.

Willard–Dempsey was a particularly brutal fight in a brutal sport. One minute into round one, the challenger landed a series of blows to the champion's body followed by a left hook that all but caved in the right side of Willard's face. Thereafter, Willard absorbed as brutal a beating as has ever been administered in a prizefight. In 1919, a fighter who knocked an opponent down could stand over him and attack as soon as his opponent's knee left the canvas. That was the modus operandi Dempsey followed. He downed Willard seven times in the first round, smashing him to the canvas again and again while the champion was in the process of rising but not yet ready to defend himself.

Willard suffered a horrible beating. After three rounds, his jaw and nose were broken. Six teeth had been knocked out. There were cuts above and below both of his eyes. "The right side of his face," Roberts writes, "looked like a peach that had been repeatedly dropped onto concrete." He could fight no more.

"I've been around twenty-five years," Max Baer said after winning the heavyweight title himself in 1934. "And I've met only one guy who could get in a room with me, lock the door, turn out the lights, and work his way out. Jack Dempsey. The day he licked Willard, I'd have been lucky to last a round with him."

Dempsey's triumph was a harbinger of things to come. The previous record gate for a prizefight had been $270,755 (generated by Johnson–Jeffries). Willard–Dempsey drew $452,224. And on a personal level, Dempsey suddenly found himself being treated very differently by the world at large.

"The first change I noticed after beating Willard," the new champion said, "was that I could talk to nice people. I hadn't met many along the line, but those I had met frightened me. It was embarrassing to say something to them and see their faces go blank, so I had learned to shut up. But suddenly, people understood me. They started laughing at my jokes. Women changed too. Every 'Hello, Mr. Dempsey' sounded real kind and interested."

Thereafter, Dempsey contracted for a lucrative circus engagement. In 1920, he ventured to Hollywood, where he received an advance plus $1,000 a week to appear in several films.

But there was a nagging issue that wouldn't go away. There were whispers, and segments of the press wouldn't let it die. The United States had entered World War I in April 1917. One month later, Congress enacted a law providing for a military draft. Physically fit men of military age were exempt from the draft if they held a job in an industry that was essential to the war effort or were the primary means of financial support for their family. Dempsey had applied for, and received, an exemption from the draft board in San Francisco on grounds that his wife (Maxine), father, mother, widowed sister, and his sister's children were financially dependent upon him. Before the war's end, he'd fought in several bouts to raise money for various Army and Navy funds. But he hadn't gone to war.

After Willard–Dempsey, Grantland Rice wrote in the *New York Herald Tribune,* "Dempsey is the champion boxer but not the champion fighter. It would be an insult to every doughboy that took his heavy pack to front-line trenches to refer to Dempsey as a fighting man. If he had been a fighting man, he would have been in khaki. So let us have no illusions about our new heavyweight champion. He is a marvel in the ring, the greatest hitting machine even the old-timers have ever seen. But he isn't the world's greatest fighting man. Not by a margin of fifty million men who stood or were ready to stand the test of cold steel and exploding shell. It would be an insult to every young American who sleeps today from the Somme to the Argonne to crown Dempsey with any laurels built of fighting courage."

Then, on January 23, 1920, the *San Francisco Chronicle* published a letter written by Maxine Cates stating that Dempsey had fraudulently evaded the draft. More specifically, Cates claimed that she had supported Dempsey with her work earnings rather than the other way around. She further claimed that she had letters from Dempsey in which he elaborated on how he evaded the draft. A heated public debate fueled by more statements from Maxine, rebuttals from Dempsey and Doc Kearns, and extensive newspaper commentary followed.

The matter was further exacerbated by a photograph. In autumn 1918, Dempsey (then a rising young heavyweight) had been asked to pose in the Sun Shipyard for a publicity photo that would be used to recruit shipyard workers. "In the shipyard," he later recalled, "I was given a pair of striped overalls and told to slip them on over my street clothes. Snap. Then I was handed a riveter's machine. Snap. Snap. Snap. And that was that. The next morning, I unfolded the newspaper and there I was, dressed in those crisp overalls with my shiny patent leather suede-topped shoes sticking out like sore thumbs."

On January 28, 1920, the New York Times editorialized, "Dempsey, whose profession is fighting, whose living is combat, whose fame is battle. Dempsey, six-feet-one of strength in the glowing splendor of youth, a man fashioned by nature as an athlete and a warrior. Dempsey did not go to war, while weak-armed strong-hearted clerks reeled under the pack and rifle; while middle-aged men with families volunteered; while America asked for its manhood. There rests the reason for the Dempsey chorus of dispraise."

One week later, Maxine Cates met with assistant U.S. attorney Charles Thomas (who had been assigned to investigate the Dempsey matter). At that meeting, she recanted her charges but it was too late. On February 24, 1920, Dempsey was indicted on a charge of conspiracy to evade the draft.

The trial began on June 8, 1920, and lasted for five days. Dempsey later called them "the five saddest days of my life." The defense established that the fighter had in fact sent money to Maxine, his parents, and other family members during the time in question and also that he had helped raise $330,000 for the government by participating in several fundraising bouts. After deliberating for less than ten minutes, the jury returned a verdict of "not guilty." But the "slacker" issue left Dempsey scarred for years to come.

Two-and-one-half months after the trial ended, Dempsey defended his championship for the first time with a third-round knockout of Billy Miske in Michigan. His purse was $55,000 (double what he made for the Willard fight). On December 14, 1920 (two months after the Walker Law legalized professional boxing in New York), he journeyed to Madison Square Garden and knocked out Bill Brennan in twelve rounds. The fight wasn't particularly profitable, but it was part of Tex Rickard's master plan.

"Rickard's goal," Roberts writes, "was to make boxing a thoroughly respectable sport that would toss together wealthy heiresses, rich businessmen, members of the middle class, and strong-armed laborers in arenas." His most notable promotions had been Johnson–Jeffries and Willard–Dempsey.

Then, in 1921, Rickard took boxing to new heights. Religious reform movements in the United States were weakening. The sport was becoming legal in an increasing number of states. Jack Dempsey versus Georges Carpentier followed.

Dempsey–Carpentier was contested on July 2, 1921, in a temporary arena at Boyle's Thirty Acres on the outskirts of Jersey City, New Jersey. More than 80,000 spectators (the largest crowd in America to witness a sporting event until that time) attended. The bout was also the first world championship match to be broadcast on radio, blow-by-blow.

"When you're fighting, you're fighting for one thing," Dempsey once said. "Money."

The live gate for Dempsey–Carpentier was $1,789,238 (more than twice the previous record for a fight and equivalent to more than $20 million today). Dempsey was guaranteed $300,000 plus 25 percent of the motion picture rights. Carpentier was guaranteed $200,000 plus the same 25 percent. Those numbers were far above anything that fighters had been paid before.

To France (and much of the rest of Europe), Carpentier was a man of destiny. He'd won the light-heavyweight championship with a fourth-round knockout of Battling Levinsky in 1920. But more significantly, he'd served in the French air force and been decorated twice for heroism in The Great War. He was handsome, graceful, intelligent, debonair, spoke reasonably good English, and was seen by the public as the most glamorous boxer ever to step into a boxing ring.

Dempsey was cast as Carpentier's opposite. "He was," Roberts writes, "the fighter who did not fight when his country most needed his services. He was dark-complexioned, his beard was coarse, his eyebrows were thick, and his face seemed cast in a permanent iron scowl. In the latter part of his career, Dempsey's reserve in public would be recognized for what it was; basic shyness. But in 1921, his reserve and awkwardness around people were interpreted as the characteristics of a mean and conceited man. There was too much of the hungry hobo about him; far too much of the animal viciousness. He wore his violence as proudly as a crown."

In other words, Dempsey–Carpentier was hero versus villain with the foreigner in the preferred role. "The Frenchman was the hero," Dempsey would say later. "I was the flat-nosed bum."

As July 2 approached, "The Fight of the Century" was the biggest story in the world. The two fighters, Roberts writes, had been "converted into cultural heroes, each representing a constituency with a set pattern of beliefs." They had become "symbols of something that transcended sports."

On the morning of the fight, a column by Grantland Rice in the *New York Herald Tribune* declared, "The greatest single day in the ancient history of an ancient sport has come at last; a day that has caught the imagination of more people from crowded centers to remote off-lying places than any single contest since the world's dim dawn."

"Never before in history," Roberts writes, "had so many famous Americans gathered together in a single place. The hoopla and ballyhoo had served its purpose. Boxing had become an American obsession. Tex Rickard had transformed prizefight promotion into an art form replete with characters, plot, and dramatic tension."

The aristocracy was represented at ringside by Vanderbilts, Rockefellers, Whitneys, Fords, Harrimans, Biddles, and Astors. Three of Theodore Roosevelt's children were there. The U.S. Senate and House of Representatives adjourned in anticipation of the event because twelve senators and ninety congressmen had tickets. The fight was also attended by a significant number of women. Ladies had been present at Willard–Dempsey but were confined to a special section. At Dempsey–Carpentier, they mingled freely with the men.

Carpentier entered the ring at 3:00 P.M. Dempsey followed. The champion weighed 188 pounds; the challenger, 172. As was the custom of the day, the champion was introduced first.

Dempsey later recalled, "Joe Humphreys picked up his megaphone and bawled, 'In this corner, weighing 188 pounds, from Salt Lake City, Utah, the heavyweight champion of the world, Jack Dempsey.' The only response from 80,000 Americans," Dempsey continued, "was a little applause and a low murmur. 'And in this corner, weighing 172 pounds, the challenger from Paris, France, Georges Carpentier.' The people went wild. It was deafening. It hurt, believe me."

The bell rang at 3:16 P.M. At 3:30, the fight was over. "Carpentier had more charm, more good manners, and more class in his dress than anybody I had ever met," Dempsey said afterward. "But I'm leveling when I tell you that it was probably the worst mismatch in the history of the heavyweight division."

The *New York Times* announced the result with a three-line headline that ran the full width of page one and devoted thirteen more pages to the fight.

"I read the stories about the fight in the next day's papers," Dempsey later acknowledged. "And I felt that I hadn't won. Carpentier was the hero of the hour. Never before had anybody seen such courage. I was just a butcher who happened to win. I was a pretty bitter fellow. No matter what you've got, you want them to like you."

After beating Carpentier, Dempsey journeyed to Europe for the first time in his life. En route to England, he wrote in his diary, "Eight years ago tonight, I thought the inside of a box car loaded with loose wheat was a fairly comfortable berth. [Now] here I am, in a beautiful room on one of the finest ships afloat, lying under a silk quilt."

The champion was well-received in London, Paris, and Berlin. In many respects, he was out of his element. Of a luncheon given in his honor by British publishing magnate Lord Northcliffe, he later wrote, "I didn't know whether to use a knife or fork. I'd wait and watch. If they noticed, they didn't let on." And although he went to the Louvre to view the *Mona Lisa*, he later confessed that he hadn't known who Leonardo DaVinci was.

But there was one area where Dempsey was on safe ground. "The most beautiful girls in the world were in Paris," he would reminisce. "It wasn't hard to meet them if you were young and heavyweight champion of the world. And I was young and heavyweight champion of the world."

After Dempsey's sojourn in Europe, the sporting public waited to see who he would fight next. One day after he defeated Willard, a statement had been issued in the new champion's name saying that he would never fight a "Negro challenger." Dempsey later told reporters that he was willing to defend his title against a person of color; Harry Wills being the most likely candidate. But Rickard and Kearns were against it, and the fight never materialized.

Dempsey declined to defend his title in 1922, preferring to engage in a series of exhibition matches. Meanwhile, Rickard was temporarily removed from the promotional scene when he was indicted on charges of taking sexual liberties with three girls, ages fifteen, twelve, and eleven. He was tried and found "not guilty," but his reputation was permanently stained.

As Rickard foundered, Doc Kearns decided to take matters into his own hands and arrange for Dempsey's next fight. In April 1923, he was approached by a group of bankers, oilmen, and cattle ranchers from Montana, who suggested that the champion defend his title in Shelby. The Montana group, bursting with civic pride, was convinced that the fight would gross in excess of $1 million.

Dempsey agreed to a fight in Shelby against Tommy Gibbons on July 4, 1923. The champion was guaranteed $300,000, although he ultimately received only $200,000 that had been put in escrow plus an estimated $80,000 in gate receipts.

Gibbons proved to be an elusive opponent. "Nailing him was like trying to thread a needle in a high wind," Dempsey said afterward. "Even though I was awarded the decision, the fight didn't do my reputation or my popularity any good."

More significantly, the fight was a financial disaster. Four Montana banks failed due to losses occasioned by the promotion. And this was before federal deposit insurance, so thousands of ordinary citizens lost their life savings.

Properly chastised, Dempsey and Kearns returned to Rickard, who mounted yet another extraordinary promotion in ten weeks time. The opponent was Luis Firpo of Argentina; big, strong, ruggedly handsome, courageous, exciting, and unskilled. Eight days after Dempsey–Gibbons, the 217-pound "Wild Bull of the Pampas" had knocked out forty-two-year-old Jess Willard in eight rounds.

Like Dempsey–Carpentier, Dempsey–Firpo captured the public's imagination. Firpo was marketed as a standard bearer for all of Latin American, while Dempsey (however disliked he might have been) was a symbol of American power.

On September 14, 1923, more than 88,000 fans jammed into the Polo Grounds in New York. An estimated 35,000 were turned away. It was boxing's second million-dollar gate. Dempsey's purse exceeded $500,000.

Once again, America's blue-blood aristocracy was at ringside. They were joined by the likes of Florenz Ziegfeld, John Ringling, and Babe Ruth.

Ten seconds into round one, a left uppercut from Firpo put Dempsey on his knees. Dempsey rose and floored Firpo seven times. Then Firpo launched a series of blows punctuated by a monstrous right hand that knocked

Dempsey out of the ring. That moment, recreated on canvas by artist George Bellows, is one of the most famous sports images of all time.

Dempsey landed in the press section; cut his lower back on a typewriter; and with the aid of one or more writers, was pushed back into the ring before the count of ten. "It was pitch dark for a few seconds," he later recalled. "Then I managed to focus on Firpo's fuzzy form. I don't remember climbing back in the ring, but I remember seeing twenty Firpos standing in front of me."

At the bell ending round one, both fighters were throwing punches with abandon. In round two, Dempsey knocked Firpo down two more times. The Argentinean was counted out at fifty-seven seconds of the round.

"A champion is someone who gets up when he can't," Dempsey said afterward.

"If they had fought on a barge like fighters used to fight on," Arthur "Bugs" Baer wrote, "Firpo would have won because Dempsey would have drowned."

After Dempsey defeated Firpo, a remarkable transformation of his image began. For four years, the American public had been locked in a love–hate relationship with the champion, but it had always known he was there. He had charisma, inside the ring and out. His rise from poverty was seen as proof of what a man could accomplish if only he were man enough to try.

Now the 1920s opened wide for Dempsey. "He was champion," Roberts writes. "But more than this, he became a product. His handshake converted into dollars and cents. His face became as familiar on stage and screen as it was in the ring."

In late 1923, Dempsey was paid $25,000 for a five-week vaudeville engagement. Then he signed a contract to star in ten films for a minimum guarantee of $1 million. The movie roles crafted a heroic, virtuous image for the champion. A "legitimate" stage role followed.

Dempsey knew he wasn't a movie actor. "When I started, I was really bad, and I never got any better," he acknowledged. As for his theatrical prowess, the fighter said, "I made good money with maybe less talent than any stage character ever. I almost ruined the American theater."

But Dempsey's position as heavyweight champion of the world, when fused with his screen career, made him seem larger than life. And he enjoyed the ride.

"After four years of unpopularity that he believed was wholly undeserved," Roberts writes, "the champion hungered for the admiration of the public. He wanted to be liked, even loved, in the same manner that the public took Babe Ruth to their hearts. Therefore, Dempsey courted the public. His accessibility and willingness to chat with anybody or sign autographs was uncommon, even for the 1920s when popular heroes were often before the public. Although he did not defend his title [for three years], he was seldom far from the minds of the millions of Americans who so keenly followed his career. From the heights of the silver screen and Broadway stage,

Dempsey's face and movements were studied by millions of people who were awed by his magnetic presence."

"This elevation to a national pedestal," Roberts continues, "had a calming effect on the champion. Instead of becoming bloated with ego, Dempsey became kinder and more considerate of others. Nothing went to his head; not success, money, or the change in his social position. He remained unspoiled, natural, and himself. The hungry, hard, mean, poorly educated Dempsey was replaced by a controlled, gentlemanly, kind, and considerate champion. If the savage in him was not tamed completely, it learned to pass invisibly before the public."

And in a remarkable turn of events, Dempsey was invited to the White House to meet with Calvin Coolidge. There, the man once vilified for evading the draft was praised by the president of the United States. It was an important moment for Dempsey, and also for the sport that had made him famous.

"The meeting marked the coming of age of professional boxing," Roberts explains. "No longer was prizefighting an unacceptable barroom sport; a contest between rough brutal men for the enjoyment of rough sadistic men. If the national symbol of the chilly Yankee ethic invited a boxer to the national home, the sport and the man had arrived."

In 1924, Dempsey moved to Los Angeles, where he quickly became one of Hollywood's most sought-after guests. Douglas Fairbanks, Charlie Chaplin, and Rudolph Valentino were among his friends. John Huston later opined, "Nobody in my lifetime had such a glory about him."

It was rumored in Hollywood that the champion was intimate with a long line of stars, including Clara Bow. Dempsey had avoided any lasting involvements with women since separating from Maxine Cates. Then he met a sensuous B-list actress named Estelle Taylor. "The hobo turned pugilist turned actor fell madly in love with the glamorous starlet," Roberts writes. "As a success symbol, she represented everything Dempsey longed for or ever hoped to obtain."

At the time of their meeting, Taylor was separated from her husband. A divorce followed. She and Dempsey were married on February 7, 1925.

The marriage was a disaster. "Miss Taylor put me into another world," Dempsey later recalled. "I tried like the devil to fit in and couldn't. Sometimes it was a little lonely being there. No snubs, really. Nobody snubs the heavyweight champion of the world. But they talked over my head a lot."

More significantly, Estelle hated boxing and boxing people. At her behest, Dempsey severed his ties with Doc Kearns (which wasn't an entirely bad thing, since Kearns was taking an exorbitant share of Dempsey's income, both in and out of the ring). The fighter tried to assimilate into Estelle's world. He was dedicated to self-improvement. But he could never fully please her. They were divorced in 1930.

Meanwhile, inevitably, there was business to be done in the ring. After three years of inactivity, Dempsey agreed to defend his crown. The opponent was Gene Tunney, a brilliant tactician. Like Dempsey, he'd defeated Georges

Carpentier and Tommy Gibbons. The lone defeat on his record was a decision loss to the great Harry Greb, who he fought five times.

Dempsey–Tunney embodied the clash of cultures that Tex Rickard loved. Tunney was from New York, a clever boxer with pretentions of intellect. Dempsey was from the west, a puncher whose battle plan was a ferocious, swarming assault.

On September 23, 1926, the staggering total of 120,757 fans jammed into Sesquicentennial Stadium in Philadelphia. Their number and the $1,895,733 in gate receipts they paid were records for that time.

Years later, Dempsey observed, "Some have said that I prayed before fights. Nonsense. I was so intense and excited that to stop and pray with people packed in the dressing room around me was the furthest thing from my mind."

Against Tunney, Dempsey didn't have a prayer. For years, the challenger had studied the champion. As a young man, he'd fought on the undercard of Dempsey–Carpentier and knocked out Soldier Jones in seven rounds. Then, instead of going to his dressing room, he'd stayed at ringside and, still in his robe, watched the main event. Thereafter, he viewed films of Dempsey countless times.

Dempsey–Tunney was scheduled for ten rounds; a distance approved by both the champion (who was giving away youth) and the challenger (who figured that ten rounds with Dempsey would be enough). At twenty-nine, Tunney was only two years younger than his opponent. But Dempsey had lived a hard life; his body had absorbed the blows of hundreds of fights; and he'd been out of the ring for three years.

Despite being surrounded by tens of thousands of people, a boxing ring can be the loneliest place imaginable. Against Tunney, Dempsey found it to be so. "From the time the bout started," he acknowledged later, "I was aware that my body and brain weren't communicating properly. I was slower than I thought, or Gene was faster. He glided around the ring like he was on ice. Wherever I went looking for him, he stuck that left of his in my face, keeping me off balance, piling up points. Now and then, he'd stop me with a stiff right. There seemed to be nothing I could do, though I tried. Tunney was so scientific a boxer that all I seemed to be able to do was to take his punishment."

Tunney thoroughly outboxed the champion and won every round. He cut Dempsey over the right eye and jabbed his left eye shut. At the bout's end, Dempsey's jaw was swollen and he was bleeding from the mouth. "I have no alibis to offer," he said. "I lost to a good man."

Years later, Dempsey would reflect back on the fight and note, "It's sad to hear the fellow with the microphone yell 'the winner and *new* heavyweight champion of the world' when you're the old one." But there was another remembrance of September 23, 1926, that the fallen champion carried with him.

"I was booed when I fought Willard, though he seemed twice my size," Dempsey observed from the vantage point of old age. "I fought a Frenchman before an American audience and was booed. I fought an Argentinean before my countrymen, and I was booed. It always dug deep and hurt terribly. But when I started to leave the ring [after losing to Tunney], something happened that had never happened to me before. To my surprise, I was loudly cheered; more than I had ever been cheered before. The people were cheering for me, clapping for me, calling out my name. I never realized how much I had hungered for a sound like that."

Dempsey had doubts about fighting again after losing to Tunney. "I was beat like no man should be beat," he later said. "I just didn't think I had enough left in my legs to catch a real boxer anymore. And I had doubts about what I could do if I did catch him."

But he did come back, meeting future heavyweight champion Jack Sharkey on July 21, 1927, at Yankee Stadium in New York before 75,000 fans. Even though it was a non-title bout, the fight generated Dempsey's (and boxing's) fourth million-dollar gate.

Sharkey dominated the early rounds. "I thought he was going to knock me out," Dempsey admitted afterward.

Then, in round seven, Dempsey landed a series of low blows. Sharkey turned to the referee to protest, and Dempsey raised his next punch (a compact left hook) to jaw level. "I hit him with one of the last good punches of my life," Dempsey said later. "It was everything I could throw. His chin was sticking out there, unprotected. I couldn't miss."

Sharkey went down, and the fight was over.

Two months later, Dempsey returned to the ring one last time for a rematch against Tunney. For only the second time in boxing's gloved era, a former heavyweight champion would be facing the man who had dethroned him.

Dempsey's purse for the first Tunney fight had been $717,000. For the rematch, he was guaranteed $450,000. Interest in the bout ran high, with the challenger given a good chance to win. After all, he was Jack Dempsey. And Tunney was the first heavyweight champion who had won the title by decision rather than knockout.

Tunney–Dempsey II rewrote boxing's financial recordbook. On September 22, 1927, 104,943 fans crammed into Soldiers' Field in Chicago. The live gate of $2,658,660 (the equivalent of more than $30 million today) would stand as a record for more than fifty years. It wasn't surpassed until Muhammad Ali and Leon Spinks fought in the New Orleans Superdome in 1978. Tunney's purse was precisely $990,445.54. After the fight, he gave Tex Rickard a check for $9,554.46 in order to receive a check for $1 million.

Dempsey was the crowd favorite. Moments before the bell for round one, referee Dave Barry called the fighters to the center of the ring for their final instructions.

After Dempsey–Willard, it had become common to require a fighter who knocked his opponent down to go to a neutral corner and stay there until instructed by the referee to return to battle. More specifically, the rules of boxing had been changed to provide, "When a contestant is down, his opponent shall retire to the farthest corner and remain there until the count is completed. Should he fail to do so, the referee and timekeeper may cease counting until he has so retired."

Against Luis Firpo, Dempsey was allowed by the referee to stand over his fallen foe and hit the Argentinean as he rose from the canvas. Thereafter, the rules were revised again and "may" became "must." The "neutral corner rule" now read, "A fighter scoring a knockdown must go to the farthest neutral corner and, if he delays, the count is not to begin until he does."

Years after Tunney–Dempsey II, Dempsey would recall Dave Barry giving instructions as follows: "Both you boys have received a book of rules of this boxing commission. They are the rules under which you are going to fight. Now I want to get one point clear. In the event of a knockdown, the man scoring the knockdown will go to the farthest neutral corner. Is that clear?"

"We nodded," Dempsey remembered.

Then Barry continued: "In the event of a knockdown, unless the boy scoring it goes to the farthest neutral corner, I will not begin the count."

Tunney dominated the early stages of the fight. "I never should have stepped into the ring that night," Dempsey later admitted. "He had me staggering and leaning against the ropes by the second round. By the third and fourth rounds, I was weary and bleeding."

Then the unthinkable happened. Fifty seconds into round seven, an old Jack Dempsey metamorphized into the Dempsey of old, landing a perfectly timed left hook to Tunney's jaw. "Everything about the punch was right," Roberts writes. "Tunney started to fall; but before he did, Dempsey hit the champion with a left–right, left–right combination, his body rotating with the punches, a metronome of destructive power."

Years later, Dempsey gave his own version of events. "I won't forget the seventh round," he reminisced. "You don't forget any second of something you waited seventeen rounds for. I got to him with a pretty good right, and then I hit him with a real good left hook. He started to go, and I hit him seven times while he was going down. I hit him with all the punches I had been trying to hit him with in the ring and in my sleep for the past year. I thought he was finished. I thought I had become the first guy ever to win back the heavyweight title."

Then Dempsey refused to go to a neutral corner and, instead, hovered over the fallen champion, waiting to strike him as he rose. "I forgot the rules," he admitted later. "I lost my head and couldn't move as the referee shouted, 'Get to a neutral corner.' I was the jungle fighter so completely set in my ways that I couldn't accept new conditions."

Five seconds elapsed before Dempsey allowed himself to be pushed to a neutral corner. Only then did Barry begin the count at "one." Films of the fight support the view that Tunney could have risen within nine seconds of the knockdown. But the fact that he had fourteen seconds to do it made life easier for him once he was on his feet again.

When Barry's count reached nine, Tunney rose and went into retreat. Dempsey was unable to catch him. Seconds before the bell ending round seven, the champion landed a hellacious body shot. "It was not a question in my mind of being knocked out," Dempsey later said of that blow. "I thought I was going to die."

In round eight, Tunney knocked Dempsey down. Then he coasted to a ten-round-decision victory.

"I'll never really know whether Gene could have gotten up [within ten seconds of the knockdown]," Dempsey said years later. "He has often told me he could have, and I have no reason not to believe him. He took the count, whatever it was. That's what any smart fighter would have done."

Eight days after the "long count" fight, Babe Ruth hit his mythic sixtieth home run. Sports were now run on the principles of big business and would be forevermore.

After the Tunney rematch, Dempsey retired from boxing. He thought he was financially secure for life. But in 1929, the stock market crashed and he lost most of his savings (more than $3 million). Between August 20, 1931, and August 15, 1932, he fought 175 exhibition bouts; sometimes as many as four a night. Then he moved to New York, and in 1935, opened a popular restaurant on Eighth Avenue across the street from Madison Square Garden. When the United States entered World War II, Dempsey was in his forties. But he enlisted in the Coast Guard, thus putting the "slacker" issue to rest forever.

After the war ended, Jack Dempsey's Restaurant moved to a new location on Broadway between 49th and 50th Streets. Dempsey loved sitting at a corner table, signing autographs and chatting with everyone who came by. "People like to touch fighters," Carlo Rotella writes. "Men clap them on the shoulder and linger over a handshake. It's like putting your hand on a smoothbore cannon and imagining you can feel resonances of a long-ago war." Dempsey graciously obliged his patrons until the restaurant closed in 1975.

On a personal level, the ex-champion married an attractive brunette singer named Hannah Williams in 1933. They had two daughters, but the marriage was stormy and ended in divorce. Dempsey vowed never to wed again and built his social life around visits to night spots like Toots Shor's, The Stork Club, El Morocco, and 21. Then, in the mid-1950s, he met and married Deanna Piattelli. They were together until his death in 1983.

Many former heavyweight champions fade from view, but Dempsey remained a public figure all his life. He was content and retained his dignity to the end. "For many years now," he said as he moved toward old age, "the American people have shown they like me in a thousand flattering ways. I'm grateful for that affection. I didn't have it when I was champion of the world. And I wanted it so very much. Ever since that mysterious swing, the American people have been wonderfully kind to me; far kinder than any man deserves."

Grantland Rice personified that "mysterious swing." In an earlier era, it was Rice who wrote, "It would be an insult to every young American who sleeps today from the Somme to the Argonne to crown Dempsey with any laurels built of fighting courage." But decades later, Rice declared, "Jack Dempsey was the finest gentleman I met in half a century of writing sports. Mr. Dempsey never knowingly hurt anyone except in the line of business."

Dempsey, for his part, responded in kind, saying, "I was a pretty good fighter, but it was the writers who made me great."

Jack Dempsey was a boxing success story. He reigned as heavyweight champion of the world for seven years; longer than anyone ever except Joe Louis (and if fragmented titles are considered, Muhammad Ali and Larry Holmes). He was a hobo who, as a consequence of the sweet science, became rich and famous and evolved into a gentleman.

"I've been knocked down too often to remember," Dempsey said late in life. "I've been knocked out. But I never lost a fight on a foul, nor was I ever thrown out of a ring for not trying." And on his seventy-fifth birthday, he proclaimed, "I can still fight right now, punch with either hand. I couldn't go very long, but I can still fight."

"Did Dempsey ever hit me below the belt?" Gene Tunney once asked rhetorically. "He sure did. But when I hit him below the belt, he never complained."

II

Curiosities, Issues, and Answers

This article, my first in 2007, began what turned out to be a series of pieces about HBO.

HBO Boxing: The Challenge

Boxing is struggling, and 2007 will bring new challenges for the sport. Showtime has publicly announced its intention to televise mixed martial arts. Meanwhile, HBO recently committed to televising three Ultimate Fighting Championship (UFC) shows during the coming year with an option for three more. HBO's current plan is to air the shows at midnight on dates still to be determined. No matter how these telecasts are packaged, ultimately they will compete with boxing.

Sources at HBO say that Ross Greenburg (president of HBO Sports) opposed the UFC deal as vigorously as possible. But in the end, he had no choice.

Ari Emanuel (a Hollywood agent on whom the character played by Jeremy Piven in *Entourage* is believed to be based) represents UFC. He pitched UFC to HBO chairman Chris Albrecht, who (in pursuit of a younger viewing demographic) insisted on the telecasts. That represented a marked shift in HBO's corporate culture. In the past, an HBO chief executive officer would not have ordered sports programming over the objection of the sports department.

During an interview last week, Greenburg declined to comment on the matter beyond acknowledging, "I wouldn't say that I'm a big fan of UFC. But when I started at HBO, I wasn't a big fan of boxing either. I recognize the fact that UFC appeals to a fan base and demographic that boxing doesn't have right now."

But Seth Abraham (Greenburg's predecessor) is less reticent, declaring, "I think it's ridiculous for HBO to televise UFC. When I was at HBO, we had discussions once or twice a year about professional wrestling. We all agreed that it would get good ratings and we also agreed that it would tarnish our boxing franchise. I feel the same way about UFC. Boxing has a storied history. When HBO attaches itself to boxing, it attaches itself to

Joe Louis, Sugar Ray Robinson, and Muhammad Ali. It attaches itself to history, achievement, and glory. UFC has none of those things and it will tarnish HBO's boxing franchise. Will UFC get good ratings? Probably. But so would naked boxing."

Be that as it may, this is a watershed moment for HBO Sports. And it comes at a time when HBO can no longer take its favored position with boxing fans for granted. Until recently, there was a presumption that, if a fight was on HBO, it was worth watching. That's no longer always the case.

The network's boxing program as a whole is getting flat. When Greenburg was executive producer of HBO Sports, he earned acclaim as an innovator in live-boxing television production. But not much new has happened since he left that position. The production values (which were once cutting edge) are growing stale. The advertising and marketing for HBO's fights are less imaginative than they should be. And replacing one or more on-screen commentators with younger "talent" won't solve the problem. To the contrary, that change most likely will only diminish HBO's aura of class.

The powers that be at HBO have to sit down with a blank piece of paper and ask themselves, "What do we want HBO Sports to look like five years from now?" And when they do, they should examine the underlying philosophy that drives their boxing program.

During Seth Abraham's tenure as president of Time Warner Sports, the network was guided by what were known internally as "the five pillars of HBO Boxing." More specifically, Abraham felt that HBO should strive to have under contract (1) the consensus pound-for-pound champion; (2) the heavyweight champion; (3) the most exciting fighter in the world; and (4) the best young fighter in the world. He also wanted (5) the fight of the year to have been televised on HBO.

Things didn't always go smoothly. "The [longterm] Roy Jones contract was a mistake," Abraham acknowledges. "I misread Roy. I thought that pride and his wanting to go down in history as one of the greatest fighters of the modern era would lead him to want more competitive fights; and obviously, he was satisfied with lesser opponents." But overall, HBO was successful in anointing stars, building them up in the public mind, and making its boxing telecasts a magnet for subscribers.

Boxing was the unquestioned centerpiece of HBO Sports during Abraham's reign. Ross Greenburg is more into diversification. Within the sports department today, Greenburg is the ultimate decision maker. Mark Taffet (senior vice president, sports operations and pay-per-view) is the pay-per-view and marketing guru. Proposals for *HBO World Championship Boxing* usually come in through Kery Davis (senior vice president, programming), who negotiates match-ups and license fees with promoters for most fights. Luis Barragan (director of programming) reports to Kery and is the point of entry for most proposals relating to *Boxing After Dark*. Barbara Thomas is the chief financial officer. Peter Mozarsky drafts contracts and interfaces with lawyers for promoters.

One thing that's missing from the equation is a forceful advocate for fans.

Lou DiBella was a senior vice president under Abraham. "There was sometimes tension between Lou and me," Seth recalls. "But Lou also had more influence with me than the other members of the team. Lou's philosophy was that HBO should make the best fights possible and that all the rest was nonsense. He and I disagreed on many things. But one of the good things that Lou did was that he was always pushing me, aggressively pushing me, to make HBO Boxing better. And Ross doesn't have anyone doing that."

Also, Greenburg is operating in a radically different financial environment from the one that Abraham enjoyed. During Abraham's tenure, HBO's chief executive officers (Michael Fuchs and, later, Jeff Bewkes) were big boxing fans. The annual budget for boxing was close to $80 million, and Seth could get additional funds when needed. The peak years were 1999 and 2000, when the all-inclusive boxing budget surpassed $120 million.

Greenburg reports to (HBO chairman) Chris Albrecht and (president) Bill Nelson, neither of whom is partial to the sweet science. The annual budget for license fees is now less than half of what it was seven years ago. And there's another fly in the ointment; pay-per-view.

Pay-per-view is here to stay. In 2006, HBO engendered 3.7 million pay-per-view buys with $177 million in gross sales. The only year with more buys than that was 1999, when the total was 4 million.

But 1999 was very different than 2006. 1999 was the year of De La Hoya–Trinidad (1.4 million buys), Holyfield–Lewis I (1.2 million), Holyfield–Lewis II (850,000), and De La Hoya–Quartey (570,000). By contrast, the only pay-per-view mega-fight in 2006 was De La Hoya–Mayorga (925,000 buys). Rahman–Maskaev was a bust with under 50,000. The other eight pay-per-view cards last year were all in the 325,000-to-450,000 range. Pay-per-view fights in that range almost always generate more money for the promoter and fighters than HBO is willing to pay for an *HBO World Championship Boxing* license fee.

Greenburg calls the expansion of pay-per-view "the biggest economic issue in boxing" and says, "I can't tell you that pay-per-view helps the sport because it doesn't. It hurts the sport because it narrows our audience, but it's a fact of life. Every time we try to make an *HBO World Championship Boxing* fight, we're up against mythical pay-per-view numbers. HBO doesn't make a lot of money from pay-per-view. There's usually a cap on what we can make. But the promoters and fighters insist on pay-per-view because that's where their greatest profits lie."

"It's a big problem," Greenburg continues. "It's getting harder and harder to put fighters like Manny Pacquiao on *HBO World Championship Boxing*. If Floyd Mayweather beats Oscar, he might never fight on *HBO World Championship Boxing* again. But if HBO stopped doing pay-per-view, the promoters would simply do it on their own [like Bob Arum did with Cotto–Malignaggi in June 2006] or find someone else who will do it for them."

Pay-per-view, of course, will be the vehicle for the May 5 super-fight between Oscar De La Hoya and Floyd Mayweather Jr. That bout will put boxing back in the media spotlight. Newspapers that haven't staffed a fight since Lennox Lewis versus Mike Tyson in 2002 will be there. But one fight won't lift boxing from its doldrums. Lewis–Tyson didn't do it, and Oscar versus Floyd won't either. As big an event as De La Hoya versus Mayweather might be, it will be over on May 6 and it will have little impact on the overall business of boxing.

That, in turn, leads to two more issues. Is HBO's "star" philosophy outdated? And if it's still viable, is it being properly implemented?

HBO wants stars. It focuses its efforts on building stars. It gives a handful of fighters exposure; gets them some wins; hopes they'll look good; and then puts them on pay-per-view. "Creating and nurturing stars," says Greenburg, "has been a key component of our philosophy for thirty years."

One can argue that building stars is what a promoter and manager (not a television network) are supposed to do. But beyond that, how many stars has HBO built in the past seven years? The truth is, apart from Oscar De La Hoya, there are no stars now in boxing. Manny Pacquiao is popular in the Philippines. Miguel Cotto has a loyal following in Puerto Rico. But most of the world (and many sports fans) have no idea who they are.

A look at HBO's 2006 schedule is instructive in evaluating the philosophy that drives the network's boxing program.

Bad pay-per-view match-ups shouldn't be a problem for fans. They simply don't have to buy them. But mediocre match-ups on *HBO World Championship Boxing* and *Boxing After Dark* are a different matter. HBO subscribers pay a monthly subscription fee and are entitled to good value for their money.

The fights on *HBO World Championship Boxing* in 2006 were pretty good, although they could have been better (more on that later). *Boxing After Dark* is a different matter. The BAD fights were a disappointment.

HBO usually pays a $300,000 license fee for *Boxing After Dark* shows ($225,000 if the promoter keeps foreign rights). Pursuant to a special contractual arrangement, Golden Boy sometimes gets $600,000. Properly spent, that money could buy wonderful fights. But HBO has consistently made the mistake of giving dates to promoters without specific fights attached.

Golden Boy got dates because HBO killed *Boxeo De Oro* (its Spanish-language fight telecasts). Bob Arum got dates because HBO used fight footage that belonged to him in a documentary series without a proper license. Lou DiBella got dates because he took a financial hit to make Taylor–Wright. The list goes on and on and it's coupled with the fact that, philosophically, HBO would rather pit a "star" against a "C-list" opponent than two "B-list" fighters against one another.

HBO televised forty-two fights in 2006. That includes eighteen fights on *HBO World Championship Boxing*, fourteen on *Boxing After Dark*, and the featured bout on ten HBO pay-per-view shows. The underdog won only five of them. That doesn't say much for the competitive level of HBO's fights.

By contrast, *Showtime Championship Boxing* televised twenty fights last year and the underdog won eight.

In sum, HBO might have televised better fighters, but Showtime televised better fights (and for a fraction of HBO's budget). The issue crystalized on December 2, 2006, when Miguel Cotto and Antonio Margarito fought on Showtime in separate bouts that will go a long way toward defining the welterweight division in 2007. That same night, on HBO, Jeff Lacy looked mediocre in squeaking by Vitali Tsypko, and Winky Wright beat up on the considerably-smaller Ike Quartey.

Insiders say that HBO paid a $4 million license fee for its December 2 telecast. Add in $500,000 for marketing and production costs and the total comes to roughly $4.5 million (more than $1 million per ratings point) for *HBO World Championship Boxing's* lowest-rated fight of the year. HBO could have doubled the license fees it pays for *Boxing After Dark* for almost an entire year for what it spent on its December 2 show. And Jermain Taylor versus Kassim Ouma (on HBO one week later), cost almost as much and didn't do much better in the ratings.

Also, keep in mind that Taylor versus Wright on June 17, 2006, was HBO's highest-rated fight of the year. The lesson is simple. Boxing fans might want to see "stars," but they want to see them in competitive fights.

HBO is in the entertainment business. In boxing, great fights are entertainment. Great performances are not. One-man-show fights get boring fast.

HBO has to get away from the star-at-any-cost mentality and televise better fights; not just fights as a vehicle for one fighter. Every fight on HBO should be good enough to stand on its own. *Boxing After Dark* should not be a developmental league for *HBO World Championship Boxing*. *HBO World Championship Boxing* shouldn't be a developmental league for HBO Pay-Per-View. Better fights will attract younger viewers in addition to more old ones.

There aren't many great fighters today, but that doesn't mean there can't be great fights. Matchmaking is an art, not a science. Fights don't always turn out the way they look on paper, but HBO is more likely to have great fights if it starts out with match-ups that are great to begin with.

Here, it should be noted that styles make fights. And one doesn't learn styles by looking up records on Boxrec.com. Micky Ward had thirteen losses in fifty-one fights. Arturo Gatti has been beaten eight times. But they gave HBO wonderful action, and not just against each other. Good fights make more good fights. And great fights create stars.

HBO calls itself "the heart and soul of boxing." It should act like it and tell promoters, "Don't bring us fights that aren't quality fights." It should tell fighters who won't go in tough, "Make your name somewhere else and come to us when you're ready to fight in a competitive fight." Regardless of what happens early in the game, most mega-fights will wind up with HBO. The network can outbid anyone for what it wants.

Looking ahead to the coming year, Ross Greenburg says, "We're going to focus on getting back to our roots and try to humanize our fighters for our audience. We're planning new image campaigns for our key charismatic fighters. We'd like to do a couple of big fights like Taylor–Wright I on *HBO World Championship Boxing*. And we'd like to make sense out of the heavyweight division, although I'm not going to tell you there's a good chance of a unification tournament because there isn't."

Then Greenburg adds words that are music to the ears, saying, "We're going to invigorate *Boxing After Dark* by loosening our commitments to promoters. Our last commitment is in June and, after that, we're going to abandon the practice of giving dates to promoters without specific fights attached. It has cramped our style and it just hasn't worked. We'll also dig our feet in a little more on mismatches and not give in to promoters, managers, and fighters who don't want to take a risk."

That's good news if HBO sticks by it. In that vein, it will be interesting to see how HBO showcases Andre Berto. Berto is a talented welterweight prospect with sixteen wins and fourteen knockouts in sixteen fights. On December 9, 2006, he fought Miguel Figueroa on *HBO World Championship Boxing*. It wasn't even a *Boxing-After-Dark*-caliber fight. Figueroa had one win in the previous two years and no business being in the ring with Berto. Andre administered an ugly beating that ended in a sixth-round knockout.

Good career guidance dictates that Berto have a number of fights against significantly weaker opponents while he's learning his craft. But those fights shouldn't be on HBO. Andre is slated to be on *Boxing After Dark* in February and again in May. Let's hope it's in competitive fights. HBO's subscribers are entitled to see good, young fighters in competitive action, not learning-experience bouts.

None of this commentary is intended as a personal attack upon anyone at HBO. The network does a superb job of covering boxing in many respects. But we in the boxing media are fans and we're advocates for fans. I'm simply saying that HBO can and should televise better fights. Many at HBO think that assessment is unfair. Let's put our conflicting views to the test.

I'd like to propose a challenge to the powers that be at HBO. Let a fan try his hand at making a fight card for *Boxing After Dark*. Give me a date with a decent lead time and a dollar number for the license fee that you're willing to pay. I'll deliver a fight card for your final approval. I won't take any payment. The process will be above-board and open.

Is making good fights on HBO's budget harder than I think it is? Maybe. Is it rocket science? I doubt it. And I guarantee you, I'll deliver fights that are better than most of what was seen last year on *Boxing After Dark*.

I don't expect HBO to take me up on this challenge. But it should. Fight fans want to see the best fights that they can possibly see on television. HBO should too.

Some Thoughts from the Hammerstein Ballroom

On February 17, 2007, boxing returned to New York City in the form of an HBO *Boxing After Dark* triple-header at the Hammerstein Ballroom.

The main event featured Paulie Malignaggi (who was in action for the first time since his June 10 loss to Miguel Cotto) against Edner Cherry.

Malignaggi came into the bout with blue hair to match his blue-and-silver trunks, blue gloves, and blue shoes (with tassels, of course). More significantly, he's a good fighter who knows what he's doing in a boxing ring. "I can't imagine how it would feel to be in the ring with a guy who can outthink me and outbox me," Paulie said recently. "That's never happened to me in a fight."

Cherry is an aggressive non-stop action fighter. But like Paulie, he lacks a big punch. And he was coming up from lightweight to meet Malignaggi at 140 pounds.

In round one, Paulie's hands were too fast and he was too fleet of foot for Cherry.

In round two, Paulie's hands were too fast and he was too fleet of foot for Cherry.

In round three, Paulie's hands were too fast and he was too fleet of foot for Cherry.

And so it went for ten rounds. Speed doesn't always kill, but it outpoints.

"It was boring at times," Malignaggi acknowledged afterward. "But I got the win."

The other bouts on HBO's Saturday-night telecast were also flawed.

Andre Berto versus Norberto Bravo was what promoter Lou DiBella would have called a "death match" if it had been someone else's fight.

Berto is an immensely talented, hard-punching young prospect with blazing hand-speed. The thirty-six-year-old Bravo (who has lost three of his last four bouts) lacks the skills to be competitive against a good young fighter.

The best thing about Berto–Bravo was that it ended quickly. Andre out-landed his foe 28-to-3 and knocked him down three times en route to a first-round stoppage. Fights like this are necessary to develop a young fighter but they shouldn't be on HBO. Either the powers that be at the cable giant knew that Berto–Bravo was a gross mismatch (in which case they shouldn't have televised it) or they didn't know (in which case they should do their home-work more diligently in the future).

Sechew Powell against Ishe Smith (which aired between Berto–Bravo and Malignaggi–Cherry) was a match-up for boxing purists. It was also a pre-dictably unsatisfying television fight. Styles make fights. And while Powell and Smith are good boxers, they're also both cautious counterpunchers. The booing by fans began in the second round and was heard sporadically throughout the bout. This observer gave Powell the nod by a 95–94 margin. The judges were unanimous in Sechew's favor.

The most intriguing issue of the night was whether HBO Sports president Ross Greenburg was watching the fights on television (neither he nor vice president Kery Davis was at ringside). The question filtered through the press row accompanied by bemused looks.

Tim Smith of the *New York Daily News* opined, "Probably not. I wouldn't."

Not to be outdone, Dan Rafael of ESPN.com offered the view, "I hope so. I'm suffering through it. So should he."

Obviously, Saturday's fight card ties into the larger issue of HBO's boxing programming.

2007 has not started well for the cable giant. Its January 20 *World Cham-pionship Boxing* show (the first of the year) featured two marquee names (Ricky Hatton and José Luis Castillo). Unfortunately, they weren't fighting each other. Instead, viewers saw Hatton against Juan Urango in a boring one-sided fight. José Luis Castillo against Herman Ngoudjo was just as boring, since Castillo wasn't in good enough shape to make it one-sided. The match-ups were designed to hype a June 23 confrontation between Hatton and Castillo, but were so sluggish that they took some of the lustre off that fight. Larry Merchant spoke for fans everywhere when he told viewers, "I have to confess, that, coming to the fights tonight, I found myself constantly think-ing, 'Why am I not coming to see Hatton fight Castillo?' "

Then, on a January 27 *Boxing After Dark* telecast, Kelly Pavlik beat up on José Luis Zertuche for eight rounds before knocking him out. In the nightcap, Jorge Arce won a twelve-round decision over Julio Roque Ler. It's a sad com-mentary on Arce–Ler that the most noteworthy thing about it was that Arce rode a horse to the ring. At no point in either fight was the outcome in doubt.

Shane Mosley against Luis Collazo on February 10 was an interesting match-up, but apparently the public wasn't interested because the ratings tanked and only 3,927 tickets were sold for the fight. The televised undercard bout between Vivian Harris and Juan Lazcano was the sort of contest that fans once saw on ESPN, not *HBO Championship Boxing.*

The powers that be at HBO Sports say they're satisfied with the way things are going. That might be because the first five months of 2007 are largely about the May 5 showdown between Oscar De La Hoya and Floyd Mayweather Jr. The network is putting a huge amount of money into a four-part prime-time "24/7" series, extensive advertising, and other promotional efforts for that extravaganza. But De La Hoya versus Mayweather won't fundamentally change the overall picture at HBO. And regardless of its impact, there's no reason that HBO (for the license fees it pays) can't give its subscribers COMPETITIVE ACTION fights on a regular basis.

As the year progressed, I had occasion to append numerous "notes" regarding HBO telecasts to my column on Secondsout.

HBO Notes

(After the March 3 match-up between Miguel Cotto and Oktay Urkal and the March 10 fight between Wladimir Klitschko and Ray Austin)

Earlier this year, I noted in a column entitled *HBO Boxing: The Challenge* that HBO televised forty-two fights in 2006 and the underdog won only five of those. That trend is continuing in 2007. Through the first ten weeks of this year, HBO has televised twelve fights. The favorite has won all twelve.

Last week, I received an e-mail from a reader who asked, "Why is it that, every time I watch a fight on HBO, everyone except maybe Max Kellerman and Fran Charles knows in advance who's going to win?"

That's a good question. The periodic promises by the powers that be at HBO about more competitive fights are starting to have all the credibility of Dick Cheney's pronouncements on the war in Iraq.

Moments before HBO's March 3, 2007, telecast of Miguel Cotto versus Oktay Urkal, Larry Merchant told viewers, "We know the result. Cotto is a 20-to-1 favorite."

This past weekend's match-up between Wladimir Klitschko and Ray Austin was worse. Prior to the bout, Lennox Lewis stated on camera that Austin "shouldn't be in the ring" with Klitschko. Merchant then added, "We wonder, does he belong on the same continent as Klitschko?" The fight that followed was an embarrassment.

HBO's riposte is, "But people will be really excited when we finally put Cotto and Klitschko in big competitive fights."

Yeah, but subscribers who pay month after month for HBO will have to shell out an additional $44.95 if they want to see the big competitive fights because they'll be on pay-per-view.

There's a new slogan in boxing: "It's not HBO; it's pay-per-view." And viewers are getting tired of it. Sources say that HBO's Cotto–Urkal card garnered a miserable 2.93 rating and cost the network a license fee in the neighborhood of $3,250,000. The numbers for Klitschko–Austin aren't in yet, but one suspects that they won't be good. Forget about the youth demographic. HBO is starting to lose the boxing fan demographic.

*(After the April 7 match-up between
Joe Calzaghe and Peter Manfredo Jr.)*

HBO throws a lot of statistics at boxing fans. Here's another statistic. It's now mid-April. HBO has televised fifteen fights on *HBO World Championship Boxing* and *Boxing After Dark* this year. And the favorite has won all fifteen.

Last weekend's doubleheader from Wales typified the non-competitive match-ups that have become synonymous with HBO Boxing. The opener was a grotesque mismatch between Amir Khan and Stefy Bull. How bad was it? As Bull ran around the ring bringing back memories of Morrade Hakkar against Bernard Hopkins, Jim Lampley told viewers, "This takes fighting to survive to an absurd level." The end came in round three.

Then Joe Calzaghe stepped into the ring to face Peter Manfredo Jr. As Larry Merchant said afterward, "Peter Manfredo is a television-made star. Joe Calzaghe is a real fighter."

The theory had been that Manfredo would fight aggressively, force the action, and make an interesting brawl out of things for as long as the bout lasted. But against Calzaghe, Peter looked like a deer caught in the headlights of a military tank. A premature stoppage by referee Terry O'Connor ended the encounter in round three. But Manfredo did nothing during the prior seven minutes to suggest that the outcome would have been any different (or much delayed) had the fight gone on.

"The difference in talent level was abundantly clear," Lampley told viewers after the stoppage. Then he suggested that the next time Calzaghe steps into the ring, he take "a real fight."

In it's last three shows, HBO has traveled to Germany, Denmark, and Wales to televise four fights. The underdog has not won a single ROUND in any of them.

*(After the April 14 match-up between
Nikolai Valuev and Ruslan Chagaev)*

The heavyweight division got a little less interesting last Saturday night (April 14) when seven-foot-two-inch Nikolai Valuev lost his WBA heavyweight belt to Ruslan Chagaev on a 117–111, 115–113, 114–114 decision.

Most of Valuev's recent opponents tried to get inside his reach. But once they did, he was able to tie them up, lean on them, and wear them down with his size.

Chagaev opted for a different strategy. He stayed outside and countered Valuev's jab with straight left hands. Valuev was too slow to be effective with right-hand leads (the traditional tactic against a southpaw). And as the fight wore on, Nikolai's lack of experience against southpaws showed.

Valuev's loss takes a potential attraction out of the immediate heavyweight championship picture. But there's a more significant story line attached to Valuev–Chagaev. This is the second month in a row that MSG Network has televised a better live fight than HBO for a fraction of the cost (MSG Network paid a $100,000 license fee for Valuev–Chagaev).

HBO's live offerings in March were Miguel Cotto against Oktay Urkal (with Edison Miranda vs. Allan Green as the opener) and Wladimir Klitschko versus Ray Austin. In each instance, HBO paid a multimillion-dollar license fee to televise the fight. By contrast, MSG Network paid a reported $50,000 in March to televise the rematch between Jean-Marc Mormeck and O'Neil Bell.

So what happened? Bell–Mormeck was a barn-burner reminiscent of the type of fight that HBO used to televise. And HBO's offerings fell flat.

That's not surprising. Prior to Cotto–Urkal, Kevin Lole of the *Las Vegas Review-Journal* branded the match-up "the type of one-sided blowout that has become an HBO staple." And Klitschko–Austin has become a magnet for mainstream media criticism of the cable giant.

"Things have reached a crisis level in the heavyweight division with the debacle involving IBF champ Wladimir Klitschko and Ray Austin," Tim Smith of the *New York Daily News* wrote afterward. "To call this a heavyweight title match would be to defame all the former champions who fought for, held, and defended the undisputed title with class and distinction. It was disgraceful for all involved; Austin for his lack of effort; the IBF for moving an unworthy challenger into the number-one spot; the promoters for perpetrating this fraud; and HBO for broadcasting the farce. Shame on them all."

Dan Rafael of ESPN.com was even more pointed in his criticism. Rafael called Klitschko–Austin "perhaps the single worst HBO show in the network's thirty-four years of televising boxing," and declared, "We all knew Klitschko–Austin was a mismatch going in, and that's exactly how it turned out. Is it too much to ask for competitive fights? Is it too much to ask that HBO stop spending its millions on sewage? It was an embarrassment to HBO. And it was a waste of time for fans."

HBO also televised the 168-pound match-up between Mikkel Kessler and Labrado Andrade in March. But it was on a tape-delay basis, the perils of which became obvious when, before the bout aired, fight fans learned that Kessler had triumphed with a 120–108 shutout on each judge's scorecard. Is it too much to ask that "the heart and soul of boxing" give its subscribers live fights?

There's a simple rule that HBO should follow. When HBO buys a fight, both fighters (not just one of them) should be an HBO-quality fighter.

HBO is now televising fights that are reminiscent of the Roy Jones mandatory days. But HBO was obligated by contract to televise Roy Jones's mismatches. Fights like Klitschko–Austin, Cotto–Urkay, and Calzaghe–Manfredo aren't required.

Bobby Goodman has been in and around boxing since the 1940s and is vice president for boxing operations at Don King Productions. "The people who run boxing at HBO," Goodman says, "make me think of a sign that Benny Friedman had on his desk."

Friedman played quarterback for the New York Giants during the Great Depression. To help make ends meet, he ran what he called a "quarterback school" for high school students. Goodman says that the sign on Friedman's desk read, "God, forgive them for they know not what they do not know."

(After the July 7 match-up between
Wladimir Klitschko and Lamon Brewster)

Earlier this year, I congratulated HBO Sports president Ross Greenburg for declining to buy the July 7 fight between Wladimir Klitschko and Lamon Brewster and wrote, "Brewster hasn't fought in more than a year, hasn't won a fight since 2005, has undergone eye surgery three times, and has gone up and down in weight like a balloon from the Macy's Thanksgiving Day Parade."

So what happened? Greenburg reversed course and bought the match-up for HBO. The subsequent May 5 kick-off press conference was a perfect metaphor for the fight that followed. The press conference was held at a steak house; they served hamburgers.

As a challenger for the IBF heavyweight title, Brewster was like a used car that has been in a wreck. You shouldn't buy it without a test drive (i.e., an interim fight against a legitimate opponent).

Against Klitschko, Lamon showed up in the ring but didn't do much else. Maybe he was in shape; but it wasn't fighting shape, given the fact that he was tired after six minutes of combat. Klitschko dominated with his jab and won every minute of every round. Brewster never mounted an assault or did anything else that seemed calculated to win the fight. Buddy McGirt (Lamon's trainer) called a halt to the proceedings after six rounds.

HBO could have taken the money it spent on the license fee and production costs for Klitschko–Brewster and applied it to some meaningful competitive fights. Instead, the network now finds itself in a situation where overspending on non-competitive match-ups has drained its budget for the rest of the year.

Boxing After Dark will be absent from the screen for three months this autumn for budgetary reasons. More significantly, after HBO's July 14 welterweight triple-header, there will be an eleven-week gap between *World*

Championship Boxing fights. *World Championship Boxing* is the anchor for HBO Sports. This hiatus is not good.

(In early September as HBO's fall season approached)

HBO Sports president Ross Greenburg ruffled some feathers with his last-minute cancellation of a promised appearance at the annual convention of the National Association of Black Journalists in Las Vegas on August 10.

New York Post columnist George Willis had coordinated a workshop moderated by *USA Today* boxing writer Chuck Johnson on the issue of "Is Boxing Down for the Count?" The panelists were to be Greenburg, Ken Hershman of Showtime, Don King, Bob Arum, Floyd Mayweather Jr., and *New York Daily News* boxing scribe Tim Smith. But on the morning of the August 10, Ray Stallone (HBO's vice president for sports publicity) sent an e-mail saying that Ross would be unable to attend due to an unspecified illness in the family.

That led to the insertion of a note entitled "Missing in Action" in Smith's August 15 column in the *Daily News*. After referring to Greenburg's "glaring absence," Smith observed, "Apparently there was no one else at HBO or Time Warner capable of discussing the network's policies and thoughts on boxing. At a conference that was important enough for two of the leading Democratic presidential candidates—Hillary Clinton and Barack Obama—to speak, HBO couldn't find anyone to represent them. That's a shame."

Several days after Greenburg's nonappearance, Smith elaborated on that theme, saying, "HBO balked at doing the panel discussion to begin with, and my sense was that they were ambivalent about coming. I won't question what I was told about an illness in the family, and I hope that everyone is healthy now. But it's hard to believe that, in a company as large as HBO, they couldn't find a substitute to attend."

The perceived snub of the National Association of Black Journalists leads to a larger issue. Some black fighters are starting to complain that they're under-represented on HBO.

Last year, Bob Arum accused the network of racism for failing to offer a date to Kelly Pavlik because Pavlik is white. "There's a perception with boxing network guys," Arum proclaimed, "that if you're a white guy, you can't fight. They judge by color."

Greenburg responded by calling Arum's comments "a disgraceful and undignified remark by a disturbed man."

But some fighters feel that there's a more traditional bias at HBO. In the first eight months of 2007, eighty-five fighters appeared on *HBO-PPV*, *World Championship Boxing*, and *Boxing After Dark*. Of those eighty-five, only twenty-six (31 percent) were black. The numbers become more skewed if Lou DiBella's cards are removed from the equation. DiBella had three dates on HBO through September 1 of this year. Ten of the fourteen fighters on his shows (71 percent) were black. Not including DiBella's three cards, there have been seventy-one fighters on HBO this year and only sixteen (23 percent) were black.

By contrast, thirty-five (50 percent) of the seventy fighters who appeared on *Showtime Championship Boxing* and *ShoBox* through September 1 of this year were black.

"Young American fighters in general are having a harder time getting on HBO than Mexican or Filipino fighters," says one observer of the boxing scene. "And that's particularly true when it comes to young African-American fighters."

It has often been said, "As the heavyweight division goes, so goes boxing." The heavyweight division hasn't been going well lately.

The Void

"The sweet science," A. J. Liebling observed, "is joined onto the past like a man's arm to his shoulder."

When Liebling penned those words, he was referring to the lineage of boxing's heavyweight champions. It was a glorious line of succession revered by fight fans with the same emotion that British royalists embrace the monarchy.

John L. Sullivan . . . James J. Corbett . . . Bob Fitzsimmons . . . James Jeffries . . . Marvin Hart . . . Tommy Burns . . . Jack Johnson . . . Jess Willard . . . Jack Dempsey . . . Gene Tunney . . . Max Schmeling . . . Jack Sharkey . . . Primo Carnera . . . Max Baer . . . James Braddock . . . Joe Louis . . . Ezzard Charles . . . Jersey Joe Walcott . . . Rocky Marciano . . . Floyd Patterson . . . Ingemar Johansson . . . Patterson, again . . . Sonny Liston . . . Muhammad Ali. . . .

These men were gods with a common bond. "Fitzsimmons had been hit by Corbett," Liebling wrote. "Corbett by John L. Sullivan; he by Paddy Ryan with the bare knuckles; and Ryan by Joe Goss, his predecessor, who as a young man had felt the fist of the great Jem Mace. It is a great thrill to feel that all that separates you from the early Victorians is a series of punches on the nose."

Even when the heavyweight champion was a fighter of limited ability, he was still the heavyweight champion of the world.

Then, world-sanctioning bodies began to proliferate and things got murky. But there was still a chain of command.

Joe Frazier . . . George Foreman . . . the return of Ali . . . Leon Spinks . . . Larry Holmes . . . Michael Spinks . . . Mike Tyson . . . James "Buster" Douglas . . . Evander Holyfield . . . Riddick Bowe . . . Holyfield, again . . . Michael Moorer . . . George Foreman . . . followed by an interregnum with Lennox Lewis emerging as the true heavyweight champion of the world.

Sadly, that lineage no longer exists. There are now four heavyweight "champions." Since Lewis retired in 2004, the depressing total of thirteen men have been anointed by the WBC, WBA, IBF, and WBO. In other words, the throne is vacant at present and will be for the foreseeable future. Greed and corruption have fragmented the crown.

The single most important thing that sports fans want is competition building to a meaningful championship.

Interest in a sport peaks during its championship season. That's when even casual observers turn on their television sets and lifelong fans are born. The National Football League has playoffs leading to the Super Bowl. Major League Baseball crests with the World Series. The National Basketball Association and National Hockey League follow similar formats. Golf captures the public imagination during the Masters and the U.S. Open. Wimbledon captivates tennis fans.

The people who run boxing have managed to deprive the sport of its signature moment: a fight for the legitimate heavyweight championship of the world.

Other sports have suffered similar lapses. The World Series was cancelled due to labor strife in 1994. There's a smudge in the National Hockey League record book where the 2005 Stanley Cup playoffs should have been. But baseball and hockey quickly got their respective houses in order, as did golf and tennis after interruptions for world war.

Yet the powers that be in boxing continue to pursue selfish agendas without regard to the overall good of the sport. And the irony is that, in the long run, their greed costs them money. Boxing's dwindling fan base and the lack of lucrative network television contracts trace in part to the absence of a true heavyweight champion. How much interest would the Olympics generate if there were four gold medalists in four separate versions of the 100-meter dash?

Boxing will not regain its status as a major sport until there's a legitimate universally recognized heavyweight champion of the world.

And in the end, it's the boxers (at least, those who are genuinely talented) who will suffer the most. The ultimate goal of any athlete in any sport is to become a true world champion. An entire generation of heavyweights is being deprived of the opportunity to achieve that goal.

This was yet another example of how the powers that be are ruining boxing.

More on the Heavyweights

Over the years, IBF heavyweight champion Wladimir Klitschko and his brother, former WBC heavyweight champion Vitali Klitschko, and have become known as good people with a social conscience.

Wladimir devotes considerable time and effort to raising public awareness and funds on behalf of the United Nations Educational, Scientific, and Cultural Organization (UNESCO). "My understanding of life changes as I see things with my own eyes," he said recently. "The world is getting smaller. We have to act differently and change our relationships to each other."

Vitali went even further, actively campaigning as a reform candidate for election as mayor of Kiev last year.

That bit of history is relevant now because Team Klitschko is currently engaged in maneuvering, that, if successful, will tarnish the Klitschko reputation forever.

On September 2, 2006, Samuel Peter of Nigeria defeated James Toney in a bout that was supposed to determine the mandatory challenger for WBC heavyweight belt-holder Oleg Maskaev. But the powers that be at the WBC ruled that the decision in Peter's favor was "controversial" and ordered the two men to fight a rematch. They did, with Peter winning convincingly on January 6, 2007.

Meanwhile, the Klitschko camp has been trying to arrange a title bout between Maskaev and one of the brothers. Initially, it wanted Peter to accept step-aside money to allow Wladimir to fight Maskaev. Samuel refused. Now Team Klitschko is urging the WBC to allow Vitali to come out of retirement and jump over Peter as the mandatory challenger by virtue of the Ukrainian being a "champion emeritus."

Asked to comment on the matter last month, WBC president José Sulaiman said, "About Vitali, because of our rules, there are now two mandatory challengers, and the WBC will have to decide which mandatory comes first. We will not take away Samuel Peter's mandatory, but we might postpone it. If you believe that is unfair, you are mistaken."

Then, on February 8, there was a meeting in New York attended by Sulaiman, Klitschko advisor Shelly Finkel, Tom Loeffler (Klitschko's promoter of record), Dennis Rappaport (Maskaev's promoter), Ivaylo Gotzev (Peter's manager), Don King, and Dino Duva (Peter's co-promoters), DKP vice president Bob Goodman, and enough lawyers to create a feeding frenzy of monstrous proportions.

The WBC, Klitschko, and Maskaev expressed the view that Klitschko–Maskaev should take place sooner rather than later. According to several meeting participants, Finkel offered $2.5 million in step-aside money to the Peter camp. In addition, if Peter stepped aside under the terms of the offer, he would be the mandatory challenger for the winner of Maskaev–Klitschko and given a fifty-fifty purse split. If the winner of Klitschko–Maskaev failed to fight Peter within 120 days, he would be stripped of his title.

However, it turned out that the offer had some loopholes that made it considerably less generous than advertised. For example, when the offer was clarified, the Peter camp was told that, if Maskaev–Klitschko never happened (let's say that Vitali is injured while training and can't compete), Samuel would receive only $500,000. Then, negotiations were put on hold while the Klitschko camp tried to find an insurer that would back a larger number.

"They're not even telling half-truths," grumbles one member of Team Peter. "Twenty-percent truths is more like it."

"That's Shelly Finkel math," says Shannon Briggs, who's still steamed over failed negotiations for a Madison Square Garden title bout against Wladimir Klitschko last year. "Shelly [the Klitschkos' advisor] told me I had the fight," Briggs continues. "He said, 'It's not 100 percent; it's 1,000 percent.' I don't know, I wasn't that good in school. Maybe 1,000 percent is less than 100 percent."

The Peter camp is uncertain as to its next step. Samuel has earned his mandatory title shot, and his attorneys are confident that they would be awarded a significant monetary recovery if the matter were resolved in its entirety in state or federal court. Their problem is that Peter signed a contract with the WBC prior to his two "mandatory eliminator" bouts against James Toney that is believed to provide for compulsory arbitration in lieu of court action should a dispute arise. Thus, if the WBC orders that the matter be arbitrated, the Peter camp would first have to go to court in an effort to void the arbitration clause.

Also, the issue of how any step-aside money would be split among Peter, Duva, and King has yet to be resolved. And there are rumors that Maskaev might not be ready to fight until June because of elbow surgery, as well as questions regarding whether Vitali is physically fit to fight twice within the span of 120 days.

If Peter steps aside, one big loser will be Don King. King is fond of saying that he has been the lead dog in boxing for more than three decades and that, "Unless you're the lead dog, the scenery never changes." The WBC–Klitschko–Maskaev–Peter confrontation is a direct test of King's influence and power. If his fighter is pushed aside, a lot of vultures will be circling.

And there's another issue regarding the Klitschko–Maskaev–Peter–WBC mess that might surface shortly. Samuel Peter is one of the two best heavyweights ever to come out of Africa (Ike Ibeabuchi is the other). Were Peter to defeat Maskaev and become WBC heavyweight champion, it would raise the profile of boxing throughout the continent and Samuel would be recognized as a hero.

How long will it be before King seizes on that fact and contrasts Samuel's African heritage with that of Klitschko, Maskaev, and WBC president José Sulaiman?

Meanwhile, the biggest loser in all of this is the public. Boxing fans bought tickets and turned on the television, not once but twice, to watch Samuel Peter versus James Toney in the belief that the winner would be the mandatory challenger for Oleg Maskaev's WBC crown. Some of those viewers, particularly in Nigeria, are ardent Samuel Peter fans.

Suppose, at commissioner Roger Goodell's urging, the National Football League announced to the world in January 2007, "We know that the Indianapolis Colts beat the New England Patriots in the AFC title game, but the Colts have accepted step-aside money to let the Patriots play the Chicago Bears in the Super Bowl."

That's what the WBC, in conjunction with the Klitschko and Maskaev camps, is now trying to lay on the public. Sleazy maneuvering like this is a primary reason why millions of sports fans have lost interest in boxing.

In recent years, mixed martial arts has become a phenomenon that the boxing world can't ignore.

A Boxing Fan Looks at Mixed Martial Arts

Today's video-game culture and increasingly violent movies have spawned a demand for entertainment that offers clearly visible mayhem.

Meanwhile, boxing is in trouble. Not many sports have a reigning superstar who has won only twice in the past four-and-a-half years and lost three of his last five outings. But that's Oscar De La Hoya's recent record.

Put the aforementioned realities together and one has an ideal environment for the rise of mixed martial arts (MMA) as a sports entertainment phenomenon.

"It's easier for the average person to identify with MMA than with professional boxing," Donald Zuckerman (an early MMA entrepreneur) said ten years ago. "There are more than 15,000 martial arts dojos in the United States, and the number of gyms devoted to boxing is diminishing. Every few years, Hollywood produces one boxing movie, but there are dozens of martial arts films annually. Most people have never engaged in a fight with regular boxing rules. But at one time or another, even if it was only on the playground in grade school, virtually everyone has engaged in some form of fighting."

A decade later, MMA is impacting today's sports culture. Type "Oscar De La Hoya" into Google and you get 1,740,000 hits. Manny Pacquiao brings in 1,180,000. Pound-for-pound king Floyd Mayweather Jr. scores 1,080,000.

Now Google the three biggest MMA stars of recent years: Tito Ortiz (761,000 hits), Chuck Liddell (701,000), and Randy Couture (650,000). Compare them with Bernard Hopkins (408,000), Wladimir Klitschko (320,000), and Kelly Pavlik (156,000).

Get the point?

The original concept behind mixed martial arts was to match combatants who practiced different fighting disciplines against one another. How would a karate expert fare against a practitioner of Brazilian jiu-jitsu? What about a kickboxer against a freestyle wrestler? However, those distinctions soon vanished and, in MMA matches today, multiple disciplines are allowed.

The rules of combat have also changed. A dozen years ago, most MMA competitions featured an anything-goes mentality. Tactics such as kicks to the groin, head butts, and pulling hair were legal. Now virtually all MMA bouts conducted in the United States are governed by the Unified Rules of Mixed Martial Arts, which specify thirty-one forbidden acts ranging from eye gouging and kicking the head of a grounded opponent to spitting and using abusive language.

The "playing field" for MMA competition varies from promoter to promoter. Some bouts are contested in a cage; others in a modified boxing ring. Rounds are five minutes in duration with a one-minute rest period in between. Championship bouts are scheduled for five rounds; non-championship contests for three. There are seven weight classes. A fighter can win by submission (when his opponent concedes defeat), technical knockout (the referee stops the contest), a judges' decision, or disqualification. In truth, once the shock value wears off, a bad MMA match gets boring quickly. But so does bad boxing.

There are times when boxing goes above and beyond sports and contributes to the elevation of society. Joe Louis and Muhammad Ali are examples of that. MMA fits into another category. To its critics, it's ugly and grotesque. John McCain has railed against it on the floor of the U.S. Senate, calling it "human cockfighting."

"In order to be an MMA champion," says Jerry Izenberg, "you need every skill that's outlawed on the planet. The very things we pride ourselves on not doing, these people elevate to an art form. I wouldn't even try to dignify it."

Emanuel Steward is in accord, saying, "Mixed martial arts is too brutal, too ugly. There's nothing beautiful about it, like a nice jab in boxing. A few years back, they invited me to watch a UFC event. But with people getting kicked in the head and punched on the ground, I walked out after the third bout. It was sickening."

Boxing fans also deride a culture that encourages MMA combatants to "tap out" (quit) and note that MMA combatants are knocked down by punches that would never put a professional boxer on the canvas.

In response, MMA adherents acknowledge that there are more broken bones and dislocations in their sport than in boxing. But they say that MMA might actually be morally superior to boxing because there are ways other than seeking to inflict brain damage on an opponent by which a combatant can win.

They also claim that their sport is safer than boxing. The four-ounce open-fingered gloves used in MMA don't allow for punching with full force.

There's relatively little leverage on punches when combatants are "grounding and pounding." And even when combatants are standing, they don't get the same leverage on punches that boxers do.

"The boxing aspect of MMA isn't the sweet science that you and I grew up with," explains Ant Evans (senior communications manager for UFC's U.K. division). "It's a more coarse version of boxing. MMA fighters have to throw punches from much further out as they have to maintain a wider distance in order to spot and defend against takedowns and kicks. Plus the traditional boxing stance positions one's weight on completely the wrong axis to defend against a takedown attempt. The feet have to be spread out a lot more to enable effective takedown defense work."

Thus, it can be argued that there are fewer catastrophic injuries in MMA than in boxing. The combatants don't punch as hard. They tap out instead of going out on their shield. They take fewer and less-concussive blows to the head in competition and in the gym. And rather than take a beating round after round, an over-matched combatant is quickly "submitted."

Also, whether or not one likes MMA, it should be conceded that the combatants are athletes with skills. The sport features disciplines within disciplines. No one can compete successfully unless he (or she) is a capable ground-fighter and can execute finishing holds.

A decade ago, there were two promoters of note in mixed martial arts struggling over pieces of a very small pie. A company called Battlecade promoted "Extreme Fighting," while Semiphore Communications marketed a brand of MMA called "Ultimate Fighting."

MMA has grown since then and is now dominated by a single brand. Ultimate Fighting has morphed into UFC and is the industry's Hertz. There is no Avis. Everyone else is Rent-A-Wreck.

The companies competing with UFC include ProElite, the International Fight League (IFL), World Extreme Cagefighting, Chuck Norris's World Combat League, Bodog Fight, Spirit XC, Strikeforce, and M1.

ProElite and the IFL are public companies. A look at their finances is instructive. In November 2006, Showtime announced a partnership with ProElite to televise live MMA events through 2009. However, ratings have been mediocre and the most recent Form 10-QSB filed by ProElite Inc. with the Securities and Exchange Commission has some interesting numbers. The company lists $30,628,263 in assets for the period ending September 30, 2007. But $12,197,363 of that total is attributed to "goodwill." ProElite's filing also reveals an operating loss of $7,345,966 for the three months ending on September 30, 2007, and an operating loss of $19,491,529 for the nine months ending on September 30, 2007. IFL has a contract with Fox SportsNet, but suffered losses of $16.9 million during the first nine months of this year.

By contrast, UFC (on the surface, at least) appears to be flourishing. The company in its present incarnation is the creation of three men.

Lorenzo and Frank Fertitta are brothers who built Station Casino (a small Las Vegas casino previously owned by their father) into the fifth-largest gaming corporation in the United States. Lorenzo is also a past president of the Nevada Resort Association (the most powerful gaming association in America). In the 1990s, he was one of the Nevada State Athletic Commission members who voted with the majority against legalizing MMA in Nevada. The best guess is that Lorenzo and Frank have a net worth well in excess of $1 billion between them.

Fast-forward to 2000. Ultimate Fighting was hemorrhaging cash and its owner told Dana White (who represented several MMA fighters) that he wanted to sell the company. White turned to Lorenzo, who had been a classmate in high school. In January 2001, the Fertittas purchased UFC for $2 million and designated White as its president, placing him in charge of day-to-day operations. The Fertittas now own 90 percent of Zuffa LLC (the company that controls UFC). White owns the other 10 percent.

During the Fertittas' first three years with UFC, the company lost an estimated $36 million. But Lorenzo was able to navigate the tricky shoals of Nevada politics to gain approval for MMA matches. Other states fell into line. And in 2004, the Fertittas and White hit upon a strategy to gain traction for their venture. They offered Spike TV an enticing package. UFC would pay all production costs for a reality show about MMA fighters who lived together and fought each other in weekly elimination bouts. Spike could have the show without an upfront payment. *Ultimate Fighter* debuted in 2006 and became the fledgling cable network's first hit. It was also an extraordinarily effective infomercial for UFC.

UFC was described this year by *Time Magazine* as "the fastest-growing sports brand in America." Its goals for the future include becoming "the next NASCAR" and the NFL of its sport. White is the public face of the company and will do almost anything to advance its goals. And while UFC might be just another investment for Frank Fertitta, it has become a way of life for Lorenzo.

UFC follows the World Wrestling Entertainment (WWE) marketing model. Fans are promised lots of action in concentrated bursts from combatants with distinctive personalities. The fights are real, but almost everything that surrounds them is scripted and the television production is tightly controlled. Because UFC is the promoter and de facto sanctioning body and has more than 300 combatants under contract, it can schedule fights on whatever dates and for whatever titles it wants.

The company offers basically the same product as other MMA groups. But the Fertittas have been willing to spend whatever is necessary to establish and market their brand. Matches have taken place in Nevada, New Jersey, California, Connecticut, Florida, Louisiana, Ohio, and Texas, and also overseas in London, Manchester, and Belfast. In March of this year, UFC purchased Pride (its primary Asian rival) for a reported $70 million.

Success sometimes breeds resentment, and UFC has its share of enemies. Rival promoters have grumbled about anti-competitive acts, such as the alleged use of financial muscle (e.g., advertising dollars), to discourage media coverage of competitors' events. They also claim that UFC marketing includes papering the house for promotions and giving cash to buyers who go to stores and purchase multiple copies of UFC DVDs. One competitor expresses his feelings with the observation, "You can't spell 'fuck' without a U, an F, and a C."

But when Chuck Liddell battled Quinton Jackson at the MGM Grand on May 26, 2007, UFC was able to boast of a sell-out with a live gate of $4.4 million. And while pay-per-view has put a damper on boxing's popularity, UFC seems to be thriving on it.

UFC promotes twelve to fourteen shows annually, all of them on pay-per-view. According to SNL Kagan (a media research company), UFC events in 2006 grossed $205 million in pay-per-view revenue compared to $177 million for HBO-PPV and $200 million for WWE.

So far, the only big revenue streams for UFC have been ticket sales and pay-per-view. The sponsors have been low-end. The company came close to breaking new ground earlier this year when it reached an agreement in principle with HBO to televise three shows with an option in the network's favor for three more. The deal was negotiated at the insistence of HBO chairman Chris Albrecht, who was seeking to attract a younger viewing demographic. HBO Sports president Ross Greenburg resisted the move. So did Sheila Nevins (the head of HBO's documentary division), who has been with the network since 1979. Nevins made an impassioned plea against UFC programming, telling Albrecht that UFC didn't "feel like HBO" and that, as a premium cable channel, the network didn't have to be ruled by ratings as a way of enticing advertisers.

But Albrecht held firm. On April 18, Dana White announced that the deal was done. "It's been a long, hard process," White told the *Los Angeles Times*. "But I'm very comfortable with where we are."

White said that the first telecast would take place during the summer. An HBO spokesperson told the *Times* that the network would select a commentating team with experience in MMA and that its regular boxing commentators were not under consideration for the job.

Then fate intervened. In the early morning hours of Sunday, May 6 (following the mega-fight between Oscar De La Hoya and Floyd Mayweather Jr.), Albrecht was arrested in the valet parking area of the MGM Grand for assaulting his thirty-seven-year-old girlfriend, Karla Jensen. According to the police report, Albrecht grabbed Jensen by the throat with both hands and was dragging her toward the hotel, when police forced him to release his grip and put him in a submission hold. Five days later, the HBO chairman pled no contest to a charge of misdemeanor battery. Under the terms of a plea-bargain agreement, he was given a six-month suspended sentence, fined $1,000, put on unsupervised probation for one year, and required to undergo domestic violence counseling. On May 9, he resigned from HBO, when the *Los Angeles Times* reported that Time Warner (the network's parent company) had previously paid $400,000 to a woman named Sasha

Emerson (Albrecht's subordinate at work and a former lover) who had accused him of choking her.

Without Albrecht running interference, the UFC–HBO agreement went down the drain over issues that revolved around the extent to which HBO would control the television production of the UFC shows it aired. Subsequent negotiations between UFC and ESPN also failed.

The Fertittas and Dana White deserve credit for building an industry. They have completely restructured MMA and turned their share of it into a highly organized, tightly controlled business. But it has to be remembered that UFC is just a promoter. A big promoter, and a successful promoter; but one promoter. That's all. UFC champions are, in essence, nothing more than "Top Rank champions" or "Golden Boy champions." And that's all they can be because combatants under contract to UFC aren't allowed to fight combatants controlled by other corporate entities.

As for the future, MMA is currently sanctioned (or has been approved by the legislature with sanction pending) in thirty-two states plus the District of Columbia. The most important jurisdiction not yet in the mix is New York, which has a statute that specifically bans MMA competition. To overturn the ban, the state assembly and state senate must pass new legislation and the governor must sign it. Toward that end, UFC has hired lobbyists to press its case. Cablevision (which owns Madison Square Garden and is the fifth-largest cable provider in the United States) is also pushing for legalization.

Another key player is Marc Ratner, who served for fourteen years as executive director of the Nevada State Athletic Commission (NSAC). In May 2006, Ratner left the NSAC to become UFC's vice president for regulatory affairs. His primary objective for 2008 is to get MMA legalized in New York. "We're the lead driver," he says. "The other organizations are just drafting on us."

Ratner acknowledges that "UFC is not for everybody." When asked how MMA stacks up against boxing, he refuses to compare the two sports. But inevitably, discussions about MMA turn to its impact on the sweet science.

UFC has a marketing line: "Boxing is your grandfather's sport." But research shows that only about 20 percent of those who attend UFC events have ever been to a boxing match, and these people tend to return to boxing. On the other hand, there's a progression from pro wrestling to the UFC that occurs when a wrestling fan is around age eighteen. If boxing could get these fans to attend a boxing match, they might like it.

But boxing keeps screwing up. It has multiple "champions" in almost every weight division. Corrupt and incompetent ring judges render decisions that alienate fans. The NFL doesn't ask for special praise when it matches the AFC and NFC champions in the Super Bowl. But boxing pats itself on the back whenever it gives fans a fight that the fans want to see. And when a big fight comes, it's usually paired with a non-competitive undercard for $44.95 or more.

HBO (which televises virtually all of boxing's major pay-per-view fights) says its studies show that undercards have little effect on pay-per-view buys.

Maybe that's because fans have been conditioned to expect lousy pay-per-view undercards. That's a great way to build a fan base: "You, the buying public, don't care what's on the undercard, so we're going to save money and show you boring one-sided fights."

MMA and the UFC don't pose a long-term threat to boxing. Boxing poses a long-term threat to boxing. If the UFC didn't exist, boxing would have the same problems that it has today.

Here, a comparison between UFC and HBO is instructive. UFC is the 800-pound gorilla in MMA. HBO is the 800-pound gorilla in boxing. Each company has an aura about it and a huge amount of money to spend.

There was a time when HBO was the closest thing that boxing had to a competent governing body. It was the driving force behind building fighters like Mike Tyson, Oscar De La Hoya, Roy Jones, Shane Mosley, and Arturo Gatti. More recently, it has enabled Golden Boy to evolve into one of the two most powerful promoters in boxing and fueled Al Haymon's managerial empire. Pro football players don't thank CBS and Fox for putting them on television. Pro basketball players don't thank NBC or TNT. But fighters always thank HBO. That makes it clear who dictates the schedule in boxing and where the power lies.

But HBO has been squandering its brand appeal. Once, fans would watch a fight simply because it was on HBO. Not anymore.

HBO is trumpeting the fact that 2007 has been a year of record-high pay-per-view buys. But it has also been a year of record-low *HBO World Championship Boxing* ratings. Moreover, there has been little correlation between the license fees that HBO pays for fights and the ratings they get.

By way of example, the network poured a $3 million license fee plus another seven figures for marketing and production into Joe Calzaghe versus Mikkel Kessler, which garnered a 2.8 rating (the lowest prime-time *HBO World Championship Boxing* rating ever). But that shouldn't have surprised anyone. The live afternoon telecast of Calzaghe against Peter Manfredo earlier in the year came in at 1.4. And the live afternoon telecasts of three Wladimir Klitschko fights held in Germany scored 2.4 (against Chris Byrd), 1.5 (against Ray Austin), and 1.7 (versus Lamon Brewster). Paulie Malignaggi got better ratings than that for a fraction of the cost twice this year on *Boxing After Dark*.

But there's another factor at work in the interplay between boxing and MMA. Years ago, boxing championed the advance of home television and closed-circuit TV. HBO, in particular, was an early leader in the marketing of pay-per-view. But boxing has lagged behind MMA when it comes to exploitation of the Internet.

At one point, the mainstream media wouldn't touch MMA, so it survived (and still does to a great degree) on publicity from cyberspace. Meanwhile, in recent years, some powers in boxing have looked down their nose at the Internet. One HBO Sports executive even proclaimed that he wouldn't return telephone calls from Internet writers. That type of arrogance is counterproductive for a lot of reasons, including the fact that the Internet attracts precisely the "young" demographic that HBO is trying to reach.

UFC is already in negotiations with Yahoo to distribute its matches over the Internet on a pay-per-view basis. Eventually, pay-per-view boxing will move to the Internet in a significant way. But when it gets there, it will find that MMA has beaten it to the punch. And the danger for HBO is that, if it doesn't change quickly, its boxing program (and much more) could be eclipsed by new technologies the same way that IBM was eclipsed by Microsoft.

HBO is important to boxing. Every time the network shoots itself in the foot, boxing bleeds. And too often lately, its aim has been off the mark.

November 17 offered a study in contrasts. That night, UFC promoted a nine-bout card at the Prudential Center in Newark, while HBO televised a *Boxing After Dark* card from Atlantic City.

The arena in Newark was already half-full at 8:15 P.M. when the first UFC bout began. Unlike boxing crowds, UFC fans tend to arrive early. That's because there isn't a red corner with all the winners in it and a blue corner with all the losers. UFC tries to avoid mismatches at every level.

A significant number of boxing writers were at the Prudential Center. The fights were contested in The Octagon; an octagonal cage thirty feet in diameter enclosed within a chain-link fence that rises sixty-nine inches above the canvas. Before each match, a short video introducing the combatants was played for the crowd. Fighters high-fived fans on the way to the ring. When the combatants were locked together in combat on the mat, the crowd watched the action on one of six large overhead screens. After each contest, the winner was interviewed over the public address system. There were no long delays between bouts.

At 10:00 P.M., after four preliminary contests, the pay-per-view portion of the card began. The arena was full. MMA, like NASCAR, is a predominantly "white" sport. Most UFC combatants are white with little or no hair on their head and a lot of tattoos. The crowd mirrored that demographic. It was overwhelmingly white with a sprinkling of Asians thrown in. With few exceptions, the only black faces were those of ushers and security personnel.

Just before the first televised bout, a UFC highlight reel was shown on the screens above. This is part of "the UFC experience." Fans await it with the same anticipation that precedes Michael Buffer's "let's get ready to rumble." During the course of the evening, there were four technical knockouts (bouts stopped by the referee) and two tap-outs. Three contests, including the main event, went to a decision. The UFC brand (not the individual fighters) was the star of the show. The announced crowd of 14,071 paid a live gate of $2.1 million.

HBO's telecast that same night began with a tape of Miguel Cotto versus Shane Mosley (which had been contested one week earlier). The two bouts televised live, thereafter, featured four foreign nationals. Abner Mares (from Mexico) met Damian Marchiano (Argentina) in a fight that figured to be a mismatch and lived down to expectations. Mares won an easy decision. Then, for viewers who were still awake (and there weren't many on the east coast since the telecast ended close to 1:00 A.M.), Joan Guzmán (from the Dominican Republic) decisioned Humberto Soto (Mexico).

But there are other comparisons that should be made between MMA and boxing. Like the sweet science, MMA is plagued by conflicts of interest and inconsistent governmental regulation.

Fighter safety is also an issue. In many jurisdictions, there are virtually no barriers to entry, and state legislatures have been lobbied in a way that has opened the floodgates to all manner of MMA toughman contests.

An increasing number of MMA combatants are now being seriously trained in the art of throwing punches on the theory that one good whack to the head can end a fight. As they grow more proficient, the number of head injuries will rise and regulators will be forced to reconsider the wisdom of requiring 140-pound boxers to wear ten-ounce gloves while 250-pound MMA combatants compete with four ounces of leather on either hand.

Illegal drugs are another problem. In most instances, drug testing is conducted by the state athletic commission that oversees a given competition, which means that, generally, there's minimal testing or no testing at all. Mixed martial arts has been described by detractors as "boxing on steroids." When steroid testing has occurred prior to MMA cards, the results have often been troubling.

And inevitably, there will be deaths. That's inherent in the nature of the sport. Recently, an MMA fighter named Sam Vasquez spent six weeks in a Texas hospital, where he was listed in critical condition and put in a medically induced coma. Two blood clots had formed in his brain and he suffered a massive stroke after being knocked out in a Renegades Extreme Fighting event in Houston on October 20. He died on November 30.

Sooner or later, UFC will experience a similar tragedy. Indeed, there's a school of thought that, while professional wrestling controls the production of its telecasts so fans will forget that wrestling is fake, UFC controls its telecasts so fans will lose sight of the true nature of the physical damage being done. UFC's cameras rarely linger on a combatant who is bleeding profusely or lying unconscious on the octagonal mat.

Moreover, there's an undercurrent of concern in the MMA industry that the audience is a UFC audience, not an MMA audience; that the audience is finite; that familiarity will breed boredom; that MMA is a bubble, and with everyone jumping onto the bubble, it will burst.

There are even those who think that UFC is starting to lose traction; that the emperor has clothes but the fabric is tearing.

More managers and agents are coming into the MMA business, which means less profit for promoters. Randy Couture is nearing the end of his career. Chuck Liddell has lost his last two fights. Tito Ortiz hasn't held a belt in four years. Few, if any, mainstream sponsors want their logo on a ring canvas that's splattered with blood.

And perhaps most significantly, on November 27, 2007, Standard and Poor's downgraded its credit rating for Zuffa LLC (the company that controls UFC) for the second time this year. The cut was the result of a weaker-than-expected corporate performance in the third quarter of 2007; the second consecutive quarter in which S&P found Zuffa's performance to be significantly below expectations. Zuffa's credit rating is now BB-minus. The rating affects $350 million in secured financing.

Debt that is rated Triple-B and higher is considered "investment quality." BB-minus debt fits into the category that is politely termed "high yield." In an earlier era, BB-minus bonds were known as "junk bonds."

There's also an issue regarding the skill level of MMA combatants. Backers of the sport are fond of saying that their top competitors would beat Floyd Mayweather Jr. and any other elite boxer in a mixed martial arts competition. But that misses the point.

Any professional golfer would beat Mayweather on the golf course. Any decent high school tennis player would outclass Bernard Hopkins at tennis. A beginning sumo wrestler would belly-bump an MMA competitor out of the ring if they were adhering to the rules of sumo wrestling. And a marginally competent club fighter would destroy an MMA competitor in a boxing match. These hypothetical match-ups involve competitors from different sports.

Today's elite boxers are the best in the world at what they do. UFC claims that it has the best mixed martial artists on the planet, but that has yet to be proved. Boxing fans still care about who's really the best in their sport, while there's a feeling that MMA champions are fungible.

How good are today's MMA combatants? At the close of HBO's telecast of Oscar De La Hoya versus Floyd Mayweather Jr., Jim Lampley declared, "There's nothing in mixed martial arts within light years of what Mayweather and De La Hoya are able to do with their hands." That view is shared by most boxing people, who believe that MMA is an inferior product that, although packaged and marketed effectively, is simply not as good as boxing.

"UFC ain't nothing new," says Don King. "They started with ultimate fighting and then they civilized it and made it into boxing. All UFC is doing is taking 200 years of rules and throwing them out the window."

Or to phrase things differently: What would happen if Bob Arum went to the Nevada State Athletic Commission and proposed boxing with a twist? To build interest in the February 16, 2008, rematch between Kelly Pavlik and Jermain Taylor, there would be a slight change in the rules. If one of the fighters knocked his opponent down, he could punch him in the head and kick him as he lay on the canvas.

This was the first in a series of articles I wrote for ESPN.com.

No One Is Enforcing the Federal Boxing Laws

Boxing is allowed to exist as an exception to state laws against violence on the premise that it will be regulated in a manner that protects the combatants physically and financially. In 1996, when it became clear that the individual states were not properly protecting boxers, congress enacted the Professional Boxing Safety Act. Four years later, that law was augmented by the Muhammad Ali Boxing Reform Act. These two pieces of legislation, taken together, are commonly referred to as the "Ali Act."

As well-intentioned as it might be, the Ali Act suffers from glaring flaws. First, it accepts the present form of piecemeal state regulation. Second, it has too many loopholes. And most significantly, no one is enforcing it. Many people in boxing today simply ignore the act's requirements. And virtually no one in a position of authority with regard to enforcement is doing anything to remedy the situation.

The Ali Act requires that each sanctioning organization file a "complete description of the organization's ratings criteria" annually with the Federal Trade Commission. In the alternative, a sanctioning body may post the information on its official website. The WBC, WBA, IBF, and WBO all purport to do so. But their actual ratings practices mock the law. An incomplete or false filing falls short of compliance.

The law mandates that, when promoting a fight, a promoter file with the supervising state athletic commission copies of all agreements to which the promoter and one or both of the boxers are parties. It also requires that the promoter disclose to each boxer "the amounts of any compensation or consideration that a promoter has contracted to receive from such match." These requirements are largely ignored.

State athletic commission personnel also violate the act when it serves their purposes. In a section entitled "conflicts of interest," the law declares,

"No member or employee of a boxing commission, no person who administers or enforces state boxing laws, and no member of the Association of Boxing Commissions may receive any compensation from any person who sanctions, arranges, or promotes professional boxing matches."

However, in Nevada, each of the state's five commissioners is given six tickets in addition to his own seat for every fight card held in Nevada. These tickets are provided by the promoter. Two of them must be ringside. The other four tickets may be anywhere in the arena that the promoter chooses. The purported goal of this rule is to eliminate the embarrassment and abuse that have come in the past from commissioners asking promoters for free tickets.

These tickets are no small matter. For De La Hoya–Mayweather, six ringside tickets had a face value of $12,000 and were being resold on the Internet and elsewhere for multiples of that amount. Also, ringside tickets can be in the first row or the last. "Anywhere in the arena" can mean more ringside tickets or nosebleed seats. That leaves a lot of room for favors.

From April 24 through April 29 of this year, more than 300 ring physicians and other state athletic commission personnel attended the WBC's World Medical Congress in Cancun, Mexico. In addition to the medical agenda, those present enjoyed fine dining, cocktail parties, golf, and other forms of entertainment. Who paid what for whom is an issue.

On May 2, 2007, the Association of Boxing Commission's (ABC) legal committee acted upon information it had received indicating that the executive directors of two state athletic commissions had attended the WBC medical congress and accepted money from the WBC to cover hotel room charges, meals, and other costs. It was also brought to the attention of the committee that the same two executive directors might have stayed at the hotel at WBC expense for an additional two days following the close of the medical congress. The matter was referred to the ABC disciplinary committee, which, five months later, still has the matter "under advisement." A number of ring physicians are thought to have benefited from similar "stipends."

Some state athletic commissions take the position that referees, judges, and ring doctors fall within the purview of the Ali Act. Others have a contrary view. However, everyone agrees that the executive director of a state athletic commission is covered by the law. Thus, it should also be noted that, at the IBF's 2007 convention in Miami Beach, one executive director was paid by the IBF to conduct a seminar (in addition to his transportation, hotel, and meals being covered). The WBA's 2007 annual convention will be held in China from October 7 through October 13. The WBC will gather in Manila from November 11 through November 16. It would be nice to think that the "conflicts of interest" provision of the Ali Act will be adhered to there, but a blurring of the lines is likely to occur.

The Ali Act also requires that states honor medical suspensions imposed on a fighter by another state. That provision, too, is violated on a regular basis.

The abuses noted above are not a complete list of Ali Act violations. They are simply examples.

Primary responsibility for enforcing the Ali Act rests with the U.S. Department of Justice and its many U.S. Attorneys' offices across the country.

Under the law, a sanctioning organization is not entitled to collect sanctioning fees if it fails to make complete and honest disclosure of its ratings criteria. That law is not being enforced by the federal government.

Under the law, a promoter who knowingly fails to make a required contract filing with a state athletic commission or fails to make a required financial disclosure to a fighter is guilty of a crime punishable by up to one year in prison and a fine of $100,000. The justice department is responsible for these prosecutions. No such indictment has ever been brought.

Under the law, any member or employee of a boxing commission who knowingly violates the law by accepting compensation from a sanctioning body or promoter is guilty of a crime punishable by up to one year in prison and a fine of $20,000. Here again, there has been no enforcement.

One should also note that, according to the Internal Revenue Service, a commissioner who receives free tickets from a promoter and gives these tickets to family members or friends (or sells them), is required to pay personal income tax on the tickets. Lots of luck on that one.

A law doesn't mean anything if nobody enforces it. Here, the thoughts of Tim Lueckenhoff (president of the Association of Boxing Commissions) are instructive.

"I can't tell you how frustrated I am," Lueckenhoff told this writer last week. "When the ABC was formed, we thought we were going to accomplish some important things, but we have no real power to deal with violations of the Ali Act. So we're in a situation now where we have this law. We're trying to uphold it. It's a federal law. And we're getting no help whatsoever from U.S. Attorneys around the country."

"There's no boxing commission in Wyoming," Lueckenhoff says. "A promoter in Wyoming was promoting fights in clear violation of the Ali Act. We sent names and dates to the U.S. Attorney in Wyoming and never got a response. We complained to the U.S. Attorney's office in Alabama about a promoter who was running illegal toughman contests there. That U.S. Attorney told us he had our complaint but wasn't going to act on it. And these aren't isolated instances. I've made at least ten referrals to U.S. Attorneys' offices around the country and haven't found anyone who's willing to go to court to enforce the law."

"Federal law requires that states honor medical suspensions imposed on a fighter by another state," Lueckenhoff continues. "It's not hard to find out if a fighter is on medical suspension. It's right on the Internet. But last year alone, there were twenty-four violations by our own member commissions that I know of. And then you have a fighter like Lamon Brewster, who's on medical suspension. He goes over to Germany and fights for a world title, still on suspension, and HBO televises it. What kind of message does that send?"

"The law simply isn't being followed," Lueckenhoff says in closing. "I wish the justice department would bring one action based on each section of the law that's being violated. Forbid one sanctioning body that's acting illegally from collecting a sanctioning fee. Shut down one promoter who's promoting illegal fights. Step in just once to punish the people responsible for knowingly allowing a fighter who's on medical suspension to fight. If that happened, people would start toeing the line. Things would change real fast. But the federal government has made it clear to us again and again that it simply isn't interested in enforcing federal law as it relates to boxing."

Thus, the question: What's the point of having a law if nobody enforces it?

During the 1990s, the New York State Athletic Commission was a cesspool of incompetence and corruption. It's a lot better now, but there's still room for improvement.

Agenda for the New York State Athletic Commission

The New York State Athletic Commission (NYSAC) has made enormous progress with Ron Scott Stevens as chairman. It might now be the best commission in the country.

With leadership comes responsibility. If the NYSAC is to remain in the forefront of boxing regulation and reform, here are a dozen things that will be required of it in the future:

1. *Conduct a serious study regarding the advisability of same-day weigh-ins and act upon it.* Early weigh-ins began as a way of getting extra television coverage to hype fights. Now they're the vehicle by which a fighter who can no longer make weight on fight night is allowed to dehydrate, weigh-in early, and enter the ring ten or fifteen pounds heavier thirty hours later. That raises health issues and also issues of equity when a fighter is considerably heavier than his opponent. With same day weigh-ins, if there's a problem, it's harder to fix. But that might not justify the charade that exists today with lightweights fighting at 150 pounds and welterweights competing at 165. I don't know what the proper resolution is, but a serious inquiry is in order.

2. *Decrease the number of mismatches.* A "mismatch" is a fight in which the skill level and physical attributes of the fighters are such that their encounter is more of a public sacrifice than a competitive sporting event. This is more than a health issue. It also relates to the integrity of the sport and the product that is sold to fans. Promoters and managers push hard for mismatches as a way of building their fighters. But the ultimate responsibility for approving fights lies with the state athletic commission, which should just say "no." It's unrealistic to expect that every

fight will be a competitive match-up on paper. But at the very least, the underdog's skill level should be such that he is expected to provide genuine problems in the ring that have to be solved.

3. *Upgrade the performance of referees and judges.* The NYSAC conducts seminars for its officials. But despite these programs, there are still some mediocre referees and judges in New York; the powers that be know who they are; and they should be weeded out.

4. *The NYSAC now requires that managers, advisers, booking agents, and anyone else who negotiates contracts for a fighter or takes a piece of the fighter's purse as his business representative be licensed.* Stevens says, "Full compliance has almost been achieved." But it hasn't been yet, and full compliance should be the goal.

5. *The law requires that numerous fight-related contracts be filed with the NYSAC.* This includes the bout contract, boxer–promoter contract, boxer–manager contract, site contract, and all television contracts. But the law isn't always followed. The imposition of significant sanctions in instances where non-compliance is found to exist would encourage full compliance.

6. *Prohibit betting on fights by licensees.* At present, there is no specific prohibition against fighters, trainers, managers, promoters, even government regulators betting on fights (including fights that they're involved with) as long as the bet is properly placed (e.g., walking into a legal sports book and betting on the fight). No one who is licensed in conjunction with boxing should be allowed to bet on any fight (and particularly not a fight that they're involved with). The ban should be policed the way Major League Baseball does it. Get caught once and you're gone for life.

7. *Continue as a strong vocal advocate within the Association of Boxing Commissions for uniform national standards with regard to medical issues.* Not every state can do what New York does (pay for MRIs and other costly medical testing for fighters). But New York should push hard for minimum national standards with regard to pre-fight physical examinations for fighters and national rules with regard to such issues as whether a fighter who has suffered uncontrolled bleeding in the brain should be allowed to fight again.

8. *Restore credibility to the New York State titles.* Too often, fights are approved as New York State "championship" bouts without being worthy of the designation. The NYSAC takes the position

that these titles create activity and excitement. And unlike the world-sanctioning organizations, the NYSAC doesn't charge a sanctioning fee. But in the opinion of many, it cheapens the belts when one or both of the combatants is a mediocre club fighter. And it's silly when an out-of-state boxer fights for a New York State title.

9. *Next year, the New York State legislature will consider legislation aimed at legalizing mixed martial arts.* Rather than sit on the sidelines, NYSAC personnel should offer their expertise in this area before the fact, not after.

10. *Other proposed legislation will seek to provide a framework for the conduct of white-collar boxing.* The NYSAC should also have input in this debate.

11. *Further explore the use of instant replay during a fight to determine (a) whether or not a knockdown has occurred and (b) whether a cut has been caused by a head-butt or a punch.* Instant replay works in other sports. It can work in boxing. There's a problem in that many fights aren't televised, which would lead to different sets of rules for televised and non-televised fights. But in non-televised fights, the alternate referee can advise the referee if he is certain that there has been a bad call. Baseball, football, and basketball officials look to each other for help. Boxing officials should too.

12. *Implement a rule that would give a fighter's cutman five minutes to stem the flow of blood from a cut caused by an accidental head-butt.* Fighters are given up to five minutes to recover from a low blow. The same amount of time should be allotted here too. The cutman would not be allowed to offer instructions, and he wouldn't be given additional time if the cut reopened later in the fight. This rule wouldn't always lead to a fight continuing. The placement and severity of a cut is often more significant than the amount of blood lost. But often, the flow of blood from an accidental head-butt unfairly affects the flow of a fight.

Bob Sheridan has a distinctive announcing style and a personality to match.

Bob Sheridan: The Voice of Boxing

Bob Sheridan was first behind the microphone for a fight in 1966. Since then, he has called more than 800 championship bouts and become an integral part of boxing's historical soundtrack. From radio to broadcast television to closed-circuit to pay-per-view; been there, done that.

Sheridan is the international voice of boxing. He's the commentator for the foreign-rights feed on most major bouts held in the United States and also for many fights overseas that are transmitted by satellite to the U.S. He was at ringside when Muhammad Ali battled George Foreman in Zaire and Joe Frazier in Manila. He has called the fights of legends like Sugar Ray Leonard, Marvin Hagler, and Roberto Duran. He was behind the microphone when Mike Tyson bit off part of Evander Holyfield's ear. In large swaths of the world, his voice is synonymous with the sweet science.

Sheridan's parents were born in 1905; his mother in County Mayo and his father in County Longford, Ireland. Both came to the United States as toddlers.

Bob was born in Boston in 1944. "None of my grandparents were educated people," he says. "But they were very family oriented and wise. My father's father, James Sheridan, was a sheet-metal worker in Boston, who died before I could know him. He passed the trade on to my father, who later became a building contractor. My maternal grandfather, Andrew Dougherty, was a farmer in New Hampshire. He knew a lot about Irish history and politics and talked endlessly to me about them."

Sheridan went to college on a baseball scholarship at the University of Miami. "Baseball was my first love," he says. He graduated in 1966, and, that summer played a few games at third base for the Miami Marlins, who were a Class-A farm team for the Baltimore Orioles. "There was never any chance I'd stay with the club," he acknowledges. "I'd been brought in to fill a spot until some kid they'd signed out of high school joined the team."

His first year out of college, Sheridan also taught physical education in the Dade County school system and hosted his own radio talk show on WDER-FM, a small station in Miami. "I bought my own airtime," he remembers. "It cost ten dollars for a two-hour slot between 6:00 A.M. and 8:00 A.M. every Sunday morning. If I sold more than ten dollars in ads, I made a profit. "

But WDER-FM led to bigger things. The general manager for the Florida Marlins was Bill Durney, who co-hosted a radio show on WGBS (a major Florida station) with Red Barber. Barber was semi-retired and living in the Sunshine State. In earlier years, he'd been a radio and television baseball play-by-play announcer of legendary proportions. Durney introduced Sheridan to Barber.

"When I was young," Sheridan says, picking up the story, "I wanted to be Babe Ruth. I had a pretty wild lifestyle, and I used to tell people that I was Babe Ruth reincarnated, except I'd been born four years before Babe died and I couldn't play ball like him. However, I did have a tremendous ability to talk, and Red hired me. At first, I lined up interviews for him and read the sports news on his show. Then my role expanded. Red taught me a lot about the business. I learned from him that it doesn't all come from the top of your head. There's research and preparation. I prepare for every fight today like it was my first. I prepare for each undercard fight the same way I prepare for the main event. I learned that from Red Barber."

Working with Barber gave Sheridan exposure throughout Florida. Then, boxing entered his life.

The first fight that Sheridan had seen in person was Cassius Clay's conquest of Sonny Liston in Miami Beach on February 25, 1964.

"Chris Dundee, the on-site promoter, called our baseball coach at Miami and asked if he could send some kids over to the arena to sell Coke at the fight," Bob remembers. "Half a dozen of us went. I think a Coke sold for a quarter back then. We each made about four dollars, but I wasn't there for the money. I was there for the fight. Clay wasn't the most popular guy in the world, but I liked him. When the main event started, I stopped selling Coke, sat down in an aisle about twelve feet from the ring, and watched the fight. Of course, none of us had any idea of the magnitude of the history that was being made."

In late-1966, Sheridan began calling Chris Dundee's fights in Miami on WGBS radio. Boxing was a popular sport back then. There were fights in town every week, and Sheridan's work became increasingly popular. "The more you do, the better you get," he says. "And as I improved, more things fell into place."

Dundee started taking Sheridan to fights out of town. He was hired to do radio color commentary for University of Miami football games. The first championship fight he called was Jerry Quarry against Jimmy Ellis for the WBA heavyweight title in 1968. Television work followed.

By the mid-1970s, Sheridan had gained a considerable following. Then his life took an unusual detour. He moved to Ireland and began raising cattle on a small farm in County Clare. "It's hard to relate to city people the pleasures of working on a farm," he says. "But remember, my grandfather was a farmer, and I loved horses and cattle."

Sheridan owned ten acres in County Clare, leased a hundred more, and at one point, had 200 head of cattle." Then the detour got stranger.

"I figured I was breeding cattle and raising them, so why not ride them," he remembers. "I tell people, I was always a bullshitter so bull riding was the next logical step. Anyway, I took up rodeo bull riding. In retrospect, it was crazy. This was before flak jackets. There were a lot of bruises and I broke my back one time at a rodeo in Arkansas. I'd fly from Shannon to the United States, do a rodeo, and fly back home again. For a while, I was Aer Lingus's number-one non-commercial account. The last time I got on a bull was in 1981 at Madison Square Garden. I got bucked off in two seconds. The shute wasn't even shut before I was off. After that, I stopped. But it was a very enjoyable period in my life. Rodeo cowboys are great athletes and fun guys to be around. The characters in rodeo are like the characters in boxing."

In late-1981, Sheridan left the cattle business and moved back to Boston. "I loved every minute of it," he says. "But land became too expensive to lease." He now lives in Las Vegas with his wife of ten years, the former Annie Kelly, who was born in County Tipperary.

"I was a hard-drinking, womanizing, single guy for a long time," Sheridan acknowledges. "I was married once before to another Irish girl, and it was a horrible marriage because I wasn't mature enough to handle it. Whatever went wrong in that one, I'll take responsibility for it. I'm a much better husband now."

In addition to being a better husband, Sheridan is also now a fixture on the international boxing scene. He's behind the microphone for forty fight cards annually, but that doesn't begin to tell the story of his travels. In one seven-week stretch last year, he was ringside for fights in Memphis, the Philippines, St. Louis, Las Vegas, Boise, and South Africa. In 2005, he visited Australia eleven times.

Here, it should be noted that Sheridan has had four heart attacks and twelve angioplasties. "I have heart attacks like other people have the flu," he jokes. But in the next sentences, he adds," Any health problems I've had are the result of genetics and eating and drinking too much. Don't blame boxing; the traveling isn't a problem. I get a bit tired sometimes, but there's always an adrenaline rush when the fights begin."

"I love boxing," Sheraton says as his thoughts return to the sweet science. "It's the purest sport in the world; it's the greatest sport in the world. And my enthusiasm for it is one of my strengths as an announcer. I'm not a journalist. I don't focus on the negative when I'm commentating. Sure, boxing has problems, but other sports have problems too. My job as a boxing commentator is to give people the facts and entertain the public. I never forget the brutality of boxing and how dangerous it is. I was tough enough to get on the back of a bull again and again. I'm not tough enough to be a fighter. But boxing takes poor kids without hope like Muhammad Ali and Mike Tyson and elevates them to a place where they're among the most famous people on the planet. And each fight is an event. Nothing excites me more than two great fighters getting in the ring for a championship fight."

"There's an old saying," Sheridan observes in closing. "If you find a job you love, you never have to do a day's work in your life. When I'm behind the microphone, I'm happy."

In recent years, there has been a decline in America's educational system. The teaching of boxing has also suffered.

Are There Fewer Good Trainers Than Before?

As sports and technology have evolved over the years, training and coaching have evolved with them. From videotape to computer analysis to sports medicine, the sources of improvement are endless. By way of example, some of the men who won gold medals in swimming at the 1960 Rome Olympics (where Cassius Clay won his gold medal) wouldn't have qualified for the women's finals at the 2004 Athens games.

It's now possible for a trainer to watch tapes of every major fighter and virtually every major fight of the past eighty years. A boxer's movement can be broken down and freeze-framed at intervals of one-tenth of a second. Yet there's a prevailing view in the sweet science today that training fighters is becoming a lost art.

"I'm managing fighters now," says Emanuel Steward. "And one of the reasons I'm still training is that there's not too many guys out there that I'd trust to train my fighters."

"The main reason that so many old fighters are successful today," adds Don Turner, "is that no one is teaching the young guys how to fight."

"Even with the trainers at the top," says Teddy Atlas, "a lot of them are in good situations rather than being good trainers."

"The proof is in the fighting," notes historian Mike Silver. "Look at the performance of today's fighters. In virtually every other sport, performance has improved significantly over the years; but not in boxing. It's obvious that the fighters aren't being trained properly."

At first glance, boxing appears simple. It isn't.

The legendary Eddie Futch once observed, "Boxing is a science. You don't just walk into a gym and start punching. Fighters are born with differences in physical ability, but you also see a big difference in their skills. That's the trainer's influence at work."

Ray Arcel (Futch's contemporary in greatness) concurred, saying, "If you take a piece of gold out of the ground, you know it's gold. But you still have to clean it; you have to polish it; you have to give it a form. A real trainer can take an amateur from his first day in the gym and give him the tools to become a champion."

Trainers, like fighters, bring their own personality and style to their task. Opinions vary as to who's a good trainer and who isn't. Most practitioners of the trade have boosters and detractors. Only a few receive universal praise. But there is general agreement regarding the qualities that are essential to being a good trainer.

First, it's not enough for a trainer to tell a boxer what to do. He has to teach him. That requires an understanding of the intricacies of boxing and the ability to communicate that knowledge in a way that it's understood. It's more than coincidence that two of the best expert analysts on television today (Emanuel Steward and Teddy Atlas) are trainers; and another trainer (Gil Clancy) led the way. "You can't just give orders," says Atlas. "You have to be able to put the knowledge and understanding that you have inside someone else's head."

"A good trainer never stops learning," says Angelo Dundee. "You have to understand that you don't know everything and be willing to go to other people for help."

"A good trainer is a good listener," says Bouie Fisher. "He spends a lot of time with his fighter and gets to know him physically and mentally."

"A trainer needs patience," says Al Mitchell.

"You have to respect your fighter," says Tommy Brooks. "Otherwise, there's no way he'll respect you."

"A good trainer is dedicated," says Joe Goossen. "It's not just the fighters who have to sacrifice."

"A good trainer leads by example," says Jesse Reid. "That means you have to be disciplined."

"A good trainer has a passion for the sport," says Naazim Richardson. "And there are times when being a trainer is like being a parent."

Teaching the fundamentals of boxing to a fighter is just one part of a trainer's job, but it's the foundation on which everything else is based. In that regard, a good trainer is a perfectionist, but one who understands the reality of boxing that his fighter will always be less than perfect.

A good trainer is also a psychologist of sorts.

"You can teach a fighter all the mechanics in the world and he still might not know how to employ them," says Teddy Atlas. "The mental toughness, the psychological things you teach a fighter, are just as important as teaching him technique. The best trainers come from a place where they had some kind of practical experience in dealing with physical threats, pressure, and fear. That's one of the things I got from Cus [D'Amato]. Cus was a genius, a mad scientist, and 100 percent committed to the sport. He was a pioneer in teaching and he understood every aspect of the game, but his forte was the psychological."

"That's one of the things that made Eddie Futch great," says Freddie Roach. "Eddie did more than just teach boxing. He knew what buttons to push to get the most out of his fighter. He got inside his fighter's head."

"You have to know when to be firm," says Pat Burns. "You have to know when to be mean; and you have to know when to be gentle. When your fighter thinks he can't do anymore, you have to get him to believe that he can. When he's exhausted and thinks he can't climb those last few steps to get to the top of the mountain, you put it in his head that, not only can he do that; if he has to, he can go down to the bottom of the mountain and climb back to the top again."

A good trainer oversees his fighter's conditioning, chooses opponents wisely, and strategizes prior to each fight. He watches his fighter's back. On fight night, he works the corner. "During a fight," Ray Arcel observed, "the trainer is the pillar of hope for every fighter. But he also has to know when his fighter has had enough and, if need be, step in to stop the fight."

Emanuel Steward and Angelo Dundee are model cornermen at work during a fight. Steward is a master at counseling strategic adjustments. Dundee is the consummate motivator. "That's what you're there for," Angelo says. "To help your guy when he needs it."

Boxing fans know the tale of Dundee exhorting Cassius Clay through the perilous fifth round of his title challenge against Sonny Liston, when an astringent trickled into Clay's eyes and impaired his vision. They're also familiar with his lighting a fire under Sugar Ray Leonard in Leonard–Hearns I with the words, "You're blowing it, son." But Dundee thinks his greatest motivational work was performed with a club fighter named John Holman.

"John was fighting Ezzard Charles [in 1955]," Angelo recalls. "Even though Ezzard was on the downside of his career, he was beating my guy pretty good. But John had this thing. All his life, he'd wanted a house with a yard and a white picket fence around it. He talked about it all the time in the gym. So at the end of the eighth round, when John came back to the corner, I told him, 'You see that guy over there. He's taking away your house with the white picket fence. Now either you knock him out or you say good-bye to that house forever.'"

Holman knocked out Ezzard Charles in the ninth round.

"If I know anything, it's how to talk to fighters," Dundee says.

Some trainers are better with boxers; some are better with punchers. Eddie Futch could train any fighter with any kind of style and do it well. One of the things he preached was, "No matter how much effort a fighter puts in, there are some things he simply won't be able to do. A good trainer doesn't try to teach a fighter more than he can learn."

"Every boxer is different," Ray Arcel said. "No two are alike. You never see the same fighter twice. If you train one fighter one way, you can't train another fighter the same way because he might not have the same ability. What's food for one is poison for another."

"A good trainer takes what his fighter has and works with it the way Charlie Goldman did with Rocky Marciano," says Don Turner. "Charlie Goldman took a guy that nobody else wanted and taught him to do what he could do best."

Dundee offers similar praise, saying, "It was sheer genius, the way Charlie Goldman built Rocky Marciano." Mike Silver proclaims, "Charlie Goldman found a block of marble in a quarry and sculpted it into *The Pieta*."

There also has to be "chemistry" between a trainer and his fighter for the relationship to work.

"Sometimes," says Freddie Roach, "you can have a good trainer and a good fighter and it just doesn't click. That's the way it was with me and Jeff Lacy."

"And you have to have fun," adds Angelo Dundee. "That's why things worked so well between me and Muhammad."

Dundee caught lightning in a bottle with Muhammad Ali. That, of course, leads to the obvious. "There's a limit on what a trainer can do to make a fighter better," says Lou Duva. "It's much easier to be a good trainer when you're working with a fighter who wants to be great. But even then, it's hopeless unless the guy you're working with has God-given talent."

George Gainsford once boasted, "I'm the greatest trainer who ever lived. I trained Sugar Ray Robinson."

The response Gainsford heard was, "George, you've had hundreds of fighters. Why aren't they all as good as Sugar Ray?" Or phrased differently; even a great trainer needs a fighter to deliver the goods. No matter how great a teacher is, not every student passes the test.

One problem boxing faces today is that, in the United States, fewer gifted young athletes than before are going into the sport. And that's true of all weight divisions, not just the heavyweights. That means there are fewer fighters in the gym for young boxers to work with as they learn their trade.

There was a time when 375 boxers trained at Stillman's in New York; and Stillman's was just one of many gyms in the city. Now Stillman's is closed and there are only 104 boxers licensed to fight in the entire state. That total includes fighters from outside New York (who must be licensed in order to fight there) and eleven women.

"In the 1930s, '40s, and '50s," says Teddy Atlas, "there were more skilled hard-working role models for young fighters to follow. Young guys would see how the great ones worked in the gym and it rubbed off on them. Plus, if you spar with the same two or three guys all the time, you don't learn as much as if you have twenty different guys with twenty different styles to learn from. All of that affects how you can train a fighter today."

It's also harder to build a great fighter when the fighter doesn't have the experience of fighting tough opponents. Gil Clancy once said, "The best learning experience is a hard competitive fight." But many of today's top young prospects won't go in tough unless it's a big-money fight. That makes it harder to teach.

And it's a common complaint that many of today's fighters simply don't listen to their trainer. Eddie Futch once famously tried to get welterweight champion Marlon Starling to pay attention to his teaching with the advisory, "Marlon, some good fighters listened."

But some don't. "You very quickly get to a point where the fighter thinks he knows everything," says John David Jackson. "In this day and age, what old person gets respect from young people?"

"You get tired of telling men to behave like men," says Atlas. "I hate to talk like that; it sounds harsh. But you get tired of reminding guys what their commitments are. One thing that drives me crazy is, if you're working on an assembly line at Ford, you don't bring your friends to the plant. But a lot of these guys think it's fine to bring their friends to the gym with them every day."

"Too many people have the fighter's ear now," says Lou Duva. "His friends are telling him one thing. His girlfriend is telling him another. The TV people are telling him he has to look good, whatever that means, to get on TV."

"I have a problem with personal conditioners taking over and getting too involved," adds Emanuel Steward. "I don't believe in it. All of a sudden, the fighter is telling the trainer he can't do something that the trainer wants him to do because he has a second workout with the conditioner later in the day. And all most of these personal conditioners are doing is reading books and experimenting on fighters. Mackie Shilstone seems to be pretty good, but most of them don't have a clue when it comes to boxing."

And there's a larger problem. Many of boxing's great trainers came out of a world that doesn't exist anymore and never will again.

There was a time when boxing developed great trainers as a matter of course. They came naturally out of the fabric of the sport and the gyms. Ray Arcel started going to the gym when he was thirteen years old. He watched, asked questions, and learned. Ultimately, he worked with twenty world champions. And that was when the words "world champion" had special meaning.

"To become a trainer in the true sense, you have to go under somebody's wing and serve an apprenticeship," says Teddy Atlas. "Years ago, guys would put in an apprenticeship with a great trainer. They helped out in the gym. Then they were a bucket carrier in the corner for fights. They worked their way up the ladder. You don't have that anymore."

"I didn't watch the fighters in the gym," says Lou Duva. "I watched the trainers; guys like Whitey Bimstein and Chickie Ferrera. Then George Benton taught me more. Tommy Brooks and Ronnie Shields learned most of what they know from George too."

George Benton learned his craft from the great trainers of Philadelphia. Emanuel Steward learned his trade from Bill Miller, Luther Burgess, and other seasoned veterans in Detroit. Teddy Atlas apprenticed with Cus D'Amato and gained further insight from Ray Arcel and Freddie Brown. Buddy McGirt was taught by Al Certo. Freddie Roach learned from Eddie Futch.

"I was a bucket carrier who hung around the gym and listened and watched," says Angelo Dundee. "I kept my eyes and ears open and my mouth shut. That's how I learned from some of the greatest trainers who ever lived. Ray Arcel, Charlie Goldman, Whitey Bimstein; those guys gave of themselves. Chickie Ferrera taught me how to tie a fighter's shoes."

But many feel that the last generation of great trainers that boxing will ever see is gone. "You have a few relationships that have kept good training from becoming entirely extinct," says Mike Silver. "But overall, it's a dying art. You don't have the concentration of activity in cities that you once had, so the knowledge that exists isn't being passed on."

"It's part of the overall picture," says Atlas. "There's less interest in the sport than there once was so the universe is smaller. There's fewer gyms where guys can learn how to become trainers. And don't forget, fifty years ago in places like New York, you had fights five nights a week. Guys got practical experience in using what they'd learned. That's not the case anymore."

"The gyms no longer function as schools for trainers," says Emanuel Steward. "We don't even have a good program to teach amateur trainers."

Another problem that plagues the training profession is an absence of standards. "A lot of guys today are just cheerleaders," says Freddie Roach. "They hang around a gym for a while, put a towel over their shoulder, and call themselves a trainer."

Teddy Atlas is in accord, saying, "There's no structure in place that demands standards. If you're a carpenter building a house, you have to be okayed by the union and build the house to building code specifications. But in boxing, anyone can call himself a trainer, so you have a lot of guys out there who are just throwing a lot of mud against the wall and hoping some of it sticks. There are so few guys who know what they're doing that it's scary. I walk into a gym and see what some of these so-called trainers are doing and I feel like screaming."

"But let's be practical," Atlas continues. "Even if you had standards—and you do have some good people who are willing to teach young trainers—it's hard to find someone who's willing to apprentice because you can't pay the bills while you're learning."

The economics of boxing hinder the development of trainers today. Except for a few guys on top, full-time trainers are a thing of the past. There's simply not enough money to go around. The sport has a handful of fighters who are well paid and a lot of fighters who make next to nothing. Ten percent of a $400 purse is forty dollars. A trainer can't take his family out for hamburgers and to the movies for that.

"Trainers used to take amateurs and build them through the pros," says Angelo Dundee. "The greatest satisfaction you can have as a trainer is when you start with a young guy at the beginning and he gets to the top. But the name of the game now for a lot of guys is to start with an already-made fighter."

"Nobody is taking the time to teach basics anymore," says Emanuel Steward. "You should start with a young fighter by teaching him about balance, distance, and movement. You tell him, 'This is how you stand; this is the way to hold your hands; this is how you move forward; this is how you move backward.' But that's boring to some people and everyone is in a hurry, so they jump right in with jab, throw the right hand, left hook."

"Developing talent isn't about making money right away," says John David Jackson. "You can ruin a young fighter fast; it takes years to build one. But fewer and fewer trainers are willing to spend years putting a foundation under a fighter because they're afraid someone will come along and steal him."

That's another part of the problem.

"A lot of trainers spend years building a kid," says Naazim Richardson. "And then a celebrity trainer steals him. It's like raising a child. Imagine if you raise a child; change his diapers; teach him to walk and talk. And then, after years of parenting, if he turns out to be the kind of person you hoped he'd be, someone comes along and tells you that he's not your kid anymore."

"Continuity is one of the keys to training a fighter," Richardson continues. "Sometimes you see a kid who has gone from foster home to foster home, and he doesn't know what it's like to have a parent. It's the same thing with a fighter who moves from trainer to trainer. But it's so bad now that a lot of trainers are afraid to push their fighter once the fighter reaches a certain level. They train to their fighter's comfort level because they don't want to lose him. The trainer is intimidated by the fighter."

Eddie Futch walked away from Riddick Bowe because Bowe wasn't willing to dedicate himself to boxing to the degree that Futch demanded of him. Things like that don't happen often anymore.

"And there's another issue," says Don Turner. "You're in a situation now with a lot of fighters where, if the fighter loses a fight, he changes his trainer. When Joe Louis was knocked out by Max Schmeling, he didn't get rid of Jack Blackburn."

Be that as it may, many of today's fighters play musical chairs when it comes to trainers. And trainers who get a lot of exposure on television tend to get a lot of fighters. That leads to another problem.

"A lot of big-name trainers today are over-extended," says Dan Birmingham. "If you have a good assistant, maybe you can train a half-dozen fighters; definitely not more. But the way it is now, a lot of name trainers are really front men. They show up in camp a few weeks before the fight; they're in the corner on fight night. But other people do the heavy lifting, which doesn't always work for the fighter."

"Emanuel Steward and I have had our differences," says Don Turner. "But Emanuel knows as much about boxing as any guy ever. Emanuel is a very, very good trainer. He just doesn't always have the time to do it right. Buddy McGirt is another guy who has a way with fighters," Turner continues. "They like him and they like the lifestyle he offers them in training camp.

Buddy understands the essence of teaching but he's over-extended. Freddie Roach does good work, but look at all the fighters he's got. Ray Arcel might have worked with twenty fighters at a time, but Ray Arcel had guys like Freddie Brown and Angelo Dundee helping him."

So, bottom line. Are there fewer good trainers now than in the past?

Probably. But two more factors should be considered.

First, as Angelo Dundee notes, "There are a lot of good trainers out there that you never hear about because they're not on television."

Naazim Richardson elaborates on that theme. "Go in the gyms and you'll see some very good trainers working with kids," he says. "They're teaching them the basics, putting a foundation under them. But the talent in that particular local area might not be good. These guys aren't celebrity trainers and they aren't working with celebrity fighters, so they don't get the attention they deserve unless one of their guys turns pro, stays with him, and makes it to the top."

Dan Birmingham was twice named "Trainer of the Year," by the Boxing Writers Association of America, in large part because of his work with Winky Wright. If Wright had never walked into Birmingham's gym, would Birmingham be any less of a trainer?

Andre Berto has been trained by Tony Morgan since the age of twelve. Jack Loew began working with Kelly Pavlik when Kelly was nine. If Berto and Pavlik make it to the top, Morgan and Loew will be hailed. But based on performance so far, shouldn't we assume that they're capable trainers?

Also, this article has been keyed to American trainers. One presumes that there are quite a few good trainers today in Latin America. Some of the European and Asian trainers are pretty good too. That's one of the reasons why so many of today's champions come from outside the United States. Some foreign fighters gravitate toward American trainers when they reach a certain point in their career. But it's local trainers who put a foundation under them.

Most people who go to school have a handful of great teachers who inspire and teach them to learn, some lousy boring teachers, and many in between. Boxing's gyms are its universities. Its teachers reflect a similar range.

I have a lot of respect for Jim Lampley. This article reflected on a difficult time in his life.

A Note on Jim Lampley

L ast summer, Jim Lampley began dating a woman named Candice Marie Sanders. Lampley is fifty-seven years old. Sanders (who reigned as Miss California in the 2003 Miss USA Pageant) was twenty-nine when they met.

Sanders became omnipresent in Lampley's life. A lot of Jim's friends and co-workers had doubts about her, but he was in love. It was a tempestuous relationship. Shortly before Christmas, they got engaged. Then, on January 1, 2007, Sanders applied for and received a temporary restraining order, claiming that Lampley had assaulted her in a domestic dispute on New Year's Eve.

The order prohibited Lampley from coming within 100 yards of Sanders or the apartment they were living in (which was in his name). It also barred him from attempting to contact her in any way or seeking to reclaim a BMW that was registered in his name but which she claimed had been given to her as a gift.

On January 3, Lampley ventured within 100 yards of the apartment. More specifically, according to sources in San Diego, he went to the landlord's office, which was within the 100-yard restricted zone. His purpose in going, the sources say, was that the landlord had notified him of its intention to evict Sanders because she was not a lawful tenant and he feared that the eviction would be construed by the court as a violation of the court order (which also temporarily prohibited him from reclaiming his apartment).

Regardless of Lampley's intentions, he encountered two police detectives, who were conducting a follow-up interview with Sanders regarding her claim of domestic violence. He was arrested for violating the restraining order and, after being held briefly at the Vista Detention Facility was released on $35,000 bail. On January 4, he issued the following statement: "I am innocent of the charge of domestic abuse that has been leveled against me and will vigorously defend myself. I have tremendous respect for the justice system as a whole and for the San Diego courts and district attorney's office specifically. I'm confident that the process will prove that I'm not guilty of this charge. I thank my friends and family for their support during this difficult time and ask for understanding and patience from the media until my legal situation allows me to discuss this in more depth."

All of us do things at one time or another in our life that are self-destructive and stupid. We also have pockets in our psyche where our private fantasies reside. One of the most painful experiences that a person can endure is when these things are made public.

From the beginning, the accusations leveled against Lampley by Sanders struck many, not so much about what Jim did (or didn't do) to Candice, as about what she could do to him. Two parallels came to mind. The first was that of Marv Albert, who fell victim to a media feeding frenzy that revolved largely around private conduct between consenting adults. The second was that of former HBO vice president Lou DiBella, who saw his reputation unfairly tarnished when he was falsely accused of taking a $50,000 bribe.

Meanwhile, Lampley was experiencing pain on multiple levels that involved the loss of someone he'd thought he loved, the possibility of serious damage to his career, and public humiliation.

None of the friends who supported Lampley during his ordeal condone the physical abuse of anyone. They simply didn't (and still don't) think that Lampley assaulted Sanders. Linda Lee (Jim's first wife and now a professor at the University of Kansas School of Journalism) spoke for many of them when she told the Associated Press, "He's like nobody else. I adore him. We've been friends since we were kids. We grew up together. We were married for a while. We're still friends. When I heard this, it was just unimaginable. I know the man; I've known him for years. He's not capable of striking a woman, in my opinion. I've never seen him strike anything or anyone. I've never seen him strike a pillow. That's not his nature. He's a very gentle man and very even-tempered."

Last Wednesday (February 21, 2007), Lampley pled "no contest" to a misdemeanor charge of violating the January 1 restraining order. He was not indicted by the San Diego County district attorney's office for assault, domestic abuse, or any other felony. The charge leveled against him was that his coming within 100 yards of his apartment (which Sanders was living in at the time) was a violation of the outstanding court order.

Following his plea, Lampley was sentenced to three years probation and fined $670 in court costs. He was also required to undergo counseling and perform forty hours of volunteer service. Sanders has until the end of the month to vacate the apartment and return the BMW to him.

Lampley's friends say that he is currently going through a period of self-evaluation and asking himself what it was that caused him to be drawn into a relationship that brought so much unhappiness to himself and to people he cares about. They believe that he will emerge from this experience as a wiser, stronger, happier person.

After this article ran on Secondsout, several readers suggested additions, which are incorporated below. Meanwhile, let it be said, no other sport is run like boxing.

If Boxing Ruled Baseball

For the past two years, in addition to his involvement with boxing, Lou DiBella has been president and managing partner of the Connecticut Defenders (a Double-A minor league baseball team). His goal is to someday be managing partner of the New York Mets.

So, what would happen if the people who run boxing took over Major League Baseball? Here's a sampling of what we could expect:

- Each state (plus Toronto and Washington, DC) would have its own commissioner, which would leave baseball with thirty teams and nineteen commissioners.
- Some state commissions would mandate the use of aluminum bats, while others would require wood.
- At least one state commission would cut the length of games from nine innings to seven as a safety measure.
- Players would walk out onto the field at the beginning of each game surrounded by family, friends, and other hangers-on.
- Instead of numbers, players would have advertisements written in charcoal on the back of their jerseys.
- Manny Ramirez would wear tassels on his socks.
- The son of the Texas commissioner would be the home-plate umpire for most high-profile home games in Arlington and Houston.
- The Cleveland Indians and Atlanta Braves would play on Native American reservations.
- Ryan Howard would abandon the Philadelphia Phillies after receiving a duffel bag filled with $2 million in cash from New York Mets general manager Omar Minaya.

- Mike Tyson would sing a profanity-laced rap version of the national anthem on opening day.
- The schedule would be made up as the season progressed. But there would be no games between the New York Yankees and Boston Red Sox because Yankees' owner Don King would only play the Red Sox if he received options on Boston slugger David Ortiz.
- As a general rule, the best teams would only play second-division clubs, which would enable them to build up their records.
- Players would openly bet on games, and the owners would use it to hype ticket sales.
- Arnold Rothstein (the mastermind behind baseball's 1919 "Black Sox Scandal") would be admitted to the Hall of Fame.
- Players would hurl ugly ethnic and sexual slurs at each other, and it would be treated as a marketing ploy.
- After each game, players on the losing side would complain bitterly that they deserved to win.
- Each team that was in first place on July 4 would be declared an "interim champion."
- Florida Marlins shortstop Roy Jones would refuse to travel north with the team to play the Phillies and would explain to reporters, "Roy doesn't want to go to Philadelphia."
- Bernard Hopkins would take a called third strike in the All-Star Game and complain about it for the rest of the season.
- The sport would have a continuing steroid scandal, but some of the users would actually be punished.
- Instead of wild-card play-off teams, there would be "mandatory" play-off challengers. Thus, the Tampa Devil Rays would finish forty games under .500 and qualify for the play offs.
- HBO and Showtime would televise the American and National League Championship Series play-off games at the same time.
- The Cleveland Indians would win the American League play-offs but be stripped of their title for failure to pay sanctioning fees and be replaced in the World Series by the "champion emeritus" New York Yankees.
- The World Series would be on pay-per-view, so as few fans as possible would see it.

This article engendered a surprisingly enthusiastic response, including several requests from publications for interviews with my mother.

My Eighty-One-Year-Old Mother Meets Don King

I have a great mother. She got married at nineteen, and I was a wedding-night baby. She isn't young anymore, but she's still young at heart.

My mother is a loyal Democrat and a cut-throat bridge player. At eighty-one, she takes a weekly class in global politics at NYU. She's inquisitive and likes life-broadening experiences. She thought it would be fun to meet Don King.

"She'll have a great time," Lou DiBella told me. "Everyone I know who wants to meet Don King walks away loving him. He charmed my mother completely."

"Tell your mother to be careful," Jay Larkin cautioned. "If you listen to Don long enough, you drink the Kool-Aid."

The meeting was arranged for October 3 at the final pre-fight press conference for King's "Faith, Hope, and Glory" card at Madison Square Garden. Samuel Peter would be defending his interim WBC heavyweight crown against Jameel McCline. That seemed like a wise choice, since it spared my mother the ordeal of listening to Ricardo Mayorga and James Toney calling their opponents "maricon" and "pussy bitch." Of course, Andrew Golota would be at the press conference as he readied to fight Kevin McBride on the undercard.

We arrived at the Garden at 11:30. My mother was wearing a "01–20-09" button in anticipation of the day that George Bush leaves office. We stopped at the security checkpoint and a guard addressed her.

"Hello, young lady."

After passing through security, we went upstairs and Joe Dwyer came over to say hello.

"Tom, I didn't know you were bringing your sister."

"I'm starting to like boxing people," my mother said.

My mother's previous experience with "boxing people" had been limited to Muhammad Ali. They met on several occasions; the first time at my apartment.

"You're much bigger than I thought," my mother told him.

"Did you call me a nigger?" Ali demanded.

"No. I said you're bigger than I thought."

Ali smacked his fist into the palm of his hand and advanced in menacing fashion. "It's not right to call someone a nigger. I'm gonna whup you bad."

Then his face broke into a smile that lit up the room.

"What a nice man," my mother told me afterward. "And handsome too."

Now she was about to meet another boxing icon. Don King, to quote Seth Abraham, "is formidable even in his sleep." Did anyone at the press conference have advice for my mother as to how to handle the situation?

"Put cotton in your ears," George Kimball counseled.

"Watch your wallet," Chris DiBlasio warned.

"Be ready for words you never heard before, and a lot of them," Buddy McGirt cautioned.

"Take your jewelry off before you shake hands with him," Ivaylo Gotzev suggested.

"You can't believe what he's saying," Lou Duva said. "And sometimes you can't even believe that he's saying what he's saying."

After checking out the room, Duva sat down next to my mother. Ten minutes of Lou goes a long way. My mother had him for the next two-and-a-half hours. "I don't fall in love with broads anymore," the eighty-five-year-old trainer told her. "I fall in love with fighters."

My mother leaned over and whispered to me, "These people are like something out of *Guys and Dolls*."

Thereafter, I introduced her to some of the fighters. She was particularly taken with Jameel McCline. "I think he's sweet," she told me. She also liked Kevin McBride, who described for her what it was like to knock out Mike Tyson.

I didn't introduce her to Andrew Golota, but explained the circumstances surrounding the riot that occurred when he fought Riddick Bowe at Madison Square Garden eleven years ago. That, of course, led to concern on my mother's part that I might be injured in a riot following Golota–McBride.

"Don't worry," I assured her. "Ticket sales are lousy. There won't be enough people there for a riot."

Then a high-pitched voice and booming laugh resounded throughout the room. Don King entered, waving multiple flags, wearing his red-white-and-blue "Only in America" jacket with rhinestones glistening beneath the television lights.

Don came over and said hello to my mother. She stared at the bling cascading down his chest.

"Is that jewelry real?" she queried.

"Oh, these are just a few doodads and baubles," he told her.

They chatted briefly, after which Don moved on to work the rest of the room. "He's larger than life," my mother observed.

The press conference began at one o'clock. King advised the assembled media, "We don't need no hyperbole; just the facts. And the facts are that this will be one of the most exciting nights in boxing history with something for every ethnic group."

That included fighters from Nigeria (Peter), Poland (Golota), Ireland (McBride), Australia (Kali Meehan), Puerto Rico (José Rivera and Daniel Santos), the Dominican Republic (Elio Rojas), and the United States (Mc-Cline and DaVarryl Williamson).

My mother sat though a parade of fighters, managers, trainers, advisers, government regulators, and Nigerian diplomats. King quoted William Shakespeare and John Donne and likened Golota to Winston Churchill. There was even a rabbi.

"Why is a rabbi talking at a boxing press conference?" my mother asked.

"Because he bought 200 tickets," I said.

When it was McCline's turn to speak, Jameel glowered at Samuel Peter and declared, "I'm a fucking beast."

"I still think he's sweet," my mother told me.

At one point in the proceedings, King introduced my mother (referring to her as "young" and "beautiful") and asked her to take a bow. She blew a kiss in his direction, which prompted him to say, "I love you, too."

Still, after ninety minutes of listening to King and company, my mother was getting bored. By 2:30, she had pretty much had it. When it was time to pose the fighters for the traditional staredown, McCline was nowhere to be found.

"He was smart and went home," my mother said.

Eventually, Jameel was located; the final photos were taken; and the festivities ended.

"So?" I asked my mother as we left. "What did you think of it all?"

"I'm not sure," she answered. "I had fun, but something is bothering me. I can't exactly put my finger on it. But I feel sad and can't explain why."

"Give it some thought."

"I guess it's that, when we were sitting there, I was thinking back to when I was young. Joe Louis was a great hero. I remember how excited everyone was when he beat the Nazi. Then I got older and Rocky Marciano was heavyweight champion of the world. Muhammad Ali was special. And even with the champions who weren't great, people knew who they were."

Now my mother was on a roll.

"What I heard today," she said, "is that there are four heavyweight champions, and Samuel Peter is another kind of heavyweight champion, and it doesn't make sense. If that's the way boxing is, no one will care."

Sometimes mothers are very smart.

By the way, now my mother wants to meet Mike Tyson.

This article was inspired by the interaction between boxing and the motion picture industry.

Hauser's Fourteen

In April 2001, I was in Las Vegas for the fight between Naseem Hamed and Marco Antonio Barrera. In the days before their encounter, the arena at the MGM Grand was taken over by Julia Roberts, George Clooney, and company, who were filming a remake of *Ocean's Eleven*.

The original *Ocean's Eleven* starred Frank Sinatra and involved a plot to rob a Las Vegas casino by causing a power blackout on New Year's Eve. The 2001 remake contemplated a similar robbery during a heavyweight championship fight. On the last day of filming, Lennox Lewis and Wladimir Klitschko stood in ring center. Thousands of extras were in the arena. Women to die for were herded around like cattle. All for scant seconds in the final cut.

It got me thinking. All boxing people have larceny in their heart. I realized that I could make a lot of money by robbing a Las Vegas casino. Discretion being the better part of valor, I put the idea aside. But with the release of *Ocean's Twelve* in 2004 and *Ocean's Thirteen* in 2007, I started thinking again. All I had to do was put together a group of co-conspirators whom I could trust. *Hauser's Fourteen* followed.

It was hard to find thirteen people in boxing I could rely on to be honest comrades in arms. But finally, I gathered a pretty good team together.

The first person I recruited to join me was Jerry Izenberg. Jerry is a genius. He bucks the system. And I like working with Jerry.

Lou DiBella was drawn to the project by the notion that he could give his share of the take to indigent boxers.

Cedric Kushner came onboard because there's nothing he likes more than a night out with the boys. I should add that Cedric was a particularly valuable addition to the team for a reason that very few people know about. For a long time, Cedric has led a double life as a government agent. In fact, several years ago, he was secretly knighted by the Queen of England for his role in recovering the Crown Jewels, which had been stolen from the Tower of London. He is now "Sir Cedric" and is rumored to have engaged in a romantic tryst with the Queen.

We needed muscle to implement the plot. Therefore, we added Arturo Gatti and Micky Ward; universally recognized as honest fighters we could trust.

We also needed someone who knows the casinos well and is welcome in them. MGM Mirage vice president Scott Ghertner was a possibility, but we were afraid that might constitute a conflict of interest since we were planning to rob Mandalay Bay. Thus, we settled on Michael Buffer. Another reason we chose Buffer was that we liked the idea of meeting for the final time before going off to rob the casino and hearing Buffer intone, "Okay, gang. Let's get ready to rumble."

Bob Sheridan was included on the theory that, if we got in trouble, the Colonel would give us a good chance of talking our way out of it.

LeRoy Neiman became the ninth member of *Hauser's Fourteen*. His diagramming of the crime scene in advance proved to be invaluable.

It was important to have someone from law enforcement with us so we could anticipate what the authorities might do to thwart our efforts. Former New York City police detective Joe Dwyer (now NABF championship chairman) was perfect for the job.

Nikolay Valuev agreed to serve as an attention-diverting decoy while the heist was underway.

On the chance that feminine wiles would be needed, we recruited HBO production coordinator Tami Cotel and Dr. Margaret Goodman. Tami is the best production coordinator in the business. And we thought it would be helpful to have a doctor in case anyone got shot.

Finally, it occurred to us that it was a good idea to have a lawyer. After all, we might get caught. After considerable negotiation, Judd Burstein took the case on a contingency-fee basis and agreed to one-fourteenth of the haul instead of his customary one-third.

I can't tell you precisely how we implemented the plot. That's because, if the authorities come looking for us, we plan to deny any involvement. However, I will say that $20 million in cash is missing from Mandalay Bay. And the next time Tami Cotel works a fight for HBO, she'll be wearing a Dolce & Gabbana gown and a diamond tiara.

Fistic Nuggets

Three years ago, I reported on Don Elbaum's efforts to promote a series of fight cards in Nevada to be known as "Bordello Boxing." Prostitution is legal in Nevada, and the plan was to promote monthly shows at an upscale brothel called Sherry's Ranch.

Things didn't work out. Advertising was considered essential to the venture, and it's illegal under Nevada law to advertise to induce people to come to a brothel.

"It's a shame, really," Elbaum said afterward, acknowledging defeat. "Boxing and prostitution is a marriage made in heaven, or wherever. The greatest thing anyone ever said about boxing is that it's the red-light district of professional sports. Red-light districts intrigue people. They don't want to be seen going in or out, but they want to be there. I love that description."

At any given time, Elbaum seems to be juggling ten balls in the air. Often, he drops nine of them. Sometimes he drops all ten. But he personifies poet Robert Browning's immortal words, "A man's reach should exceed his grasp or what's a heaven for?"

Elbaum is always pursuing a dream. When he was fifteen, he left home to join a carnival.

"It was summer vacation," he recalls. "School was out, and a carnival was passing through town. It had throwing balls through a hoop, popping balloons, everything you can think of. One of the games was, you chose a number and they spun a wheel and, if your number came up, you won a doll. The girl spinning the wheel was the daughter of the guy who owned the carnival, and she was drop-dead gorgeous beautiful. I spent eight hours talking with her. I went home that night and told my parents that I was leaving home to join the carnival. My father understood; my mother had a different view. But I did it and ran a penny-pitching game with the carnival for a month. The owner's daughter and I really hit it off. I had a ball."

The following summer, Elbaum left home again; this time, to play an Indian in a wild west show. "The owner of the show was named Wild Bill," he remembers. "I can't remember his last name. He had a beautiful daughter too, but I was less successful with her than with the carnival owner's daughter."

Since the failure of bordello boxing, Elbaum has continued chasing rainbows. His most notable recent venture was trying unsuccessfully to convince Oprah Winfrey to serve as the ring announcer for a fight card at the Blue Horizon. He's always "working on a few things."

• • •

No report on the subject of boxing and prostitution would be complete without a tip of the hat to Cedric Kushner. Where women of the night are concerned, the promoter is something of a ladies man. "One way or the other, you pay for it," Cedric observes. "I just pay more directly."

Kushner has a ceiling on what he will pay for services. "The end result is the same," he posits, "so why pay more?" The following stories are told without passing judgment and with Cedric's permission.

In July 2001, Kushner was at Caesars Palace in Las Vegas to promote the heavyweight match-up between Michael Grant and Jameel McCline. Two nights before the fight, Craig Hamilton (Grant's advisor) was playing blackjack in the casino when an attractive woman in her early twenties walked over and stood behind him.

"Anyone could see what was going on," Hamilton recalls. "She was wearing an extremely revealing dress. I was up three or four thousand dollars, so there was a big pile of chips on the table in front of me."

Kushner came over and asked Hamilton, "Would you mind telling me what the story is with the girl behind you?"

"You figure it out," Hamilton responded. "She's about thirty years younger than I am; she's dressed like a hooker; and I have a big pile of money in front of me."

"Would it be possible for you to make an inquiry on my behalf?"

So Hamilton turned to the woman and said, "Look, we both know why you're here. I'm not interested, but my friend is. How much?"

The woman examined Kushner and answered, "Three hundred for an hour; seven hundred for the night."

That put the ball on Cedric's side of the court. "With all due respect," he told her, "there's nothing I can do during the course of an entire night that I can't do in an hour."

And they went off to the elevator together.

But Kushner's encounters with women of the night have not been without risk. Once, in Atlantic City, he brought a hooker to his room and awoke the following morning, groggy and disoriented. She'd put "knockout drops" in his drink and stolen his watch, wallet, and everything else of value.

The lesson most people would learn from that experience is, "Don't bring a hooker to your hotel room." The lesson Cedric learned was, "When I bring a hooker to my room, I shouldn't drink anything that I haven't followed with my own eyes from source to mouth."

Thus, several years later, Kushner was robbed again. This time, it happened in Las Vegas. The hooker put knockout drops on her nipples.

"There's one thing you have to agree with," Cedric says, reflecting back on those experiences and his history of ups and downs in boxing. "I'm the same guy no matter what happens."

• • •

Former Time Warner Sports president Seth Abraham is known in boxing circles as the architect of HBO's boxing program. But in his youth, Abraham had an in-ring experience of his own.

"I was ten years old," Abraham remembers. "It was at a sleepaway camp in Monroe, New York. One afternoon, the counselors organized a boxing tournament. I was matched against a camper named Mark Slate. He hit me, and it made me so angry that I threw a huge roundhouse left [Abraham is a southpaw] that, by chance, landed right on his nose."

What happened next is instructive.

"The gloves were the size of pillows," Abraham says. "It was almost impossible to hurt someone with them, but the punch hit Mark just right. Blood started pouring from his nose. And I was so upset by the sight of it that I fainted."

"Two fantasies were destroyed that afternoon," Abraham acknowledges. "My young fantasy of becoming heavyweight champion of the world and my mother's fantasy of her son becoming a doctor."

• • •

A tip of the hat to Larry Holmes, one of the greatest heavyweight champions ever. Last month, Holmes attended the Great Sports Legends Dinner that's held annually to raise money for The Buoniconti Fund to Cure Paralysis. Other attendees included John Elway, Magic Johnson, Mark Messier, and Gary Player.

Then there were the second-tier sports celebrities, including New York Knicks guard Nate Robinson. At one point, Holmes and Craig Hamilton found themselves talking with Robinson.

"I hope you're not embarrassed," Robinson told Holmes. "But I don't know who you are."

"I'm not embarrassed," the legendary champion responded. "But you should be."

• • •

Believe it or not, Paulie Malignaggi has a shy side.

In November 2002, I was in Atlantic City for the second fight between Arturo Gatti and Micky Ward. Paulie (who was relatively unknown at the time) was slated to fight Paul Delgado on the undercard. Gatti had just finished a sitdown in a conference room with a small group of media. Paulie had come in to listen and was standing off to the side.

"Arturo is my hero," Paulie told me.

"Have you met him?"

"No."

"C'mon. I'll introduce you."

Gatti was warm and welcoming. Paulie was respectful. They chatted for several minutes.

"That made me feel good," Paulie said afterward. "He treated me like I'm somebody. He's a really nice guy."

. . .

The saga of Don Elbaum continues.

On March 17, 2007, Elbaum found himself at the Grand Casino (a Native American venue in Hinckley, Minnesota). There's a lot of friction these days between Native American tribes and Scott LeDoux (executive director of the Minnesota State Athletic Commission). In fact, LeDoux has gone so far as to warn his officials that he will look askance at their working shows at certain tribal casinos.

Elbaum was at the Grand Casino as an "adviser" to Joey Abell, a twenty-five-year-old heavyweight from Minneapolis with a 13–1 record and thirteen knockouts.

"Joey is like a young George Foreman," Don boasts. "He punches like a freight train. And things being the way they are, it doesn't hurt that he's white."

What made the March 17 fight card unique is that Elbaum refereed all six contests, including Abell's bout.

"I was very fair," Elbaum reports. "Joey fought a guy named James Gerstein and knocked him down three times in the first round. Then I stopped it. There was a little bit of a storm over my being Joey's adviser but not much. And there was another fantastic fight on the card. Zach 'Jungle Boy' Walters and 'Gentleman' James Johnson really got into it. James hit Zach in the balls, and Zach complained, 'He hit me low.' So I told Zach, 'Then you hit him low.' What a fight."

"Half of the referees today don't know what they're doing," Elbaum advises. "Believe me, I'm a good referee."

. . .

And more on Cedric Kushner—

During a press gathering at a Manhattan restaurant to promote an upcoming Cedric Kushner Gotham Boxing card, the conversation turned to the awards that had just been announced by the Boxing Writers Association of America.

Fighter of the Year, Manny Pacquiao . . . Trainer of the Year, Freddie Roach . . . Manager of the Year, no award.

"Who's Noah Ward?" Cedric queried. "I've never heard of him."

The moment brought to mind the famous Abbott and Costello baseball routine, "Who's On First?" But the best line of the evening came from David Tua. When the five-foot-nine-inch heavyweight was asked whether he could overcome his height and reach disadvantage in a fight against seven-foot-two-inch Nikolai Valuev or six-foot-six-inch Wladimir Klitschko, Tua answered, "No problem. It's like dating a taller girl. In bed, you're the same size."

. . .

It has long been suspected in some circles that WBC championship belts are for sale. Now comes proof positive. The WBC Merchandising Europe website is selling the belts to the public for 2,348 pounds sterling (the equivalent of $4,635). According to the site, this is the "exact belt that the champions receive."

Would the National Football League sell exact replicas of the Vince Lombardi Super Bowl trophy to the public? I doubt it. Would the St. Louis Cardinals make extra World Series rings to sell on the side? I think not.

The WBC website says that the belts are "made from highest quality green leather inlaid with gold." It doesn't say what kind of gold or whether the belts are tarnished.

Fistic Notes

In 1973, Elton John advised the world, "Saturday night's alright for fighting; get a little action in." Now Saturday is the only night on which mega-fights are held.

It wasn't always that way. For the first half of boxing's history under the Marquis of Queensberry Rules, the live gate was the economic force that drove the sport. Big fights were held in major cities. Men (the crowds were overwhelmingly male) would leave work and go to the fight before going home. Thus, the biggest fights were virtually always on a weekday night. By way of example, John L. Sullivan versus James J. Corbett (Wednesday), both Dempsey–Tunney fights (Thursday), and Louis–Schmeling II (Wednesday) were mid-week encounters. Louis–Schmeling I was slated for a Thursday but was delayed for twenty-four hours because of rain.

Then closed-circuit television become a force and, where mega-fights were concerned, mid-week continued to reign. Saturday was "date night" while Monday through Thursday were available for a "boys night out." And more significantly, theater owners didn't want a big fight to take place on a Friday or Saturday night. Attendance at movies was poor during the week, so those nights could be set aside for boxing. But shut out movie-goers on a Friday or Saturday night? No way.

Thus, all of Muhammad Ali's fights against Sonny Liston, Joe Frazier, George Foreman, and Larry Holmes were contested on a Monday, Tuesday, Wednesday, or Thursday. Similarly, Sugar Ray Leonard's three biggest closed-circuit bouts (Leonard–Duran II, Leonard–Hearns I, and Hagler–Leonard) were mid-week encounters.

Then two more forces came into play. Casinos started paying huge site fees for mega-fights with the intent of luring high-rollers in for an entire weekend, not just a weekday night. And the advent of pay-per-view made Saturday-night mega-fights possible. Boxing was no longer dependent upon the willingness of theater owners to open their doors. Boxing fans could be charged for watching a fight at home.

Now, as a matter of course, every major fight is on a Saturday night. Is a mid-week mega-fight feasible today? A big-city arena like Madison Square Garden could host an event on the scale of Lewis–Tyson on a "work night" and the live gate would be fine. However, pay-per-view sales would probably suffer.

The west coast is now a major factor in pay-per-view buys. And the three-hour time difference between east and west makes a mega-fight on a "work night" impractical. Pay-per-view telecasts typically start at 9:00 P.M. EST, 6:00 P.M. PST. That means, on a Monday through Friday night, most west coast viewers wouldn't be home from work when the first bout started. On the east coast, the main event wouldn't begin until after 11:00 P.M. And no matter how one juggles the timing, there would be a problem.

Also, watching a pay-per-view fight today is often a group experience with four or five fans getting together to party and share the cost. That's a lot easier to orchestrate on a Saturday night.

Mid-week mega-fights are a thing of the past.

• • •

In the past, I've recounted the memories of boxing personalities regarding the first professional fight they ever saw. The recollections of four more individuals who have left their mark on the sweet science follow:

SYLVESTER STALLONE: "A lot of people are surprised by this, but I never went to a fight before I wrote *Rocky*. I was always either doing other things or was too poor to go. But I started at the top. The first fight I went to was Larry Holmes against Ken Norton [on June 9, 1978] at Caesars in Las Vegas. What a great fight! It was toe-to-toe action. And to be honest, if I'd seen that fight before writing *Rocky*, the movie might have been a little different because one of the things that struck me about Holmes–Norton was the audience participation. In the fight scenes in *Rocky*, we focused on the fighters and their corners. But at Holmes–Norton, I realized that the crowd is a character in itself."

MATTHEW SAAD MUHAMMAD: "It was at the Blue Horizon in Philadelphia. I was seventeen years old. My amateur coach took me, and the fighters were punishing each other like rock 'em, sock 'em robots. It was like Hollywood. No normal man could take that kind of punishment. But they had victory in their eyes, and I could see that the desire to win lessened the pain they felt. My coach said to me, 'This is what it's going to be like if you turn pro. To win, you'll have to condition yourself physically and mentally. Do you think you can do this?' And I told him, 'Whatever it takes, I'm going to do this. I can take the punishment. I can take the pain.' "

SHANNON BRIGGS: "I was a kid, seventeen years old, learning how to box at the Starrett City Boxing Gym in Brooklyn. My coach, Jimmy O'Pharrow, took me and some other kids he was working with to Yonkers. We drove there in a big white Cadillac with a blue top. I don't remember anything about the fights, but I remember meeting Renaldo Snipes, who was in the crowd. I weighed around 170 pounds at the time, and he seemed like a giant to me. This was after he'd fought Larry Holmes, so he'd been within one punch of being heavyweight champion of the world. He wished me good luck, and it was like 'wow.' I was in awe of him. I wasn't thinking about fighting as a pro back then, but it was a nice experience."

DAN BIRMINGHAM: "I went with my amateur trainer, Art Mayorga. Art was from Youngstown, Ohio, where I grew up. He'd been one of Sonny Liston's sparring partners. After he retired, he trained kids in his basement. The walls were the ropes, so we learned to stay in the center of the ring. I started boxing with him at 112 pounds and finished at 160. My record was 35-and-7, but I never turned pro. Art took me to church every Sunday, and I went because he always bought me breakfast afterward. The first pro fight he took me to was in 1968 or 1969 after I'd been fighting for a few years. There were three brothers—John May, James May, and Tommy May—who fought in Youngstown. Two of them were on the card. To me, it was more of a bonding experience with Art than it was about going to the fights. I remember, he talked about his experiences in boxing and guys he'd known like Billy Conn and Sandy Saddler. Art died a few years ago and I still think about him. Just when I think I remember everything he taught me, something else surfaces in my mind.

• • •

How bad are the opponents that Joe Mesi has been fighting lately?

Last Saturday night (April 14, 2007), Mesi knocked out Ron Johnson at the Hughes Center in Russellville, Arkansas. Knockouts are nothing new for Johnson. He has been stopped seventeen times. The novelty here is that he was knocked out by a heavyweight.

You see, Johnson began his career as a junior-middleweight. Two fights ago, he was competing at 165 pounds.

Mesi also fought in Russellville last year, when he knocked out Dennis Matthews who was 9-and-27 at the time. Matthews is now 9-and-30 and on a ten-fight losing streak.

Joe's other comeback opponents have been Ron Bellamy (who was carried from the ring on a stretcher in two of his previous three bouts before facing Mesi); Stephane Tessier (now 3-and-12 and on a ten-fight losing streak); Jason Weiss (a novice with four pro fights); and George Linberger (who was knocked out in one round by Butterbean).

Jack Mesi (Joe's father and manager) says that his son shouldn't be blamed for the poor quality of opposition in his most recent fight. "We found out at the last minute that there was a change in opponents," Jack said the morning after. "I didn't know anything about this guy [Johnson] until the bell rang."

But Johnson was a substitute for Marvin Hill who, in thirty-two outings, has beaten only three opponents with a victory to their credit. And Hill has been knocked out in the first round six times.

Mesi is expected to ask the New York State Athletic Commission to restore his boxing license later this year. In support of his application, he will cite his six consecutive comeback victories. New York should stand firm in support of its policy that fighters who have suffered uncontrolled bleeding in the brain should not be allowed to fight again. Meanwhile, Arkansas and the other jurisdictions that have allowed Mesi's recent fights should reevaluate their standards.

• • •

One of the endearing things about boxing is the range of characters who find a niche in the sport. Put Tomas Mendoza on that list.

Mendoza was born in Guadalajara, Mexico, in 1957. He came to the United States in 1975 and took a job as a construction worker in Chicago. He now owns his own company and does contracting work for homes and small businesses.

Mendoza's claim to boxing fame is that he's often seen on television, waving the flag of a fighter's country as he leads the fighter to the ring. The first time he did it was for Willie Salazar, when Salazar fought Danny Romero in Las Vegas in 1995.

"Salazar was from Mexico," Mendoza recalls. "I just wanted to be close to a fighter. They are my idols. I asked him if I could do it, and he said yes."

Romero was 25-and-0 at the time. Salazar was a shopworn 41–21–1 and had been knocked out thirteen times. But in a bout later designated as *Ring Magazine's* "upset of the year," Salazar stopped the favorite in seven rounds.

After that, a lot of fighters thought of Tomas as a good luck charm.

Mendoza still lives in Chicago. The list of fighters he has carried the flag for includes Oscar De La Hoya, Floyd Mayweather Jr., Bernard Hopkins, Jermain Taylor, Miguel Cotto, Shane Mosley, Vitali Klitschko, Wladimir Klitschko, and Nikolai Valuev.

Mendoza buys his own flags. He has about thirty of them. He pays his own way to fights and, often, doesn't know whether he'll be allowed to carry a flag into the ring until the day of a fight.

"If I could have carried the flag for anyone in history," Mendoza says, "it would have been for Joe Louis when he knocked out Max Schmeling. I would have been very proud to do that. And in my heart, I wish I could have carried the flag for Roberto Durán. He was my greatest hero. I never had the chance to carry the flag for him. But a great moment for me was, one time, I met him.

And my hero, the great Roberto Durán, knew who I was. He said to me, 'Hello, Mr. Flag-Man.' "

. . .

On April 6, New York governor Eliot Spitzer nominated Melvina Lathan to serve as a commissioner of the New York State Athletic Commission. Ms. Lathan, according to a press release issued by the governor's office, is an artist, photographer, costume designer, and sound designer. She is also an active ring judge, having worked eighty-two world championship fights.

In recent years, the NYSAC has become a leader in the effort to make boxing a safer, more honesty-run sport. One assumes that Ms. Lathan will follow that lead and refrain from judging further fights.

The Muhammad Ali Boxing Reform Act (in a section entitled "Conflicts of Interest") states: "No member or employee of a boxing commission may belong to, contract with, or receive any compensation from any person who sanctions, arranges, or promotes professional boxing matches."

The applicability of this provision to Ms. Lathan is obvious. Depending on the magnitude of a fight, ring judges receive as much as $7,500 for an evening's work. That's in addition to first-class travel and a pretty good seat on fight night. But these assignments are dependent upon the goodwill of promoters, world-sanctioning bodies, and others whom Ms. Lathan will be expected to regulate.

It would be a clear violation of the Muhammad Ali Boxing Reform Act (to say nothing of New York law) for Ms. Lathan to judge fights in or out of the State of New York.

. . .

On March 3, Roman Greenberg won a ten-round decision over Michael Simms to raise his record to 25–0 with seventeen knockouts.

The twenty-four-year-old Greenberg is a rarity in boxing. He's white, Jewish, a heavyweight, and an Israeli citizen. He also brings to mind a quote from Mark Twain, who wrote, "Wagner's music is better than it sounds."

Like Wagner's music, Greenberg is better than a lot of people think he is. He has fast hands, moderate power, and reasonably good defensive skills (but drops his right hand at inopportune moments leaving himself open to a quick left hook). He has yet to face a world-class opponent, but his record against the usual suspects is comparable to the performances of better-known fighters.

Greenberg knocked out Marcus McGee in four rounds. McGee went the distance with Jameel McCline, Malik Scott, and Michael Grant, and lasted into the eighth round against Sultan Ibragimov. Similarly, Alex Vassilev went the distance with Nikolai Valuev, Sergei Liakhovich, and Vassiliy Jirov. Roman stopped Vassilev in six stanzas.

Greenberg's stoppage of Vassilev earned him the IBO Inter-Continental heavyweight title, which he defended successfully against Alexei Varakin. "But I read recently that someone else was fighting for it," Roman says, "so I guess I vacated it or was stripped. To be honest, I don't know which."

In the dressing room before his fight against Michael Simms, Greenberg displayed all the urgency of a fighter who was readying for a sparring session. He chatted amiably with the members of his team, New York State Athletic Commission personnel, and anyone else who happened by.

"I try to relax before a fight," Roman says. "It's no good working myself into a state. By the time I get to the arena, I've thought about the fight a lot. I know what I have to do. In the dressing room, I want to take my mind off it for a while. If I think about it too much, I'll become a nervous wreck."

Simms is a slick counterpuncher, who came into the bout with a 19–6 record and thirteen knockouts. He's reluctant to take risks and has never been stopped. Roman made the fight (such as it was), using his jab effectively and doing some good body work with his right hand. Then he got into a comfort zone, stayed there, and cruised to a 99–91 victory on each judge's scorecard.

As for what lies ahead, Greenberg is likeable and well-spoken; traits that mean nothing once the bell rings. And there's danger in the fact that he appears to be too trusting in the ring. He pulls out of clinches with his hands low, leaves himself unnecessarily vulnerable to headbutts on the inside, and drops his guard at the bell ending each round.

Also, Greenberg has the reflexes of an elite athlete but not the body type. That's partly because he only recently began paying proper attention to conditioning and diet; and it's partly Mother Nature's doing. The bottom line is that he has 17 percent body fat (which trainer–manager Jim Evans hopes to reduce significantly this year). Unless corrective action is taken, he might find that some opponents are simply too physically strong for him.

"I want to fight for one of the four major belts within the next few years," Greenberg says. "Right now, I think that Waldimir Klitschko is the best of the heavyweights. Maskaev and Briggs won't be there for long. Valuev is underrated as a boxer. I would love to fight him."

One can envision a bout between the six-foot-two-inch Israeli and the seven-foot-two-inch Russian being marketed as "David against Goliath," but Roman has a different view. "Greenberg against Valuev sounds better to me," he says.

• • •

On the literary front—

Muhammad Ali Handbook by Dave Zirin (MQ Publications) begins with considerable promise. Zirin is a talented counterculture sports journalist with a creative eye. In the book's introduction, he writes, "Ali's past has been edited and reedited almost beyond recognition. An Ali school of falsification has been running at full throttle since 1996. That year, the champ, his hands trembling, lit the Olympic torch. The connection between Ali and his audience crackled and sparked a renaissance of interest. Sadly, the response to this revived fascination was a plethora of books and retrospectives swamped with obfuscation, spin, and slander."

"The dominant discourse," Zirin continues, "runs through the 'Sanitize Ali' movement. The emissaries of this group present the champ as a harmless symbol. He is now deemed safe for public appearances, Super Bowl commercials, and political photo ops. He can be feted at the White House by George W. Bush. The other approach comes from the 'Smear Ali' crowd. This is represented by a new cottage industry of books that attempt to prove that Ali was 'an unapologetic sexist and unabashed racist' who was 'bad for America.' Both wings of the Ali School of Falsification share a common aim: the obliteration of who he was and his incalculable effect on the social movements, emerging mass culture, and global media of his day."

Thereafter, the reader is treated to a nicely put together collection of photos and quotations. But too much of Zirin's work is a rehash of statements from previous Ali books.

The most interesting portions of *Muhammad Ali Handbook* are transcripts of interviews that the author conducted with Robert Lipsyte and Dave Kindred (two author–journalists who covered Ali during and after his ring career). The text of several other interviews (including one with this author) are also included.

Lipsyte's thoughts are particularly insightful, reminding us that, before he was a social, political, and religious figure, Cassius Marcellus Clay Jr. was a fighter.

"He was a jock," Lipsyte says of Ali. "He started boxing when he was twelve years old. It was the total focus of his life. His high school diploma was a gift because they didn't want to stand in the way, so they didn't bother him with all the niceties of education like learning how to read. So here is this typical jock, totally focused on one thing. He just had to box. Totally absorbed in his own career. Illiterate, ignorant. Then he comes back from the Olympics and he's bought by the plantation owners of Louisville [the Louisville Sponsoring Group]. Now he's really a hired piece of meat. He's in the warm. He loves the fame. He loves the joy of it. He's a seeker, though. Something's missing in his life. He wants something larger but he's still an ignorant kid, not the Muhammad Ali of our dreams."

One wishes that Zirin had opted for more original research and analysis like this and less cut-and-paste from earlier works. With all his talent, he hasn't put his best foot forward with *Muhammad Ali Handbook*.

• • •

Boxing's Top 100 by Bill Gray (Blue Lightning Press) purports to be an accurate pound-for-pound ranking of the greatest champions of all time based on irrefutable statistics rather than subjective analysis. Gray took 700 champions and fed 29 categories of statistical data into a computer.

Sugar Ray Robinson is ranked first. Well and good. But after that, things start to get crazy.

Virgil Hill is ranked seventeenth on the list of greatest pound-for-pound fighters of all time. Other curious appearances in the top 100 include Juan Coggi, Leo Gamez, Marcel Thil, Fabrice Tiozzo, Luis Estaba, Chana Porpaoin,

Bruno Arcari, Markus Beyes, Nicolino Loche, Dennis Andries, and Jorge Castro.

By contrast, Joe Frazier is #400 in Gray's pound-for-pound rankings; Sonny Liston, #422; and James J. Corbett, #522.

Looking at individual weight classes; Tommy Burns is ranked eighth among the heavyweights, ahead of Rocky Marciano, John L. Sullivan, Jack Johnson, Jack Dempsey, Mike Tyson, Gene Tunney, James J. Jeffries, Joe Frazier, Sonny Liston, and James J. Corbett. Floyd Patterson, by the way, is also ranked ahead of Liston. Go figure.

In the middleweight division, William Joppy is ahead of Jake LaMotta.

José Nápoles is listed as the second-greatest welterweight of all time. Tommy Freeman gets higher marks than Ray Leonard, Thomas Hearns, and Mickey Walker.

Having fun? Okay, here's more. Benny Leonard (#139 in the overall pound-for-pound rankings) is the twelfth-ranked lightweight, two spots behind José Luis Ramirez.

The book makes a valid point in observing that many people who wax eloquent about the fighters of old never saw them fight. No film footage of John L. Sullivan in the ring exists. There is only fragmentary footage from three Joe Gans bouts and two Stanley Ketchel fights. Thus, John Benson's introduction to the book is on solid ground when it states, "The usual boxers are included in every book because they are famous, and they are famous because they have been included in every book. Once a boxer was excluded from the dominant popular thinking about greatness, his relegation to oblivion became permanent. He couldn't be reconsidered for the label of 'great' because he wasn't included in any of the books about great boxers."

But let's be reasonable. Gray should have reprogrammed his computer.

There's some interesting trivia and raw statistical data in *Boxing's Top 100*. But if this is computer technology, give me old-fashioned subjective analysis. Ranking fighters across the ages is an art, not a science.

• • •

Tiger Flowers has been largely forgotten. The Georgia native was the first African-American boxer to hold the world middleweight championship and the first after Jack Johnson who was allowed to fight for a world title in any weight division.

Flowers threw punches in bunches from a southpaw stance. He won his crown by defeating Harry Greb at Madison Square Garden on a fifteen-round decision in February 1926; beat Greb again six months later; and lost the title to Mickey Walker in December on what most observers agreed was an unusually bad decision.

Flowers was hailed by black Americans for his ring triumphs and embraced by white southerners because he was a "good Negro." That is, he was viewed as "a harmless man–child; cheerful, unobtrusive, and loyal, who knew his place." Following his untimely death in 1927 (caused by surgery to remove scar tissue from around his eyes), the *Atlanta Constitution* reported,

"Many thousands of white and colored citizens assembled to assist in the funeral services. No greater and more impressive obsequies for a colored citizen have ever been witnessed in the south."

The Pussycat of Prizefighting by Andrew M. Kaye (University of Georgia Press) treats Flowers's career as a prism through which to understand the racial climate and customs of the early twentieth-century South. The writing is often dry with the flavor of a doctoral dissertation. Also, one of the sources that Kaye relies upon is the notoriously inaccurate "autobiography" of Muhammad Ali (written by Richard Durham). That raises nagging questions regarding the reliability of some of Kaye's other sources.

But the book is thought-provoking and intelligent. That's particularly true of the Introduction, which reflects on the role of prizefighting in American society and posits, "No nation has extracted as much meaning from prizefighting as the United States. The direct confrontation of two men with different backgrounds held before vast partisan audiences has on occasion graphically converted a conflict of values into a palpable physical struggle."

• • •

The Half-Life of an American Essayist by Arthur Krystal (David R. Godine) is a collection of pieces that run the gamut from ruminations on sin to the development of the typewriter. Two of the essays—"An African-American in Regency England" (which first appeared in *The New Yorker*) and "Boxers and Writers" (in *Harper's*) deal with the sweet science.

"An African-American in Regency England" (the better of Krystal's two fistic essays) recounts the two heavyweight championship fights between Englishman Tom Cribb and Tom Molineaux. Little reliable biographical information about Molineaux exists today. What is known is that, one week before Christmas 1810, 10,000 spectators gathered in the rain on Copthall Common, Sussex, to watch Cribb defend his crown.

"There had been anticipated contests before," Krystal writes. "But none like this. Cribb versus Molineaux was the first great sporting event of the modern era, the one fight that everyone who was anyone had to attend."

It was also a time when, in Krystal's words, "Most Britons tended to equate the mettle demonstrated in the prize ring with the courage demanded on the battlefield." But this particular encounter ran contrary to logic. "A black man challenging for the title? And an American to boot? It defied the natural order. It was as if a tallish citizen of Baghdad had deplaned in Chicago in 1999 and proceeded to taunt Michael Jordan, demanding he play him one-on-one."

The fight lasted fifty-five minutes with an out-of-shape Cribb winning under dubious circumstances. "Molineaux was allowed to fight," Krystal notes. "He was just not allowed to win." Pierce Egan later wrote, "It will not be forgotten, if justice holds the scales, that [Molineaux's] colour alone prevented him from becoming the hero of that fight."

Nine months later, a rematch was contested before 20,000 spectators on the outskirts of London. This time, Cribb had trained properly and Molineaux

404 / Fistic Notes

hadn't. After nineteen minutes of battle, the Englishman emerged victorious. Seven years later, Molineaux was dead at age thirty-four.

•   •   •

God In My Corner (Thomas Nelson Publishers) is George Foreman's guide for living within the context of his religious beliefs.

I've interviewed George with regards to values on numerous occasions. The most notable of these interviews was recounted in an article entitled "Two Conversations with George Foreman" that I wrote six years ago. In it, I noted, "We live in an age when many believers of all faiths assert that their way is the only road to heaven. George has a contrary view."

I then quoted George as saying, "Someone who has no faith in God should be embraced, not with doctrine, but with love . . . A preacher can preach without a tongue and without a Bible by simply doing good works . . . Good is good, whether or not one believes in Jesus. To be good is to be saved . . . If I treat everybody nice, that's religion."

George was criticized in some circles for voicing those thoughts. The next time I saw him, he thanked me for writing the article. "I had something I wanted to get off my chest and I'm glad I said it," he told me. "No one religion has a monopoly on God's love."

I'll leave the evaluation of the religious views expressed in *God In My Corner* to others. As an aside, I'll add that I'm skeptical of George's claim (voiced in the book) that he lost to Muhammad Ali in Zaire because he was drugged by his trainer. But I don't question the sincerity of George's religious beliefs.

God In My Corner contains thoughts that are worth reading; some because they'll make a reader reflect seriously, others because they'll bring a smile. A few of my favorites are:

- "I grew up believing that hamburgers were only for rich people."
- "Mom told me it was better to walk away from a street fight than to get killed. She often cautioned, 'It's better to say 'There he goes,' than 'There he lays.' "
- "People will pull out a cigarette and ask, 'Do you mind if I smoke?' But I've never heard anyone ask, 'Do you mind if I cuss?' You can't ask to be seated in a non-cursing section at a restaurant."
- "I believed in God. I just didn't believe in religion. I didn't love anybody but myself."
- "Phonies and hypocrits will always be involved in religion, but that doesn't mean that Jesus isn't real."
- "Life is a privilege."

•   •   •

The Legality of Boxing by Jack Anderson (Birkbeck Law Press) views the sport in its historical context; studies its legality through the ages; evaluates the dangers that it poses to participants; and weighs the current state of the law in light of the philosophical and ethical questions raised by these dangers.

Anderson posits that boxing's protection under the law springs from a long-ago time when (like archery, jousting, and other combat sports) it was directly related to community survival and the preparation of young men for war. Boxing today, he continues, "is granted an exemption from the ordinary law of violence on the grounds that it is a well- and self-regulated sport entered into by mature consenting adults whose intentions, while physically invasive, are essentially sporting in nature."

But as Anderson notes, boxing's current regulatory framework is woefully inadequate. Fighters are largely unprotected. The sport simply isn't regulated properly.

The Legality of Boxing isn't for the casual reader. At times, the writing is tedious (most legal tomes are). But it's also thoughtful and of particular interest when Anderson turns to the philosophical and ethical issues that surround the fundamental nature of boxing.

Anderson respects boxing's "nuanced levels of discipline, skill, and courage." He also concedes that injury and death are an inevitable by-product of other sports like automobile racing, mountaineering, and football (all of which, in some ways, are more dangerous than boxing). But he notes the testimony of Baroness Lena Jeger, who, during a 1995 debate, told the House of Lords, "When I was rock-climbing and hanging from the end of a rope, the chap at the top did not cut the rope to make me fall. My fall would not be caused deliberately. That is the difference. Boxing is the deliberate causing of injury."

Therein lies the rub.

"It cannot reasonably be denied," Anderson writes, "that the objective of professional boxing is the infliction of bodily harm. Boxers come to hurt and spectators come to see it. The most efficient means of victory in a boxing match is to render one's opponent unconscious. The aim is to hurt your opponent to such an extent that he is unable to defend himself [and then you can hurt him even more]."

Thus, the words of George Lundberg, former editor of the *Journal of the American Medical Association* (quoted by Anderson): "It is morally wrong for one human being to attempt intentionally to harm the brain of another. The major purpose of a sports event is to win. When the surest way to win is by damaging the opponent's brain and this becomes the standard procedure, the sport is morally wrong."

That's something to think about during the ongoing debate over the future of boxing.

• • •

And something else to think about . . .

Boxers carry a heavier psychological burden than other athletes. That burden is inherent in the nature of what they do and also the impact of a loss, physically and financially, upon them. Yet there is negligible psychiatric support for fighters. Team athletes have it; Olympic athletes have it. Fighters don't.

They should.

. . .

I guess I've made it to the big time. A "bad" signature of mine is on eBay. It's on a document that also has a "bad" signature of Muhammad Ali (which is why it's on eBay to begin with).

Earlier this summer (July 18, 2007), "item number 220135656368" was listed with "the World's Online Marketplace." The "item title" is "Muhammad Ali book with signed note to Dick Schaap." The listing reads as follows:

"Offered is a hardcover book, *Muhammad Ali: His Life and Times,* by Thomas Hauser. Simon & Schuster, 1991, 544 pp. This biography doesn't take the normal course. The story of Muhammad Ali's life is told by those who know him, with the interviews chosen and arranged by the author. One of those people was Dick Schaap, who met the young heavyweight before his flight to Rome for the 1960 Olympics. The two remained friends long after . . . The note that comes with this book is a thank you note, most likely for the memories Dick contributed. The 'thank you' is typewritten and does not mention Dick by name. I imagine all the contributors received such a note. It is on stationery which simply says 'Muhammad Ali' at the top, and is signed by Ali and Thomas Hauser. Condition is very good, but the front free-end page is not properly pasted to the spine. The dust jacket has some scuffing. The note is folded once, and not perfectly. Other than these flaws, I find none."

A scan of the note is included with the listing. The "buy it now" price is $175 plus shipping. The book purports to come from the estate of Dick Schaap. I'll assume it does, although I'll also assume that Dick's family has nothing to do with this listing.

Here's the rub. The "note" is a photo-copy, not an original.

During my research for *Muhammad Ali: His Life and Times,* I interviewed close to 200 people. When the book was published, Simon & Schuster sent copies to most of them. It seemed a bit much to ask Muhammad to sign 200 "thank you" letters. So a letter was typed on Muhammad Ali stationery. Ali and I signed it. Simon & Schuster then made copies of the letter and included a copy with each book.

I have the original letter in my personal collection of Muhammad Ali memorabilia. The stationery is gray and "Muhammad Ali" is emblazoned across the top in maroon. The letter is signed by Muhammad and myself. We each used a felt-tip pen with blue ink.

The item offered for sale on eBay is entirely in black, white, and gray. It's hard for me to believe that the seller thinks the signatures are originals. Maybe he or she does. And in fairness to him or her, the eBay item description never says that the signatures are originals rather than copies. But hardcover editions of *Muhammad Ali: His Life and Times* are available online for as little as one dollar plus shipping. So it wouldn't be unreasonable for someone who pays $175 for "item number 220135656368" to assume that Ali's signature on the note is original.

Craig Hamilton is one of the foremost boxing memorabilia dealers in the United States. Several years ago, he complained, "There's a ton of phony merchandise out there. Most of it is bad autographs. eBay is the area of prime offense. It's the cesspool of sports collectibles. The listings on eBay simply aren't screened sufficiently, so it's a true place for the buyer to beware. The bad material on eBay flows like a rancid tide."

As Hamilton warned: Buyer beware.

I believe that all of us have an obligation to speak out on issues of importance.

More Important Than Boxing: 2007

We don't stop being citizens when we enter the world of sports. With that in mind, once a year I use this space to address issues that are more important than boxing.

Democracy should be practiced, not just celebrated. One of the most troubling aspects of George Bush's tenure in office has been his assault on the judicial underpinnings of American democracy. Despite his rhetoric, Mr. Bush has dishonored the fundamental traditions of American justice. Anyone who isn't outraged at what he has done isn't paying attention.

U.S. Attorneys who refuse to conduct criminal investigations in accord with political commands from the White House have been removed from office.

Lewis "Scooter" Libby (Dick Cheney's former chief of staff) was convicted of perjury and obstruction of justice after lying to federal agents and to a grand jury that was investigating the leak of the name of a CIA operative. He was sentenced to thirty months in prison; but before he could be incarcerated, Mr. Bush commuted his sentence. The commutation had all the earmarks of buying Libby's silence. Thanks to the president, Mr. Libby (who committed a crime that bears directly on national security) served less time in jail than Paris Hilton.

But the most grotesque aspect of the Bush administration's distortion of justice has been its repeated violation of constitutional rights and reliance upon torture as a tool in the "war on terror."

There was a time when the United States stood as a beacon of hope for the proposition that human rights are deserving of respect. Article 3 of the Geneva Conventions of 1949 (to which the United States is a signatory) prohibits "mutilation, cruel treatment, and torture" in addition to the "humiliating and degrading treatment" of detainees. In autumn 2007, the United States Supreme Court ruled that military detainees in the "war on terror" must be treated in accord with the Geneva Conventions. In response, Mr. Bush issued an executive order of dubious legality that simply reclassified the detainees.

The Bush administration now takes the position that detainees can be held indefinitely and do not have a right to contest their detention in federal court or before another neutral decision maker. Suspects are imprisoned in undisclosed locations without counsel or notification to their families. Many of them are interrogated in secret prisons in Afghanistan, Thailand, and Eastern Europe, where their captors rely on interrogation techniques developed by the governments of Egypt, Saudi Arabia, and the former Soviet Union. These techniques include waterboarding, sleep deprivation, prolonged exposure to extreme temperatures, and beatings.

The Bush administration's guidelines for officially sanctioned torture allow for everything but "extreme acts causing severe pain of the sort that accompanies serious physical injury leading to death or organ failure." In other words, it's permissible to break someone's leg with a crowbar. That might be an "extreme act causing severe pain of the sort that accompanies serious physical injury" but it wouldn't necessarily "lead to death or organ failure."

One can make a rational argument in support of the use of torture in certain limited, clearly defined, closely regulated instances. Suppose, for example, the authorities know that a nuclear weapon is about to be detonated on American soil and believe that a detainee has information, which, if revealed, could preclude the carnage. The dialogue regarding a hypothetical situation of this nature would be similar in many respects to the debate over capital punishment.

The argument against capital punishment is twofold: (1) there are those who think that it debases any society that employs it, and (2) an innocent person might be executed. I personally believe that there are instances when capital punishment is warranted. Many people take a contrary view. But under American law (at least, in theory), there is a clearly defined process that must be followed before a death penalty is administered.

By contrast, under present circumstances, the utilization of torture by our government appears to be arbitrary. Not only does it debase our society, there is also a legitimate fear that innocent people are being tortured and killed.

It would be comforting to think that the men and women responsible for interrogating detainees in the "war on terror" are capable operatives with sound judgment. But what we know about the Bush administration offers scant hope in that regard.

The centerpiece of the "war on terror" has been the invasion of Iraq. The rationale for the invasion keeps changing. First, we invaded Iraq because Saddam Hussein was purportedly building weapons of mass destruction. When that charge proved false, the war became about "bringing freedom to the Iraqi people." By that logic, we should also invade China to bring freedom to the Chinese people. Now, we're implored to "stay the course" in Iraq because it's important to stay the course.

There will be no "victory" for the United States in Iraq. Iraq barely functions as a country anymore. It's a bloody conglomeration of local militias, warlords, terrorists, the U.S. military, the Iraqi military, and other disparate forces. The only remaining questions are how many more lives will be lost, how much more money will it cost, and how bad the damage to our long-term interests and standing in the international community will be before we withdraw.

That was made clear by General Ricardo Sanchez (former commander of American forces in Iraq), who told a gathering of military reporters last month (October 2007) that the Bush administration's handling of the war was based on "a catastrophically flawed, unrealistically optimistic war plan that has led to a nightmare with no end in sight. There has been," General Sanchez said, "a glaring and unfortunate display of incompetent strategic leadership" by leaders who have been "derelict in their duties" and guilty of a "lust for power."

The following is a sampling of mishaps (characterized by total incompetence) that have come to light since I wrote about the invasion of Iraq in this forum one year ago:

- The Bush administration flew nearly $12 billion in shrink-wrapped $100 bills into Iraq and distributed the cash with inadequate controls over who was receiving it and how it was spent. The cash weighed 363 tons and was sent to Baghdad for disbursement to Iraqi ministries and U.S. contractors. A good portion of it was retained for private personal use or fell into the hands of terrorists. As Henry Waxman (chairman of the House of Representatives Committee on Oversight and Government Reform) queried, "Who in their right mind would send 363 tons of cash into a war zone?"
- The Special Inspector General for Iraq Reconstruction reported to Congress that only 12,000 of the 500,000 weapons given to the Iraqi Ministries of Defense and Interior by our government since the invasion are being properly tracked. In other words, hundreds of thousands of weapons (including grenade launchers, machine guns, and assault rifles) could be anywhere and in anyone's hands. Thereafter, in one of its last acts, the Republican-controlled 109th Congress passed (and George Bush signed) a military authorization bill that terminated the Office of the Special Inspector General for Iraq Reconstruction.
- The Bush administration launched a website called "Operation Iraqi Freedom Document Portal" to propagate the argument that Saddam Hussein had, in fact, been planning to build weapons of mass destruction. The launch came over the objection of Director of National Intelligence John Negroponte. The site was closed in

November 2006 after International Atomic Energy Agency officials complained that the documents on it went beyond anything else that was publicly available in constituting a basic guide to building an atomic bomb.

In sum, the Bush Administration has an extensive record of mismanaging the "war on terror." Thus, the question: "How many innocent people have been tortured and killed by our government?"

We'll never know, because the hidden nature of the interrogations and torture keep "bad decisions" from coming to light.

George Bush should not have been put in the position of responsibility and power that he has abused for almost seven years. But rather than dwell on the past, let's give practical application to the issues raised by this article. Why not subject the Bush administration to the same standard of "justice" that it has applied to others?

On July 9, 2007, George Bush invoked a claim of "executive privilege" in response to requests for information by two Congressional committees that were investigating the firing of nine U.S. Attorneys. More specifically, the White House refused to comply with subpoenas for relevant documents and blocked two presidential aides with knowledge related to the firings from testifying before Congress.

Why bother with subpoenas and lengthy court proceedings? Bring former Attorney General Alberto Gonzalez before Congress and beat the information out of him.

Come to think of it, Congress could impeach and convict the president and vice president using the same process. Arrest Mr. Bush and Mr. Cheney. Hold them incommunicato in a secret prison without access to a lawyer. The pre-trial discovery would be enlightening. One can only begin to imagine the wrongdoing that would be revealed after waterboarding, sleep deprivation, and brutal beatings. The Bush administration says that these interrogation techniques are reserved for "high value" detainees. But who's more "high value" that George Bush and Dick Cheney? We might even get some photographs of the president and vice president nude on their hands and knees, each one with a dog collar around his neck and a woman soldier holding the leash.

The impeachment trial would be conducted in secret. As for the sentence; given Dick Cheney's much-publicized heart condition, he probably wouldn't make it that far. But Mr. Bush seems to be in pretty good shape. Life imprisonment or the death penalty? What do you think?

Some bleeding-heart liberals and card-carrying members of the American Civil Liberties Union might find fault with interrogation and a trial of this nature. But I'm sure that patriotic Americans wouldn't object.

PS: Words like "torture" and "beating" have become so common in usage that we tend to read through them. They sanitize the violence. So let's think in terms of you, the reader. An interrogator punches you flush on the tip of your nose, flattening it against your face. You still haven't told him what he wants to know. You might not even know it, but he thinks you do. Or maybe he's just a sadistic bastard. So he shoves slivers of metal beneath your fingertips.

Hey, as former secretary of defense Donald Rumsfeld blithely said about the mounting death toll in Iraq: "Stuff happens."

Several days after this article appeared, James Toney called me with one final thought. "The writers can say all they want to about how bad the heavyweights are today," James told me. "In the old days, the writers were better too."

The Heavyweights Rate the Writers

It has become accepted sport in the boxing industry for writers to trash today's heavyweights. With that in mind (and on the theory that turnabout is fair play), I asked some of the more-criticized heavyweights of recent years to evaluate today's boxing writers. Their thoughts follow:

SHANNON BRIGGS: "Oh, man. I'm so glad you asked me that question. The writers are always writing that boxing is a dying sport, and they're one of the reasons it's dying. They're always ragging the fighters and ragging the sport. A lot of them, especially on the Internet, don't know two cents about boxing. They're not even real writers; they work at Wal-Mart. It's a hobby for them. They write whatever they want to write without knowing the facts. They wouldn't be taken seriously in any other sport. But because there's so little about boxing in the newspapers, people read them. It hurts the sport; it hurts the fighters as individuals. And a lot of the newspaper guys aren't much better. Just because you write for a newspaper doesn't mean you know anything about boxing. It's easy to say, 'This guy got knocked out and he's a bum,' but most of them don't have a clue about what it means to be a fighter. If I'm grading the boxing writers today, I give them an 'F.'"

JOHN RUIZ: "I've been hit more by the writers than I've been hit in all my fights. With some of them, it seems like they think that, if they write negative things, they'll get more attention. It hurts personally. It hurts financially. And they don't care. It's been a tough road for me. I had some setbacks. Then, finally, I beat Holyfield, and all the writers did was come down on me. I don't mind criticism, but it should be fair and done with knowledge of what you're writing about. Most of the writers never picked up a pair of gloves in their life. They act like it's easy to fight. 'Oh, he should have done this; he should have done that.' They don't understand. It's not easy; it's a war in there. Before you criticize an athlete, you should try his sport yourself. Let some of these experts get in a boxing ring. One round would be enough. That would teach them respect. I'd like to see them try even to walk around for three minutes holding their hands up and see how tired their arms get. Some of the writers are good; but most of them, I'd give an 'F.' "

HASIM RAHMAN: "I've said lots of times that it's too easy to be licensed as a professional fighter. There are guys who should never be allowed in the ring, but fighters like me get to fight them to build a record when we're coming up. It's a flaw in the sport. And it's the same thing with boxing writing. Some of the writers are very knowledgeable, but a lot of them know nothing. All they do is repeat gossip and jump on the bandwagon. I don't take their criticism personally. I'm a Baltimore Orioles fan. If I'm not pleased with the way they play, I speak my mind. I might rip the Orioles but they're still my team. So I'd say it's okay for writers to criticize but they should get the facts right. It's not rocket science. Get the facts right. If I was grading the boxing writers, I'd say the grades run from 'A' to 'F' with the average at 'C.' "

JAMES TONEY: "Most of the writers are fucked up and messed up. They don't feel good about themselves, so they take it out on someone else. They write shit about you. And then, when they need you for a story, they're all smiles and excuses and 'Oh, James; I didn't mean it that way.' You didn't mean it that way? Kiss my ass, motherfucker. What they write don't hurt me, but it pisses me off. You got guys 300 pounds writing, 'James Toney is out of shape; James Toney has a belly.' Look in the mirror, you fat motherfucker. An 'F' is too good for them. Most of the writers, I'd give an 'F-minus.' "

And a grace note from the last man to be universally recognized as the true heavyweight champion of the world . . .

LENNOX LEWIS: "It's hard for me to rate the writers today because I haven't been reading them lately. When I was boxing, I read what they wrote to see how they were interpreting me. Some got it and some didn't. It was frustrating at times because writers have a platform. A lot of people believe that what they read in the newspaper is one hundred percent true, and it's not. Some writers get their facts wrong. Others are unable to move beyond their biases. Once they've accepted a fighter, he's a hero; and if someone challenges their hero, he's a bum. There are some very good writers; but overall, I'd give the boxing writers an 'F.' "

I won't say that this article goes to the heart of boxing. But after it was posted on Secondsout.com, there was favorable comment from all segments of the boxing community.

Tempest Storm

She's seventy-nine years old now and lives in a one-bedroom apartment in East Las Vegas, the industrial part of town. Defying age, she has managed to remain both shapely and slender. She's charming and disarming with an air of refinement and still has long fiery-red hair.

It's May 1, 2007, four days before Oscar De La Hoya versus Floyd Mayweather Jr. In another part of the city, high rollers are descending upon the casinos in anticipation of The Big Event. Power brokers are spreading their wings. There's glitz everywhere.

Trust me, the lady understands power and glitz. She was intimate with John F. Kennedy and Elvis Presley. Check her out on the Internet. Google her (and oogle her) at your pleasure. There was a time when she was embedded in the sexual fantasies of literally millions of men around the world.

Tempest Storm was born in rural Georgia on February 29, 1928. Her mother and stepfather were sharecroppers. She grew up picking cotton and lived in a shack without indoor plumbing or electricity. The name given to her at birth was Annie Blanche Banks.

Annie matured physically at an early age. When she was thirteen, five young men (including the local sheriff's son) gang-raped her. A year later, her stepfather wanted the same thing. "I woke up one night and he was on top of me," she says. "That night, I told myself, 'I've got to get out of here.' I have very few memories of my childhood. It was a horrible life, and I've blocked out a lot of what happened to me when I was young."

Annie ran away from home at age fourteen, rented a room for a dollar a night, and took a job waitressing for $10 a week plus tips. The authorities threatened to return her to her parents, so she married a man she barely knew (a soldier on furlough named Rural Giddens). Several weeks later, she left Giddens and started waitressing again. At age sixteen, she married for the second time, to a soldier named Jack Locke. That marriage lasted a year.

After the collapse of her second marriage, Annie worked in a jewelry store, a hosiery mill, and a diner. When she was nineteen, a man she waited on occasionally in the diner asked if she'd like to go to California with him. "When do we leave?" she responded. They lived together in Hollywood for two months. Then he tried to shoot her because he suspected that she was cheating on him, and she was on her own again.

Annie's dream was to break into show business, but there were problems. Her teeth were crooked; so much so that she was reluctant to smile. She had no acting experience. And at the modeling agencies, she recalls, "I was a joke, a freak [five-feet-six-inches tall, 135 pounds] with a forty-inch bosom that would never fit into their high-fashion dresses."

At age twenty-one, she took a job as a cocktail waitress at a lounge called The Paddock, which had drinking and dancing up front and bookmaking in back. A customer suggested that she audition for an opening in the chorus line at the Follies Theater in Los Angeles. She'd be one of many women on-stage. She wouldn't have to take her clothes off.

Annie started dancing for $40 a week, but the $60 a week that the strippers made was enticing. And Lillian Hunt (who produced the show) saw gold in her body. At age twenty-two, Annie took her clothes off onstage for the first time. The deal was sealed by Hunt's offer to pay to have her new recruit's teeth straightened and capped.

"This is show business," Annie told herself. "And I've always wanted to be in show business." Right before her first performance au natural (a five-minute number), Hunt instructed, "No matter what happens, keep going." Soon after, Annie took the stage name "Tempest Storm." In 1957, it became her legal moniker.

"Being in burlesque meant being pursued by men," Tempest recalls. "Famous men; rich men; guys next door. And all of them wanted one thing: Sex."

Tempest's first "celebrity romance" began when Mickey Rooney visited her backstage after she'd been dancing for two months. "Mickey was a big star," she wrote in her 1987 memoir. "If he wanted to take me out, I knew what it could do for my career. Being seen with him meant bits in gossip columns, photos in magazines, perhaps breaks in other types of show business. I was learning how to handle my career, how to use the press to further my reputation and enhance my image. There's much more to a career in burlesque than performing. I'd reached a point where I needed to be seen with name entertainers, to be talked about, to be publicized."

"Mickey took my arm and escorted me through the people backstage," Tempest remembers. "I could feel their eyes on me, and I knew they were thinking, 'There goes Rooney with another conquest.' But that's exactly what I wanted; for them, for everyone, to talk about Tempest Storm."

They went to bed together on their second date. "In his suite," Tempest later wrote, "he wasted little time. He mixed me a drink, which I really didn't want, put a record on the phonograph, and waltzed me around the room. Within a few minutes, we were in bed."

The next day, their relationship was the subject of a gossip item in the *Los Angeles Mirror*. Three weeks later, Rooney gave her a full-length mink coat ("a mink coat that said I'd hit the big time"). The liaison lasted for three months. Then Rooney went on to other women.

"He wanted something from me, but I also wanted something from him," Tempest concludes. "The world of show business can be a tough world. It's important to know how to protect yourself and your interests."

After the fling with Rooney ended, Tempest journeyed north to perform as the star attraction for six weeks at the El Ray Theater in Oakland (her first gig as a headliner). The job paid $350 a week. She dyed her brunette hair red and bought her first car, a 1951 Cadillac convertible, with the help of the manager of a local car dealership (who had seen her perform).

In 1953, she married again; this time, to a bartender named John Becker, who performed as a singer and burlesque straight man under the stage name Johnny Del Mar. Becker was physically and verbally abusive. The low point in their marriage came when Tempest threw a pair of scissors at him ("I grabbed them and tried to stab him, but he jumped out of my reach so I threw the scissors at him.") They were divorced on Valentine's Day 1955. Thereafter, Johnny returned the favor of the scissors by trying to run Tempest's car off the freeway in Los Angeles.

Meanwhile, onstage, Tempest was developing a philosophy for her performance art. And she was becoming a star.

Burlesque in the 1950s was often upscale entertainment. It was performed in elegant theaters, not just clubs and bars.

"I wanted to be a class act," Tempest says. "I wanted to entertain, but I also wanted to be a lady about my act. Sexy, yes. Teasing, yes. Vulgar, never. And I worked hard to develop an act that set me apart from other dancers in the business. A lot of people thought it was easy work, but it wasn't. I took some ballet lessons when I started. Later, I had a choreographer and surrounded myself with high-quality musicians. I rehearsed a lot and spent a fortune on costumes. Success doesn't just happen in burlesque any more than it just happens in any other form of show business. You have to create your own style and your own way of entertaining people. You have to work at becoming a star, onstage and off. I was good copy for the gossip columnists; I had a great rapport with them; but that will carry you just so far. I was always using my imagination to develop an act that was classy and original. I never allowed my personal struggles to undermine the fantasies that people had when they came to watch me perform. The adult entertainment business today is awful. It has no class. They call lap dancing and pole dancing 'the new burlesque,' but that's not burlesque as I knew it. Those things are just raunchy. If I was twenty years old today, I'd do something else. But for me, the key to it all was that I enjoyed performing. Onstage, I was always happy; I became a different person. When I was onstage, in my mind, I was a little girl, all dressed up and gorgeous."

After Tempest and John Becker divorced, she returned to the celebrity dating scene. "I was single, sexy, and yearning for the good times that would make up for all those hard years back in Georgia," she wrote in her memoir. "Nothing could have pleased the lonely daughter of a sharecropper more than to have her childhood dreams of show business and romance come true, and for me they had."

The next celebrity Tempest dated was Hugh O'Brien. ("His sensitivity was especially important to me in the difficult time after my divorce. He made me feel so special and secure.") Then Nat King Cole entered her life. ("He told me that I was the most beautiful woman he'd ever known. Our lovemaking was vibrant, warm, and wonderful. When I was with him, I felt truly connected to another human being, safe at last from the terrible loneliness of my life. Never had a woman found herself so suddenly awake and living all her romantic dreams come true.")

But two problems intruded on the relationship. First, Nat King Cole was black at a time when an interracial relationship, if it became public knowledge, could damage both parties. And second, he was married. Thus, "the good-bye of star-crossed lovers."

Also in 1955, while performing at the Casino Royale in Washington DC, Tempest met a young senator from Massachusetts named John F. Kennedy. He attended her show two nights in a row and, the second night, she accepted an invitation to visit him at his table.

"He was charming with a wonderful sense of humor and very handsome," Tempest recalls. "The people who were with him left us alone to talk, and we made a date for the following evening, which was my night off. I knew he was married, but he told me that he and his wife were unhappy together."

Thereafter, a relationship developed. "He was a lot of fun to be with," Tempest says. "When he was elected president, I was in seventh heaven."

And then there was Elvis Presley.

"Elvis liked younger women but he made an exception for me," she says with pride.

They met in 1957, when Elvis was twenty-two and Tempest was twenty-nine. He had entered mainstream American culture one year earlier when he appeared on *The Ed Sullivan Show* and topped the charts with "Heartbreak Hotel," "Don't Be Cruel," "Hound Dog," and "Love Me Tender."

The union of the two iconic personalities occurred in Las Vegas at The Dunes, where they were performing independently of one another. It was suggested that they pose for a publicity photo together.

"Even with his dark skin," Tempest later wrote, "Elvis blushed deeply when he saw me. I could tell he was trying not to look at my plunging neckline."

Later that day, the telephone in her room rang.

"Miss Storm," the hotel switchboard operator advised, "Mr. Elvis Presley would like to talk to you."

They met again.

"There's something we have in common," Tempest told him. "Members of the opposite sex lust after us. They don't understand that what we do onstage is an act, a performance."

Thereafter, they became intimate.

"I wanted the satisfaction of knowing that I was adored by America's hottest sex symbol," Tempest acknowledges. "And he was the most interesting younger man I ever knew."

But Elvis's manager ("Colonel" Tom Parker) didn't like their seeing each other.

"If you keep hanging around that stripper woman, those screaming teenagers are going to quit screaming," Parker told Elvis. "And when they stop screaming, they'll stop buying your records, and then where the hell are you going to be? Back in Memphis driving a goddamn truck."

"Elvis decided that The Colonel was right," Tempest recalls. "He was afraid that being linked to a stripper would ruin his career, so it ended between us."

When was the last time she saw Elvis?

"In the early 1970s," she answers. "I went to see Perry Como at The Hilton [in Las Vegas] and, after the show, I went backstage. Elvis was there and so was Pat Boone. Perry asked me, 'Tempest, I used to be a barber. Is that really all your hair?' I told him, 'Perry, everything about me is real. If you don't believe me, ask Elvis.' Elvis turned and said, 'Well, it's time for me to go.' But he stayed."

"I was devastated by Elvis's disintegration," Tempest says. "I still dream about him sometimes. There's one song—'Are You Lonesome Tonight?'— every time I hear Elvis singing it, I feel like crying."

"It was hard sometimes, the way people thought about me," she admits. "I tried to do what I did with class so people would respect me. But I knew from the beginning that there was a stigma. Some people look down on burlesque dancers like we're prostitutes. I wanted Elvis to respect me for the person I was instead of thinking that I was only a stripper. But that's not the way he felt."

Still, in the world of burlesque, Tempest Storm was becoming royalty. By the late-1950s, she was making $3,500 a week. "Rich men showered me with diamonds and furs and cruises," she recalls. Michael Wilding, Vic Damone, and Sammy Davis Jr. became lovers. She lived in Hollywood next door to Marilyn Monroe. "When Marilyn sang "Happy Birthday" for the president at his birthday party [at Madison Square Garden in 1962], I thought it was terrific," she says.

In 1959, Tempest married again; this time to singer Herb Jeffries. And again, the result was disaster. "I always demanded respect in my professional life," she acknowledges. "But in my personal life, I didn't demand it often enough. The men I married always ended up treating me like dirt.

Herb was lazy and jealous. He told me once, 'You're in a degenerate business.' I said, 'Excuse me. You're driving my car and sleeping in my house and living off me.'"

In 1962, Tempest filed for divorce; then learned that she was pregnant. She and Herb reconciled, and a daughter (Patty) was born. After that, Tempest went back to work. After three separations, she and Herb were divorced.

Life went on. There were more lovers and more performances. And finally, there was validation as a performing artist. On March 23, 1973, at age forty-five, Tempest Storm became the first (and to this day, only) "stripper" to perform at Carnegie Hall.

"I was a little cocky that night," she says. "Someone asked how I felt about performing at Carnegie Hall, and I told him, 'I feel like Muhammad Ali. I'm The Greatest.' But that night was important to me. I felt that the audience appreciated the art of my performance. They understood the choreography and skill and hard work that were involved. When they applauded me, they were applauding my talent."

Tempest Storm never retired from the burlesque trade. In 1999, at age seventy-one, she performed at a thirtieth anniversary celebration for the O'Farrell Theatre in San Francisco. Mayor Willie Brown issued a proclamation designating the occasion as "Tempest Storm Day." In a review of her performance, the *San Francisco Chronicle* proclaimed, "When Storm takes something off—her gown, one of several bras, or multiple bottom layers—she's likely to put something else back on. She bares her breasts and almost everything else, and pulls a white boa from the wings to play peekaboo with what's left. Her skin sags a little here and there. Her movements can get a little creaky. But she hasn't lost an ounce of know-how."

In 2005, Tempest was onstage in Nashville and San Francisco. "I did about twenty minutes and got a standing ovation," she reports. "I'd still work every week if there was a place to work."

But the past few years have been hard. Tempest's world fell apart in 2001 with the death of a man she loved and was engaged to marry. Soon after, a business representative misappropriated most of her financial assets. Circumstances forced her to live in a trailer for several years. Then she moved to Las Vegas.

Her apartment is small but immaculately kept. The white rug and white furniture are spotless. A photograph of Tempest with Elvis Presley and other reminders of her career line the walls. An elaborately published pictorial work entitled *The Big Book of Breasts* is prominently displayed on the coffee-table in front of her sofa.

"There's ten pages on me in there," Tempest says. "Would you like to see them?"

She also has a full binder of old photographs and news clippings that she shows to chosen guests.

"I keep myself busy," she says when the conversation turns to her life in Las Vegas. "I read a lot and go out to dinner sometimes with friends."

She seems a bit lonely. She also seems like a kind person with a good heart.

"You were born on a leap day," she's told. "February 29, 1928. That means, next year, you'll be twenty."

"In my dreams," she says with a laugh.

Tempest enjoys her status as a sexual icon in what now seems to have been an innocent age of sex. She rose to prominence before the pill changed lovers' habits; when *Playboy* was cutting edge and married couples on TV sitcoms slept in separate beds. Sexual icons limited their performances to stage and screen rather than running amok through society like Anna Nicole Smith.

That time is long gone. So are the most prominent men who marked Tempest's life. John F. Kennedy, struck down by an assassin's bullet at age forty-six. Nat King Cole, dead of cancer at forty-five. Elvis Presley, a bloated caricature of himself, dead at forty-two. But she looks back on her life with satisfaction and believes that there are still good times ahead.

On occasion, she's reflective. "Except for the men I married, I think I've made good choices," she says. "I don't blame myself for the first two marriages. I was very young then. As for the others, maybe I was punishing myself for something. Maybe I got involved with so many married men because, on some level, I told myself, 'This way, I won't be hurt.' Maybe I chose burlesque because of what happened to me when I was young. When you're onstage, the men in the audience can look but not touch. And I got unconditional love from my audience. In a lot of ways, I'm quite conventional. I wasn't a drinker. I was around all kinds of drugs but I never did them. I've led a pristine life except for my dancing and my men. That's where my wildness comes out."

"I was a wealthy woman," Tempest continues, still reflecting on the past. "That's gone now, but I can deal with it. If I have any regrets, it's that I didn't do more to pursue a career in acting. Acting was my dream. Sometimes I wish that, when I got famous, I'd been strong enough to break away from the nice clothes and fancy jewelry and glamour and risk everything to get into acting. That's what I would have done if I'd chosen my profession instead of my profession choosing me. But there are no complaints. I wanted to be a star. I worked my way to the top of the burlesque world and I stayed there. Nobody lasted in the business as long as I did. I like to think that my talent and my personality led people to respect me. I'm sure that some did and some didn't."

In her sunset years, Tempest Storm has the satisfaction of knowing that, for millions of men who never knew her, she'll be an object of desire forever.

"I've had a great ride," she says. "I didn't miss anything. Not bad for a sharecropper's daughter from Eastman, Georgia."

If There's Free Food, Grab It

There's a centuries-old proverb, "Whose bread I eat, his song I sing."

Howard Cosell used to declaim, "You can buy the writers for a ham sandwich."

"With some writers, it's in their DNA," says former Boxing Writers Association of America president Bernard Fernandez. "If it's free, they have to eat it."

Put those thoughts together and you have what some think is Rule One for being a boxing writer: "If there's free food, grab it."

"It's not new," says Bobby Goodman of Don King Productions (DKP). "The writers could always eat. In the old days, you used to hear, 'Feed me to read me.' Lester Bromberg, who wrote boxing for the *New York Post*, was a notorious eater," Goodman reminisces. "One time, my father [publicist Murray Goodman] set Lester up in an eating contest. They brought out what looked like a whole side of beef. Lester ate and ate and ate some more. And then he got sick as a dog. That was a memorable moment."

"Everybody likes a good meal," says Alan Hopper (director of public relations for DKP). "And when you serve food at a press conference, the writers show up on time."

"There are times when it seems like half of my being is about what kind of food and which restaurant," says Debbie Caplan, who is following in her father's footsteps as a boxing publicist. "Sometimes the turnout for a press conference is dictated by the restaurant, not the fight."

"Over the years, I've heard more complaints about the food than the fights," adds father Bill. "You can announce that two undefeated champions are fighting each other. And afterward, if you ask people what they thought about the press conference, you're likely to hear, 'So-and-so gave us roast beef and turkey, and you only gave us roast beef.' Sometimes I think the writers are frustrated food critics."

As a general rule, kick-off press conferences are held at the fight site or in a restaurant that bears some relationship to the card. If two Mexican fighters are facing off in the main event, the media isn't invited to a Japanese restaurant.

Promoter Lou DiBella makes a point of holding press conferences for Dmitriy Salita's fights in kosher restaurants because Salita is an Orthodox Jew. Beyond that, DiBella notes, "It's no accident that most of the press conferences for my Broadway Boxing series are at Gallagher's Steak House. The majority of guys writing boxing today are young kids with no money. The free meal, particularly if it's a steak at Gallagher's, is an inducement."

Different promoters feed the media differently. For a big fight, things start with the kick-off press conference.

Years ago, when Don King had an office on the top floor at Rockefeller Plaza, he regularly held press conferences in the Rainbow Room. Now King's catering varies; but almost always, the food is superb.

"The thing that I appreciate most about Don," says Alan Hopper, "is that he understands public relations. Don never says, 'Give them coffee and muffins because it's cheaper.' Don wants everything to be first-rate. The food at some of his press conferences is Roman in its excess."

"Don King has everybody beat," confirms HBO's "unofficial ringside judge" and culinary connoisseur Harold Lederman. "When Don goes all out, no one else in boxing comes close. There's so much food at some of his press conferences that you think you're at a bar mitzvah."

HBO vice president Mark Taffet maintains that the "all-time greatest food at a press conference" was served when Jerry Perenchio promoted Oscar De La Hoya against Javier Castillejo. The kick-off press conference was held at the St. Regis Hotel in Beverly Hills. A dozen chefs wearing high white hats were on duty. "The food was so good and there was so much of it," Taffet recalls, "that we couldn't get anyone to leave the dining area and come into the press conference. Finally, we literally had to close down the buffet table."

At the other end of the spectrum, *New York Daily News* boxing scribe Tim Smith harkens back to Roy Jones versus Eric Harding, which was promoted by Murad Muhammad. "We were in New Orleans, one of the best food towns in the country," Smith says. "I came to the press conference hungry. This was a big-time fight, and I had high expectations. Boy, was I wrong. All we got were peanuts, pretzels, and soda. Murad was pinching pennies on that one."

That's understandable. Last year, Murad hosted a press conference at Gallagher's to kick off Evander Holyfield versus Fres Oquendo. When lunch was done, he had to give the maître d' three different credit cards before one cleared.

Press conferences at Madison Square Garden are catered in-house and follow a formula of deli sandwiches, wraps, salads, chocolate chip cookies, and brownies. "I love the cookies," says Hopper.

Virtually all press conferences are dry. But that didn't stop a group of writers who attended a press conference at Tavern on the Green in New York from running up a $400 bar tab and telling the bartender to charge it to HBO. "I was with HBO at the time," DiBella remembers. "But the press conference was the responsibility of Main Events. I gave the bill to [Main Events vice president] Carl Moretti and told him, 'This is your problem, not mine.'"

Sometimes the food served at a press conference isn't for the media. When George Foreman began his comeback, he was defensive about his age and weight. Bob Arum, who was promoting Big George at the time, recalls, "I told him, 'George, if you're defensive about it, things will only get worse. You have to make a joke out of it.' George is a smart guy," Arum continues. "He understood the point. So at the next press conference we did for him, I had a waiter bring a platter piled high with cheeseburgers to George at the dais. The press loved it; it made all the TV stations. And it became a signature part of George's press conferences after that."

In the days immediately preceding a big fight, the culinary scene shifts to the on-site media center. Nostalgia flows when veteran boxing writers talk about the food at Caesars Palace in Las Vegas during the glory years.

Bill Caplan looks to the east coast and recalls, "The best food I remember was when George Foreman fought Evander Holyfield in Atlantic City. Donald Trump was very much into the fight. He had a chef in the media center every minute it was open. George came in every day just to see what they were serving."

When Lennox Lewis and Mike Tyson fought in Memphis, Tennessee, media day for Team Tyson was held at Fitzgerald's Casino in Tunica, Mississippi, where the press was kept in a holding area in ninety-five-degree heat for forty-five minutes while Tyson finished a private workout. Thereafter, Iron Mike hit a speed bag for several minutes, toyed briefly with a slip-bag, and left without saying a word. No food (or water) was served.

One day later, Lewis made a lot of friends when he hosted a media luncheon in the grand ballroom at Sam's Town Casino. There were flowers on the tables, harp music in the background, and a memorable buffet.

But the following year, there was grumbling when Gary Shaw took over as Lennox's promoter for Lewis versus Vitali Klitschko in Los Angeles. After repeated complaints from the media that they weren't getting enough to eat, Debbie Caplan decided to host a barbeque at her home. Those who were privileged to attend still talk fondly about it.

There's an odd juxtaposition in the fact that, at a time when fighters often are struggling to make weight, there's so much food in the media center. One student of the scene notes, "You can always tell what's being served by the stains on Mike Katz's shirt and the crumbs in his beard." Meanwhile,

Richard Sandomir of the *New York Times* observes, "When Roberto Duran sees a media center buffet, he says 'mas.' "

Here, it should be noted that there are times when jostling for position on the food line in the media center resembles "Manos de Piedra" fighting on the inside. Boxing historian Herb Goldman once got into a heated shoving match as he neared the buffet table. "Some jerk was trying to make his presence felt," Goldman recalls. "It wasn't really about the food."

Meanwhile, Dan Rafael thinks back to September 2004, when the media was at the MGM Grand for the mega-fight between Oscar De La Hoya and Bernard Hopkins and a press release went out heralding a Friday-night press conference for the rematch between Shane Mosley and Winky Wright.

"The Wright–Mosley press conference was at Mandalay Bay," Rafael remembers. "And the way they got the writers over there was to put on the press release in big capital letters, 'FREE SHRIMP.' "

The situation is summed up by Bernard Fernandez, who opines, "Bernard Hopkins claims that he hasn't eaten a donut in twenty years. He'll never make a boxing writer."

Then comes fight night.

At Madison Square Garden, if the fights are in The Theater, there's no food other than what's sold at the concession stands. If the card takes place in the main arena, there's an $8 charge for a modest buffet dinner with all proceeds going to the Garden of Dreams Foundation.

Mandalay Bay traditionally serves hot dogs, chili, nachos, and Dove bars on fight night. "If you eat enough Dove bars," Fernandez says, "you overlook the fact that they're only giving you hot dogs, chili, and nachos as the entrée."

Publicist Fred Sternberg recalls working Mosley–Wright I at Mandalay Bay and, shortly before the fight, seeing Jack Mosley in the media center getting a hot dog. "I remember asking myself, 'Shouldn't he be in the dressing room with his son?' " Sternberg notes.

The MGM Grand traditionally puts out an elaborate fight-night buffet replete with roast beef, salmon, chicken, several kinds of pasta, salads, cakes, pies, fresh fruit, and tiramisu.

But you can't please everybody. On the night of De La Hoya–Mayweather, one writer complained to MGM vice president Scott Ghertner that there weren't any Dove bars.

Some writers have been known to toke on a joint before going to the media center to indulge a desire for munchies. As for alcohol, publicist John Beyrooty recalls, "We used to have beer in the press room on fight night at The Forum, but we had to stop because a couple of guys got drunk." Mandalay Bay discontinued the practice of serving beer in the media center on fight night for the same reason.

Meanwhile, there's a downside to all the free food that's given to boxing writers. Someone has to pay for it.

Gallagher's Steak House charges promoters $54 per person (including tip and tax) for a full steak meal. At the Copacabana (another favored New York location), it's $40 a person but the promoter is charged $2,500 for audio–visual equipment. Madison Square Garden's deli package is $25 a head. The Rainbow Room charges $10,000 for the room, $3,000 for audio–visual equipment, and $60 per person for food.

At the Las Vegas hotel-casinos, who pays how much for what is determined by the structure of the deal between the site and the promoter. Media center fare during fight week can range from coffee and tea to elaborate buffets for breakfast, lunch, and afternoon break.

Golden Boy CEO Richard Schaefer reports that, during fight week for De La Hoya–Mayweather, the cost of feeding the media exceeded $100,000. "The food is a courtesy and a convenience for the writers," says Schaefer. "But there are times when putting the menu together is like planning a wedding."

Sometimes the courtesies are abused. Dan Rafael saw a prominent boxing writer walk into the media center at the MGM Grand with a small gym bag and leave with two six-packs of soda and a dozen candy bars.

John Beyrooty recounts an incident that occurred when he was overseeing publicity for Forum Boxing. "Our cards featured Mexican fighters, so we made a point of offering good Mexican food at our press conferences," Beyrooty recalls. "One day, a guy came in with his mother, filled two plastic containers to the brim, and was walking out to his car when I stopped him. What made it particularly offensive is that they were walking out with the food before the press conference even started."

And there's another problem. The free food attracts the writers but it also brings in a lot of freeloaders.

"There's a problem today," says Bobby Goodman, "because it's not clearly defined who's a boxing writer. Years ago, you knew who the legitimate guys were and you were honored to have them. But things are different now."

Ed Keenan is the guiding force behind EMC, which handles media relations, credentials, and other services for many of today's big fights. As such, he's often responsible for organizing press conferences.

"It's hard to keep track of all the people who say they write about boxing," Keenan acknowledges. "In the beginning, it was okay when they showed up for media lunches but now it's getting out of hand. The Copa has a guy who stands at the front door with a clicker and counts the number of people who come in. Gallagher's counts plates. At the ESPN Zone [another favored site], they give out wristbands. The cost adds up. If you have fifty people who don't belong, that can add $2,000 to the bill, sometimes more."

"Also, people who don't belong take up space," Keenan continues. "They make it hard for the legitimate writers to get access to the fighters. Under a hundred people work in the upstairs room at Gallagher's. But if you go over a hundred, things get tight. When Don King held a press conference at Gallagher's for Briggs–Liakhovich, 140 people showed up. Every time someone walked in the door, a waiter ran up to him with a plate so they could charge another $54. It was so crowded that I had to eat in the kitchen."

On July 31, 2007, Lou DiBella held a press conference at Tavern on the Green to announce the middleweight championship fight between Jermain Taylor and Kelly Pavlik. The room was jammed; in part because those present thought they'd be getting a free lunch. Instead, they were given what one disgruntled attendee called "rabbit food" (cut vegetables and fruit).

"After seeing who was there, I'm happy I didn't do a full meal," DiBella said afterward. "The real boxing Internet sites are carrying the game right now. I have no problem giving the people who work for them a free meal. But there are also a lot of hobby websites and bullshit blogs that aren't worth the price of a lunch. And quite frankly, there are people who come to my press conferences who I've never seen a word from."

So what happens next?

Alan Hopper says, "I love the freeloaders; they fill up the room. A publicist's greatest nightmare is that the room will be empty. On a marginal event, the freeloaders help."

But most promoters don't have Don King's budget for food. And one can envision a time in the not-too-distant future when promoters only allow invited guests to attend their press conferences and put teeth in that requirement.

"You don't have outsiders freeloading like this in any other sport," says Dan Rafael. "I don't see why we should have it in boxing."

Boxing has enough problems without inaugurating a new economic model that further alienates its fans.

Ticket Scalping and Boxing

There's a time-honored promotional tactic in the entertainment industry. Create a buzz that an event is where everyone wants to be; and suddenly, because of the buzz, everyone wants to be there.

When Floyd Mayweather Jr. fought Ricky Hatton in Las Vegas on December 8, tickets for the fight had a face value of $1,000, $750, $600, $300, and $150. Golden Boy (which promoted the fight) announced prior to the public sale that there would be a limit of two tickets per customer. On September 17, it proudly proclaimed that tickets had sold out within thirty minutes of their being made available to the public and that the live gate would be $10.5 million.

But a key fact was left out of the PR blitz. More specifically, Mayweather–Hatton was the first fight (and possibly the first major sports event ever) for which the primary means of ticket distribution was "scalping." Well over half the tickets for the fight were sold to a select few individuals, who resold them at a significant premium (often to brokers, who sold them yet again to the public).

Ticket scalping has long been part of the culture of boxing. But for the most part, it has been limited to ringside seats and implemented largely through personal contacts. The magnitude of the scalping for Mayweather–Hatton was unparalleled in its scope and, in some instances, implemented in a far more sophisticated manner than in the past.

Richard Schaefer (CEO of Golden Boy) says that the MGM Grand (which hosted the fight) wanted to buy 8,000 tickets but was limited to 5,000. Most of these were distributed within the MGM–Mirage empire and given to high-rollers.

Golden Boy (depending on whom one talks with) retained between 1,500 and 1,800 tickets, which were divided among sponsors, HBO, other business associates, and the like. Between 200 and 500 tickets went on direct sale to the public.

That leaves roughly 9,000 tickets. Schaefer says that these were divided evenly between the Mayweather and Hatton camps, which were entitled by contract to purchase 4,500 tickets each at face value. Nevada State Athletic Commission records show that, in addition to whatever other sum might have been paid by the Hatton camp to Golden Boy, $3.1 million was deducted from Hatton's purse for the purchase of tickets.

Bob Arum describes what happened next as "creative marketing that allowed certain people to sell thousand-dollar tickets to morons for ten thousand dollars." Or phrased differently; large blocks of tickets were sold at a premium to brokers, who in turn resold them to the buying public.

The Hatton camp is believed to have sold many of its tickets at a 30-percent markup. The Mayweather camp is thought to have had a more sophisticated and more profitable resale operation.

Ken Sulkey of Las Vegas is vice president of the National Association of Ticket Brokers. "The difference between this and other fights," says Sulkey, "was the British invasion. There were a few people with a lot of tickets who capitalized on the opportunity. Brokers paid between $3,000 and $5,000 for ringside seats depending on location. Generally, we work on a 25-to-30-percent mark-up, so a choice ringside seat might have sold to the public for as much as $6,500. I heard stories about tickets selling for $10,000," Sulkey notes. "But I doubt that more than ten or twenty tickets sold in that price range."

Ticket scalping with front-office complicity is common in sports. Brokers have arrangements with team personnel in each of the major sports leagues. The most-coveted and most-feverishly scalped tickets are for the Super Bowl.

A small percentage of Super Bowl tickets (slightly more than 1 percent) are sold directly to the public. Generally, the National Football League retains about 25 percent of the seats (largely for corporate sponsors and other business partners). The two teams competing in the game split about one-third of the tickets. The host franchise gets roughly 5 percent. The other NFL teams divide approximately one-third of the tickets between them. Each team determines for itself how its tickets will be allocated. The remaining tickets are distributed to league executives, players, coaches, and a few lucky others.

The first Super Bowl was played in the Los Angeles Coliseum in 1967 before 61,046 fans and 32,000 empty seats. Times have changed. Choice seats for the Super Bowl now sell on the open market for between $7,500 and $10,000. Scalped tickets often find their way into travel packages. It's easy to include a ticket with the package and overcharge for everything else.

The NFL requires that all players, coaches, and club personnel who receive Super Bowl tickets sign a release stating they will not sell the tickets at a profit. In March 2005, Minnesota Vikings head coach Mike Tice admitted to league security investigators that he had scalped part of his ticket allotment for the February 2005 Super Bowl and was fined $100,000. However, it's widely believed that some NFL owners also sell Super Bowl tickets at a premium. "Mike Tice got hit because he was a coach," says one person with in-depth knowledge of ticket-brokering. "There are two sets of rules. Coaches and players can't do that sort of thing. Owners can."

Let's draw two distinctions between tickets for the Super Bowl and tickets for Mayweather–Hatton. First, scalping was the *primary* means of ticket distribution for Mayweather–Hatton. And second, the Super Bowl (unlike boxing's big events) is available free of charge on television. Anyone who wants to can watch it. Fans who didn't have tickets for Mayweather–Hatton had to pay a suggested retail price of $54.95 to see the action.

Keep in mind, ticket-scalping plans can implode. When Lennox Lewis and Mike Tyson fought in Memphis in 2002, it was announced that all 19,185 tickets had been sold. Then brokers who had been shut out of the initial ticket distribution were approached by other brokers with tickets to sell. Some brokers even forfeited deposit money rather than pay full price for tickets that had been assigned to them. Then it was announced that 1,000 previously unavailable tickets would go on sale to the public. The official explanation was that additional seats were freed up once the television production set-up in the arena was finalized. Ten days before the fight, the sellout fantasy bubble burst when 3,500 newly released tickets went on sale to the public. On fight night, $1,400 seats were available on the streets of Memphis for $500, and $900 tickets could be bought for $300.

Mayweather–Hatton had no such problems. But the manner in which tickets were distributed for the fight raises some interesting issues.

For starters, there's a 4-percent ticket tax in Nevada. Thus, Bob Arum observes, "What's really going on here is that the state is being paid a ticket tax on a substantial number of tickets that is significantly below the real value of the tickets. The state tax authorities should look into this situation very carefully. The face value of the tickets is a charade."

Moreover, let's assume that, pursuant to contract, a fighter's camp pays $3 million for tickets with a face value of $3 million but the real value of the tickets is $9 million. Should the $6 million differential be treated as part of the fighter's purse for tax purposes? And if not, isn't any resale profit on the tickets at every level fully taxable as ordinary income?

Also, there are strong public-policy arguments to be made against the way in which Mayweather–Hatton tickets were distributed. It's understandable that the MGM Grand would buy a large number of tickets to give away to high-rollers. Golden Boy obviously needs tickets for sponsors and other business partners. And a fighter's camp is entitled to a certain number of tickets for personal use.

But let's start with the obvious. Neither Floyd Mayweather or Ricky Hatton invited 4,500 friends and business associates to the fight at a cost in excess of $3 million. And to anyone who heard the crowd singing, "There's only one Ricky Hatton," it didn't sound as though the Mayweather camp bought tickets to ensure that Floyd's fans would be there.

Something is very wrong when scalping becomes the primary method of ticket distribution for a fight. A boxing match is a public event, and tickets should be available to the public at face value. The sport's current economic model is bad enough without making ticket scalping an integral part of it. This is one more example of boxing treating its fans badly.

Nevada already has a prohibition against more than 4 percent of the tickets for a boxing match being given away without the approval of the state athletic commission unless the promoter pays what otherwise would have been the ticket tax on the extra complimentary tickets. Perhaps the commission can also place limits on the resale of fight tickets by licensees or mandate that a certain percentage of tickets for each event go on sale to the general public.

A regulatory body shouldn't set ticket prices. But it does have a responsibility to the public to see that ticket distribution is transparent and fair. In the case of Mayweather–Hatton, it wasn't. Also, tax collection is one of the main functions of the Nevada State Athletic Commission. And in the case of Mayweather–Hatton, there's a question as to whether all appropriate taxes were collected.

It's possible that nothing improper was done here. But the NSAC should have a full understanding of "who, what, how, when, where, and why." The commission should conduct a thorough review of ticket distribution for Mayweather–Hatton with anyone who received a large block of tickets being called to testify.

Big fights should be a time when boxing is more fan-friendly, not less. It's not in the public interest or the best interests of boxing to perpetuate this situation.

I think that this was the most important article I wrote in 2007.

Larry Merchant and HBO

The recent contract negotiations between Larry Merchant and HBO offer insight into several facets of the relationship between boxing and the media.

As virtually every boxing fan knows, Merchant's previous contract with HBO expired on June 1, 2007. It was widely anticipated that, thereafter, his employment would be terminated by the network. But after much drama, he was offered and signed a new agreement that calls for him to remain with the cable giant until May 31, 2009. HBO has an option to extend his services through May 31, 2011.

HBO Sports president Ross Greenburg declined a request to be interviewed for this article. But many present and past HBO employees were willing to talk about the matter on condition of anonymity, while others agreed to speak on the record.

Merchant is a calming presence, not the sort of person one would expect to find at the center of a storm. He's seventy-six years old and has called more than 600 fights during his twenty-nine-year career with HBO. He has never been a traditional television commentator. At his core, he's an old-time, old-line, old-school journalist with ink in his veins. He has never promoted himself as a show business personality. His responsibility, as he sees it, is to commentate insightfully on HBO fights. He's quiet and well-mannered, a voice of reason who tells it like it is when the emperor has no clothes.

Most viewers like Merchant; some don't. But everyone agrees that he speaks the truth as he sees it. Seth Abraham (former president of Time Warner Sports and the original architect of HBO's boxing program) calls Merchant "one of the pillars of HBO's boxing franchise" and "the conscience of HBO boxing."

"Over the years," Abraham says, "Larry's contribution to HBO has gone far beyond his work behind the microphone. Even though Lou

[DiBella] wore a diamond stud in his ear, Lou was a suit when he was making fights for HBO. Lou was management. And Larry was never a suit. He was an ombudsman, a voice for the fan, and a reliable, knowledgeable sounding board for everything we did."

It's not often that the public figures one looks up to in youth turn out to be as decent and honorable as they appeared to have been when viewed through adolescent eyes. But as new generations of journalists and TV personnel have become Merchant's co-workers, they found him to be a man of integrity and grace. His presence in the sweet science gives boxing and everyone associated with it a bit more dignity and class.

In late 2005, Ross Greenburg began planning to remove Merchant from his role as lead analyst on HBO's *World Championship Boxing* and pay-per-view fights. His primary motivation is said to have been a desire to appeal to a younger audience demographic. Toward that end, Greenburg met with Max Kellerman (now thirty-three years old). In March 2006, a contract was signed. Informed sources say that it called for Kellerman to serve as lead analyst on all *Boxing After Dark* telecasts and perform desk duty on selected pay-per-view events through May 31, 2007. Thereafter, Max would assume Merchant's role as lead analyst on all *World Championship Boxing* and pay-per-view shows. The contract runs through May 31, 2010. Kellerman received in the neighborhood of $10,000 for each *Boxing After Dark* telecast. When he stepped into Merchant's shoes, his salary was to rise to approximately $550,000 a year.

In 2003, Showtime brought Al Bernstein in to fill a vacancy in the lead-analyst position on *Showtime Championship Boxing*. Before Bernstein was hired, Jay Larkin (then the head of Showtime Boxing) sat down with blow-by-blow commentator Steve Albert and asked him how he felt about the move and what he thought the chemistry between him and Bernstein would be like. Albert responded enthusiastically.

There is no evidence that Greenburg had a similar conversation with Jim Lampley regarding his partnering with Kellerman. To the contrary, replacing Larry with Max was Greenburg's call, plain and simple. Informed sources say that he did it with relatively little staff input and against the wishes of most of the people who deal with boxing at HBO.

Moreover, as one current HBO employee observes, "If you've promised a person's job to someone else, the only honorable thing to do is pick up the phone and tell him; or better yet, tell him face-to-face. And that's particularly true when the person you're terminating is Larry Merchant, who has been with you for twenty-nine years."

But that call wasn't made. And ultimately, Merchant was left dangling for months while his future remained in doubt.

Multiple sources say that it wasn't until November 2006 that Merchant was advised that his role on *World Championship Boxing* and pay-per-view fights as he knew it was about to be terminated. At that time, Greenburg offered him a slot on *Boxing After Dark* and unspecified "other duties" at a 70-percent cut in pay.

Merchant was prepared to begin the process of stepping back to make way for a successor, but not to the degree that Greenburg wanted. He pressed for clarification of just what those "other duties" would be and learned that they were largely illusory. In essence, Greenburg simply wanted him to trade jobs with Kellerman.

Merchant suggested a variety of alternatives, one of which conformed to Greenburg's desire to have him give up *World Championship Boxing* and pay-per-view fights. Larry said he would become the lead analyst for *Boxing After Dark (BAD)* if he could also be the matchmaker for *BAD*. He felt that HBO could, and should, be making better fights that it was. But Greenburg rejected the offer, saying that HBO's management team was perfectly capable of making good fights. Ross also voiced the view that it would be improper for one person to make and then commentate upon fights, despite the historical precedent of Gil Clancy, Ferdie Pacheco, and Alex Wallau doing so at CBS, NBC, and ABC, respectively.

Thereafter, other than offering a bit more money, Greenburg refused to budge and Merchant readied to leave HBO. It wasn't a negotiating ploy on Larry's part; he wasn't posturing. He felt unwanted and thought it was time to go.

"I don't blame Max," Merchant told intimates. "Every job in television is open to competition. This isn't about Max. It's a decision that Ross made with regard to me. He never told me why he was doing it. I'm sure he'll be asked at some point and he'll say something like, 'Larry was here for twenty-nine years and we love him but we have to look to the future.' "

"I'm not going to dodge the reality of what's happening," Merchant continued. "Change of this nature causes anxiety, but I feel good about myself and I'm optimistic about the future. I have a lot of good memories. When I look back over the years, that run in the eighties with Leonard, Hearns, Hagler, and Duran was fantastic. Holmes–Cooney was a fascinating event. Tyson–Douglas, Holyfield–Bowe, Gatti–Ward, Barrera–Morales, those fights were extraordinary. But all good things come to an end."

On February 28, 2007, Greenburg and Ray Stallone (HBO's vice president for sports publicity) met with Merchant in Los Angeles to discuss how his departure from the network would be handled from a public relations point of view.

"They were in a very self-protective mode," Merchant said afterward. "Ross wanted to be seen as the good guy who asked me to stay on. They handed me a written outline of how they hoped I would explain this to the media; the idea being that HBO offered to keep me on in a slightly different role but that I wanted to go in a different direction. It was corporate-speak and ignored the reality that Ross made it very clear to me by his words and actions that he wanted me out. I said I'd think about it. We agreed that Taylor–Spinks [on May 19, 2007] would be my last fight. Then they asked what sort of pomp and circumstance I wanted at the end, and I told them that I didn't want a grand tour. Whatever I do, I'll plan it myself."

Thereafter, Merchant drafted some farewell remarks that he intended to share with viewers on May 19. When asked, he told Rick Bernstein (executive producer of HBO Sports) that he did not want an on-air tribute at the close of the telecast.

Then the landscape shifted. Word began to leak out that Merchant wouldn't be continuing at HBO, and there was an outpouring of emotion from the boxing community. It came from fighters, writers, managers, promoters, television personnel, and fans. There was anger over his imminent departure, coupled with respect for Merchant himself.

"Ross didn't have a clue as to the backlash he'd get because he doesn't understand boxing fans or most of the people in boxing," says one HBO insider. "He had no idea how many people would stand by Larry, and he had no idea that there would be such a negative reaction to Max."

"I'm disappointed," said Seth Abraham. "Larry and I were together for twenty-five years and I consider him a friend, so I'm not a dispassionate observer. But having Larry or not having Larry doesn't change the audience demographics. And a broadcast team is just that. It's a team. Larry makes everyone else on the team better. He asks the right questions. He has the right follow-up. He never tries to be bigger than his fellow commentators. The question is not whether Max is better than Larry. The question is, 'Will Max make the team better?'"

"Just because you're the head of a department doesn't mean that you have a monopoly on brains," Abraham continued. "Sometimes you have a monopoly on shortsightedness and stupidity. That's one reason I've always liked consensus. When I was at HBO, I had the final vote, subject at times to the approval of [CEOs] Michael Fuchs and Jeff Bewkes. But there were occasions when I would think one thing and Ross, Lou [DiBella], Mark [Taffet], and even [financial officer] Barbara Thomas would have a different point of view. When that happened, I'd go into Bryant Park, sit down with a cup of cappucino, and ask myself, 'Why do these very intelligent people have a view that's different than mine?' And often— not always, but often—I'd come around to their view. Larry brings so much to the telecast. He'll be missed in many ways. If I were the president of HBO Sports—and I'm not, it's Ross's decision to make—I would renew Larry's contract."

Blow-by-blow commentator Jim Lampley also sang Merchant's praises. It's axiomatic in boxing that styles make fights, but styles also make announcing teams. The chemistry between Lampley and Merchant is superb; a blend of fire and ice. The one time that Lampley and Kellerman had been paired (on HBO's October 14, 2006, telecast of Joe Calzaghe versus Sakio Bika), the on-air chemistry between them had not been good. There were fears that replacing Larry with Max could wind up being the equivalent of trying to shove a square peg into a round hole.

Lampley spoke of Kellerman in complimentary terms but had special praise for Merchant. "Larry is not replaceable," Jim said. "He's unique in the history of our sport in terms of his integrity. The term 'truth-teller' is often used. It's the kind of flattery that anyone would like to hear, but to say it about Larry is to say it in the purest possible sense. Larry has never shilled for a moment. He has never bent to corporate will for a moment. Whether dealing with a fighter, a promoter, a corporate executive, a major sponsor, anyone; he has never said a word that he didn't firmly believe was the truth. I can only hope that someday, somewhere in my career, I can look at myself and, in my heart of hearts, believe that I'm as courageous as Larry. He inspires me every day that I work with him and he will continue to inspire me after he's gone."

Others were less charitable in viewing the situation. "I don't understand who Ross thinks he's appealing to with this move," said one industry insider. "I keep hearing, 'Younger demographic! Younger demographic!' Let's get real. Does Max appeal to young urban blacks? You've got to be kidding. Young women? I don't think so. The NASCAR crowd? No way. Instead of pandering to a younger demographic that he doesn't understand, Ross should try appealing to a boxing demographic. Better fights will attract more viewers."

Meanwhile, Kellerman was in a difficult situation. The lead analyst position on *World Championship Boxing* was his dream job and he was on track to get it. But the issue of Merchant's termination was making Max a lightning rod for criticism of HBO, and he was being attacked on both a professional and personal level.

"Max is a provocateur, not an analyst," said one member of HBO's production team. "To be an analyst, it's not enough to be able to talk. You need judgment and maturity and you have to know what you're talking about. There are times when Larry pauses on air to search for the right word. That's not age. That's thinking before he speaks instead of shooting off his mouth."

On a February 17 *Boxing After Dark* telecast, Kellerman likened Paulie Malignaggi to Billy Conn. As reported by Internet writer Charles Jay, "Max proceeded to make this comment about Malignaggi as the self-proclaimed 'Magic Man' entered the ring: 'He's an ethnic white guy, fights in the Northeast, doesn't hit with a lot of power, and so inevitably he reminds me of the great Billy Conn, light-heavyweight champion, who gave a very good showing against the great Joe Louis, a heavyweight, much like Malignaggi gave a very good showing against Miguel Cotto at junior-welterweight.' "

"INEVITABLY he reminds you of Conn?" Jay wrote. "I had no idea of the inevitability of that comparison. That's kind of like saying that, because they're both loud, obnoxious, and Jewish, Kellerman should be compared to Howard Cosell."

Actually, most people who meet Kellerman and talk with him one-on-one find him rather likable, whereas Cosell was even more abrasive and unpleasant in person than he was on television. Also, Cosell frequently sought to undermine his commentating partners, while Kellerman does the opposite. By way of example, Lennox Lewis says, "From the very beginning, Max has done everything he could to make me feel more comfortable behind the microphone."

Regardless, Max has lobbed quite a few hard verbal shots at targets on the air. And in boxing, when you throw punches, punches come back.

"Replacing Larry Merchant with Max Kellerman is like replacing Jack Nicholson with Jack Black," Ron Higgins of the *Memphis Commercial-Appeal* wrote. "Kellerman has zero journalistic background and is just another blabby radio-talk-show host whose schtick plays well on TV for the attention-deficit-disorder demographic of video-game zombies who prefer their knowledge in five-second sound bytes."

Doug Krikorian of the *Long Beach Press-Telegram* declared, "In what has to be one of the most misguided decisions in sports television history, HBO president Ross Greenburg has decided not to renew the contract of his longtime boxing analyst, Larry Merchant, and replace him with Max Kellerman. Omigod! What is Mr. Greenburg thinking? If he wanted a clown, I'm sure there are plenty available at Ringling Bros. and Barnum & Bailey Circus that are a lot more entertaining than Max Kellerman. Kellerman has a superficial knowledge of boxing, makes a lot of noise, and offers the kind of opinions one routinely hears in places like beer bars, fraternity houses, and barber shops. Greenburg is insulting the intelligence of his audience."

But no critic was more persistent than Bob Raissman of the *New York Daily News*, who, in a series of columns, attacked Kellerman for "smug rants designed to pander to the coveted younger demographic," and proclaimed, "Replacing Larry Merchant with Max Kellerman would be like replacing Picasso with the guy who sells the velvet Elvises outside of Graceland. MeMax's greatest asset is his ability to self-promote. He has fooled more than a few TV and radio suits, who again prove that having a brain is not a prerequisite for becoming a network sports executive. If HBO honchos dump Merchant in favor of Kellerman, it will signal a lowering of journalistic standards, which have always separated HBO Sports from all other TV sports operations."

The situation reached critical mass in Las Vegas during the week leading up to Oscar De La Hoya versus Floyd Mayweather Jr. Greenburg had wanted to replace Merchant with someone who would elicit a reaction from the media and fans, but this wasn't the reaction he wanted.

"Ross is all alone on this one," one HBO insider said. "Kery Davis, Mark Taffet, Rick Bernstein, Barbara Thomas; everyone thinks he's making a mistake."

The HBO bubble that Greenburg lives in was bursting. His decision to terminate Merchant's tenure was being attacked as evincing a lack of respect for boxing fans and boxing. It was suggested by one observer of the scene that HBO launch a new TV reality series entitled *Greenburg–Merchant–Kellerman 24/7*.

One moment spoke volumes. Several days before De La Hoya–Mayweather, Greenburg came into the media center at the MGM Grand Hotel and Casino, walked past dozens of writers and other "boxing people" without a word, and sat down next to former Los Angeles Dodgers manager Tommy Lasorda. By virtue of his position as president of HBO Sports, Ross was the most powerful person in the room. But he didn't seem to like the people he was sharing the room with very much.

Meanwhile, an extremely troubling issue had arisen. Earlier that week, Greenburg had been interviewed by Michael Hiestand of *USA Today* with regard to Merchant's contract status.

"Larry is still throwing a ninety-five-miles-per-hour fastball and hitting the corners," Hiestand quoted Ross as saying. "We'd never give him a reduced role. We're working to hammer this out."

The words, "We'd never give him a reduced role," were at odds with the truth.

Time Warner (HBO's parent company) is a media–entertainment conglomerate with a long tradition of journalistic excellence. *Time Magazine* and CNN are among its component parts. Closer to home, HBO prides itself on its journalistic integrity. That's the philosophy behind its boxing telecasts and shows like *Real Sports*.

For the president of HBO Sports to be quoted in "America's newspaper" and for that quote to be false was disheartening to a lot of people at HBO.

Then everything changed. Depending on one's point of view, either Greenburg blinked or had a change of heart.

On Friday, May 4 (the day before De La Hoya–Mayweather) Ross asked to have breakfast with Merchant at the MGM Grand and made an unexpected offer. His proposal was for a two-year contract with options at HBO's election for two years more. Merchant would work all of HBO's pay-per-view boxing cards (an estimated six per year) and half of its *World Championship Boxing* shows (Larry would choose which ones). His role on the telecasts would be the same as in the past. Other details (including salary) were ironed out at a May 8 meeting in New York when Merchant was in town to tape commentary for the network's replay of De La Hoya–Mayweather.

Merchant considered the agreement to be fair and was pleased with it. Then, a week later, he received unsettling news in the form of a telephone call from Rick Bernstein. Bernstein had been a strong advocate for Larry within HBO. Indeed, some people had begun referring to him as "the janitor" because, in the words of one co-worker, "he's trying to clean up the mess that Ross has made."

Bernstein told Merchant that there was a snag. Greenburg had thought he could persuade Kellerman to accept a lesser role on *World Championship Boxing* and pay-per-view fights and continue as the lead analyst on *Boxing After Dark*. But Max was objecting to Larry's new contract on grounds that he had a contract of his own and expected it to be fulfilled. Short of that, Kellerman was demanding parity with Merchant in assignments and refusing to work *Boxing After Dark* subsequent to May 31 because it wasn't required by his contract.

"HBO has gotten locked into bad long-term contracts with fighters in the past," marveled one network executive. "But this is the first time that HBO has gotten screwed on a long-term contract with an announcer."

Regardless, Greenburg was now backing away from the agreement that he and Merchant had reached. If Larry's new contract was to be finalized, he would have to accept a lesser number of fights than previously agreed to and would no longer have the right to choose which fights he worked.

Intimates say that Merchant was shaken and angered by the new turn of events. "This knocks me for a loop," he said. "I was prepared to leave. I had come to grips with it emotionally. And now, to be told that we have a deal for me to stay on and, less than ten days later, to be told that the terms of the deal are changing; I'm not happy about it at all. In the three decades that I've been at HBO, nothing like this has happened to me before and I'm not aware of it happening to anyone else."

Once again, Merchant's status was in limbo. Taylor–Spinks came and went. Larry finished the telecast not knowing whether he'd sit behind an HBO microphone again.

Then another precinct was heard from. At the kick-off press conference for his upcoming fight against Alfonso Gomez, Arturo Gatti was asked what he thought about Merchant's possible departure. Gatti has fought under the HBO banner twenty-one times. Only Oscar De La Hoya and Roy Jones Jr. have made more appearances.

"I wouldn't want to speak to nobody but Larry Merchant after a fight," Arturo opined. "Some people don't like him. I like him because he's real. He's got balls to say it. If Max Kellerman goes to HBO, HBO is gonna go to shit."

Still, time was running out. May 31 came and went. Now a new deadline loomed. On June 8, the Boxing Writers Association of America was to present Merchant with the James J. Walker Award for "long and meritorious service to boxing." The next night, Miguel Cotto versus Zab Judah would be televised from Madison Square Garden on HBO Pay-Per-View. The announcing team for that fight was still undetermined.

More negotiations followed. HBO refused a request from the Kellerman camp that it sweeten Max's contract by relaxing an exclusivity provision that precludes him from appearing on ESPN. Merchant made several concessions with regard to terms that Greenburg had initially promised but later withdrew.

Finally, on June 8, HBO issued a press release announcing that the network and Merchant had agreed to a new contract. "We are delighted to have one of sports television's most respected broadcasters continue to call them as he sees them," the release quoted Greenburg as saying. "Larry is an institution at HBO. Sharing the workload with Larry will be Max Kellerman, which essentially gives us two formidable broadcast teams on *World Championship Boxing*."

Informed sources say that Merchant's contract with HBO provides for the following: (1) Merchant will work half of all *World Championship Boxing* and up to six pay-per-view shows per year; (2) to ease *Boxing After Dark's* transition to a new announcing team, he will work two *BAD* shows each year; and (3) he will have first priority on all fights outside of the United

States. Beyond that, HBO will determine which shows Larry works after "meaningful consultation" between him and Rick Bernstein.

As for how things will play out, Merchant and Kellerman are said to have overlapping expectations. But each of their contracts is "pay or play" (an industry term that means that HBO can apportion air dates between them as it sees fit as long as it pays them).

It would be unfair to Kellerman to judge his work against the standard that Merchant has set. Max should be allowed to rise or fall on his own merits. But he'll be under a lot of pressure in the months ahead. And by refusing to work *Boxing After Dark*, he has created an opening for whoever fills *BAD's* lead-analyst slot. As Earnie Shavers once said, "When you marry your mistress, you create a vacancy."

Meanwhile, HBO has a new set of problems as a result of the resolution of L'Affaire Merchant. An announcing team is a network's representative to the viewing public and, where boxing is concerned, the only constant the public sees from show to show. HBO is now in a situation where its flagship product (*World Championship Boxing*) has a schizophrenic identity. Some football teams have a quarterback controversy with two guys switching back and forth. HBO is on the brink of a lead-analyst controversy that will aggravate some viewers and create a certain amount of internal discomfort.

Greenburg's critics say that his handling of the situation typifies a larger malaise within HBO's boxing program. Dan Rafael wrote recently that Ross "bungled the entire Larry Merchant affair from Day 1, handling contract negotiations with his irreplaceable star analyst like a rookie instead of a seasoned executive." One member of HBO's production crew likens Ross's championing of Kellerman to Coca Cola's ill-fated product improvement ("new Coke") of the 1980s.

And more than a few feathers were ruffled on June 8 when the annual Boxing Writers Association of America awards dinner took place. Showtime CEO Matt Blanc and Ken Hershman (who runs that network's boxing program) were there to see Steve Albert receive the Sam Taub Award for excellence in broadcast journalism (which was bestowed upon Merchant in 1985). Larry, as noted earlier in this article, was honored on June 8 for his long and meritorious service to boxing. Greenburg chose not to attend the dinner.

Still, as Seth Abraham notes, "One of the marks of good leadership is the ability to recognize that you've made a mistake and the willingness to change course. I think it's to Ross's credit that he took a step back, reevaluated the situation, and changed his mind as far as Larry's future at HBO is concerned."

That brings us back to Merchant. On June 9, HBO asked if he would be willing to cover its June 16 *Boxing After Dark* card at Mohegan Sun in Connecticut. Larry agreed and, the following weekend, flew from California to the east coast, did the show, and (on two hours sleep) flew back to California. At age seventy-six. That's a team player, the guy Greenburg wanted to terminate.

Merchant is satisfied with his new contract. "It worked out as well as I could have hoped for under the circumstances," he says. "It's a fair deal. It gives me time to do a few more things, personal and professional, that I want to do and keeps me involved with boxing. I'm satisfied."

Then Merchant is asked what he thinks will happen with boxing at HBO over the next few years.

"I don't know," he answers. "One or two guys can change everything. And those guys can be in the ring or out of it."

Thomas Hauser is the author of thirty-six books. His first book, *Missing*, was nominated for the Pulitzer Prize, Bancroft Prize, and National Book Award, and served as the basis for the Academy-Award-winning film starring Jack Lemmon and Sissy Spacek. *Muhammad Ali: His Life and Times*, Hauser's most celebrated work to date, is widely regarded as the definitive biography of the most famous man on earth. In 1998, Hauser and Ali were named as co-recipients of the Haviva Reik Award for their efforts to combat bigotry and prejudice. In 2004, Hauser was honored by the Boxing Writers Association of America, which bestowed upon him the Nat Fleischer Award for Career Excellence in Boxing Journalism.

796.83   Hauser, Thomas.
HAU
          The boxing scene.

$23.95 pb   3/9/09

	DATE	

BAKER & TAYLOR